UNTOLD COMIC TALES FROM THE HIT TV SERIES ON THE CW

RIVERDALE®

ALL-NEW STORIES

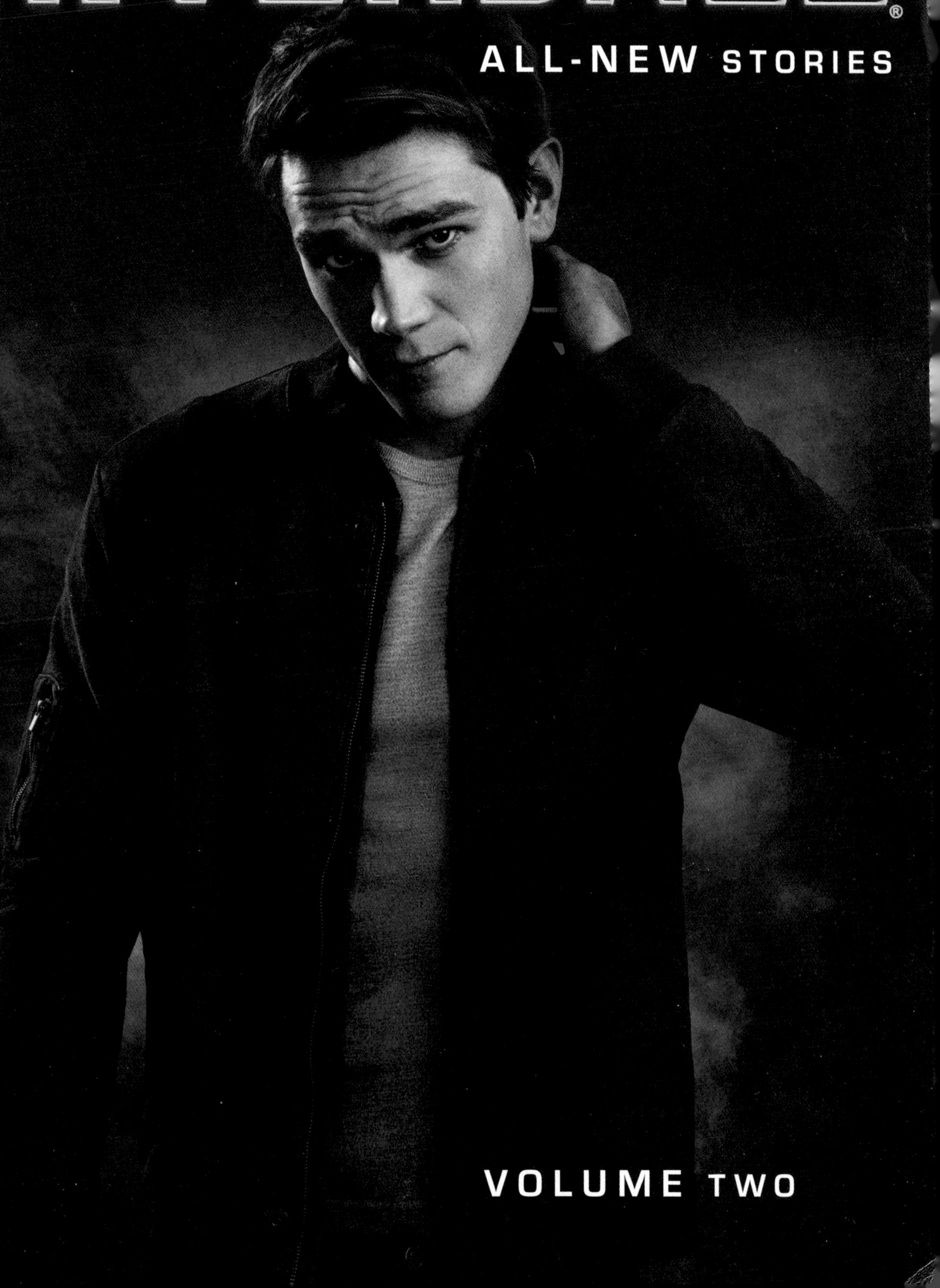

VOLUME TWO

UNTOLD COMIC TALES FROM THE HIT TV SERIES ON THE CW

RIVERDALE®

STORIES BY:
ROBERTO AGUIRRE-SACASA

WRITTEN BY:
AARON ALLEN, WILL EWING,
MICHAEL GRASSI, ROSS MAXWELL,
BRIAN E. PATERSON
& TESSA LEIGH WILLIAMS.

WITH ART BY:
JOE EISMA, THOMAS PITILLI,
JANICE CHIANG, JOHN WORKMAN
& ANDRE SZYMANOWICZ.

CHIEF EXECUTIVE OFFICER/PUBLISHER:
JON GOLDWATER

CHIEF CREATIVE OFFICER:
ROBERTO AGUIRRE-SACASA

EDITOR-IN-CHIEF:
VICTOR GORELICK

LEAD DESIGNER:
KARI MCLACHLAN

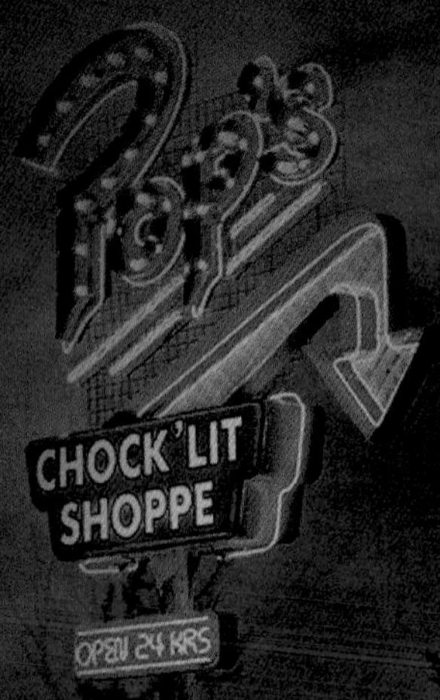
Pop's
CHOCK'LIT SHOPPE
OPEN 24 HRS

All photos courtesy of The CW/Warner Bros.

As you're reading this, the final episodes of *Riverdale* Season 2 will be airing on the CW network. And, wow, what a ride it's been! To call the experience a "phenomenon" would be a huge understatement. The show has captured the attention of fans around the world, and had a huge impact on pop culture.

If you've been following along with the series, you'll know how intense these past two seasons have been—from mysterious deaths, forbidden romances, deadly crimes and familial drama—*Riverdale* knows how to keep you at the edge of your seat while reminding you why you love these iconic characters. It's edgy while still having heart. It's gripping. It's *fearless*. Most importantly, though, it's Archie.

"Fearless" was the mantra I used when I took over the company about ten years ago and realized the brand needed a top-to-bottom refresh. "It's gotta be Archie" was an equally important concept—because no matter the changes or new directions, the characters still had to feel and be themselves. The strategy worked. Since my first days at the company, we've made a lot of bold changes that breathed new life into the characters. With each new twist or idea, we'd push the envelope just a bit more and more and, in doing so, I realized the true expanse of amazing things we could do here at Archie. No matter what situation the characters were placed in, be it supernatural horror or psychological drama, people would still know it's Archie. Everyone knows and loves the kid.

That's why *Riverdale* works so well. People care about these characters, they recognize them; they root for them even when it seems like the odds are against them. That's due in large part to the creative genius of Archie Chief Creative Officer and showrunner Roberto Aguirre-Sacasa, who cares so deeply about the Archie characters. When I read the first script, I knew that it was the final touch needed on the reinvigoration of the characters and brand—he took them to a totally new place, but the integrity remains intact from what you would expect from all of the characters from 75 years ago.

Now, wrapping up season 2, *Riverdale* continues to present to the world the notion that Archie Comics have a wide, diverse and multifaceted library of characters. People outside of the comic industry are finally starting to take notice—we're working on a brand new *Chilling Adventures of Sabrina* series for Netflix, and there's certainly more to come. It's taken time, but with a lot of hard work, Archie is relevant again; not just a retro concept. And this is just the start of the Archie Revolution.

—Jon Goldwater

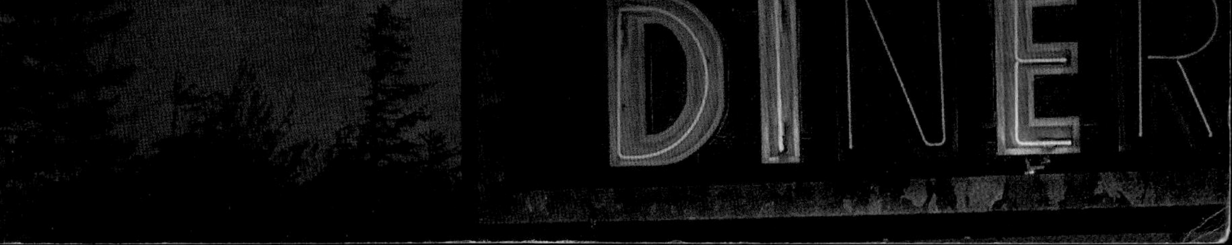
DINER

ISSUE FOUR

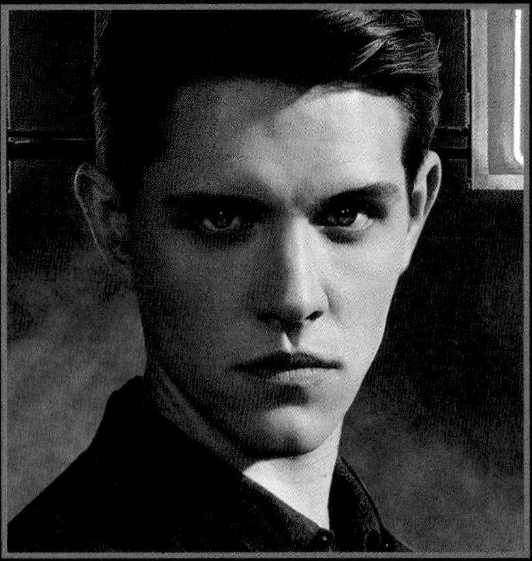

WE NEED TO TALK ABOUT KEVIN

WRITER:
MICHAEL GRASSI

ART:
JOE EISMA

COLORS:
ANDRE SZYMANOWICZ

LETTERS:
JOHN WORKMAN

STARRING
KEVIN KELLER

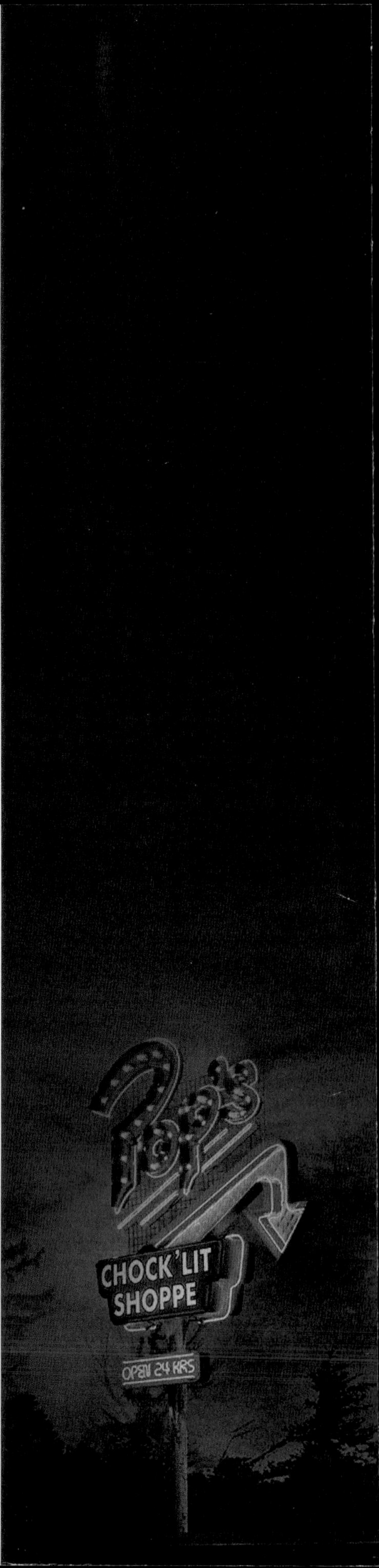
CHOCK'LIT
SHOPPE
OPEN 24 HRS

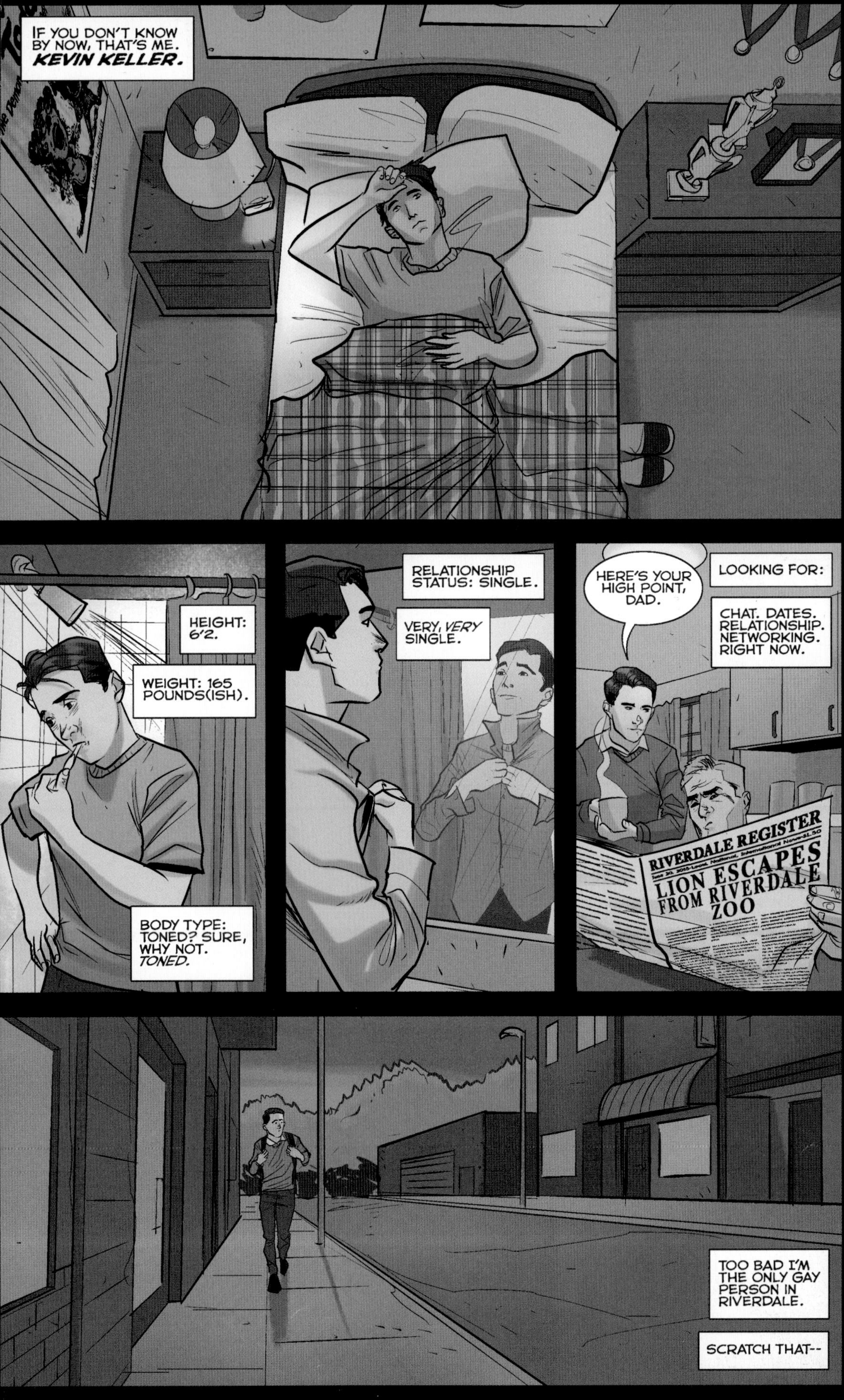
IF YOU DON'T KNOW BY NOW, THAT'S ME. *KEVIN KELLER.*
HEIGHT: 6'2.
WEIGHT: 165 POUNDS(ISH).
BODY TYPE: TONED? SURE, WHY NOT. *TONED.*
RELATIONSHIP STATUS: SINGLE.
VERY, *VERY* SINGLE.
HERE'S YOUR HIGH POINT, DAD.
LOOKING FOR:
CHAT. DATES. RELATIONSHIP. NETWORKING. RIGHT NOW.
RIVERDALE REGISTER
LION ESCAPES FROM RIVERDALE ZOO
TOO BAD I'M THE ONLY GAY PERSON IN RIVERDALE.
SCRATCH THAT--

I'M THE ONLY *OPENLY* GAY PERSON IN RIVERDALE.

FOR INSTANCE...

THE MANAGER OF THE USED BOOKSTORE *HAS* TO LIKE GUYS.

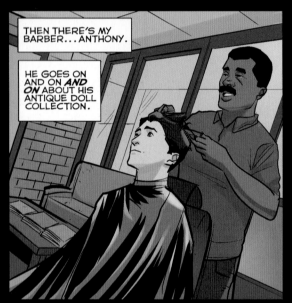

THEN THERE'S MY BARBER...ANTHONY.

HE GOES ON AND ON *AND ON* ABOUT HIS ANTIQUE DOLL COLLECTION.

AND THE FLORIST, BETH, FLIRTS WITH *ALL* OF HER FEMALE CUSTOMERS.

OH, AND THEN THERE'S--

THE POPCORN GUY AT THE BIJOU.

LARGE WITH EXTRA BUTTER LAYERED IN, JUST HOW YOU LIKE IT!

THANKS...

THE MAILMAN.

MORNING, KEVIN!

(OKAY, MAYBE THAT ONE'S JUST WISHFUL THINKING...)

HECK, YOU NEVER KNOW, POP TATE COULD BE GAY.

SAY HELLO TO YOUR DAD FOR ME, KEVIN.

I DON'T *ACTUALLY* THINK HE IS. BUT THAT'S MY POINT...

GETTING THROUGH EACH AND EVERY DAY WITHOUT *KNOWING* IF THERE'S SOMEONE ELSE OUT THERE LIKE ME...

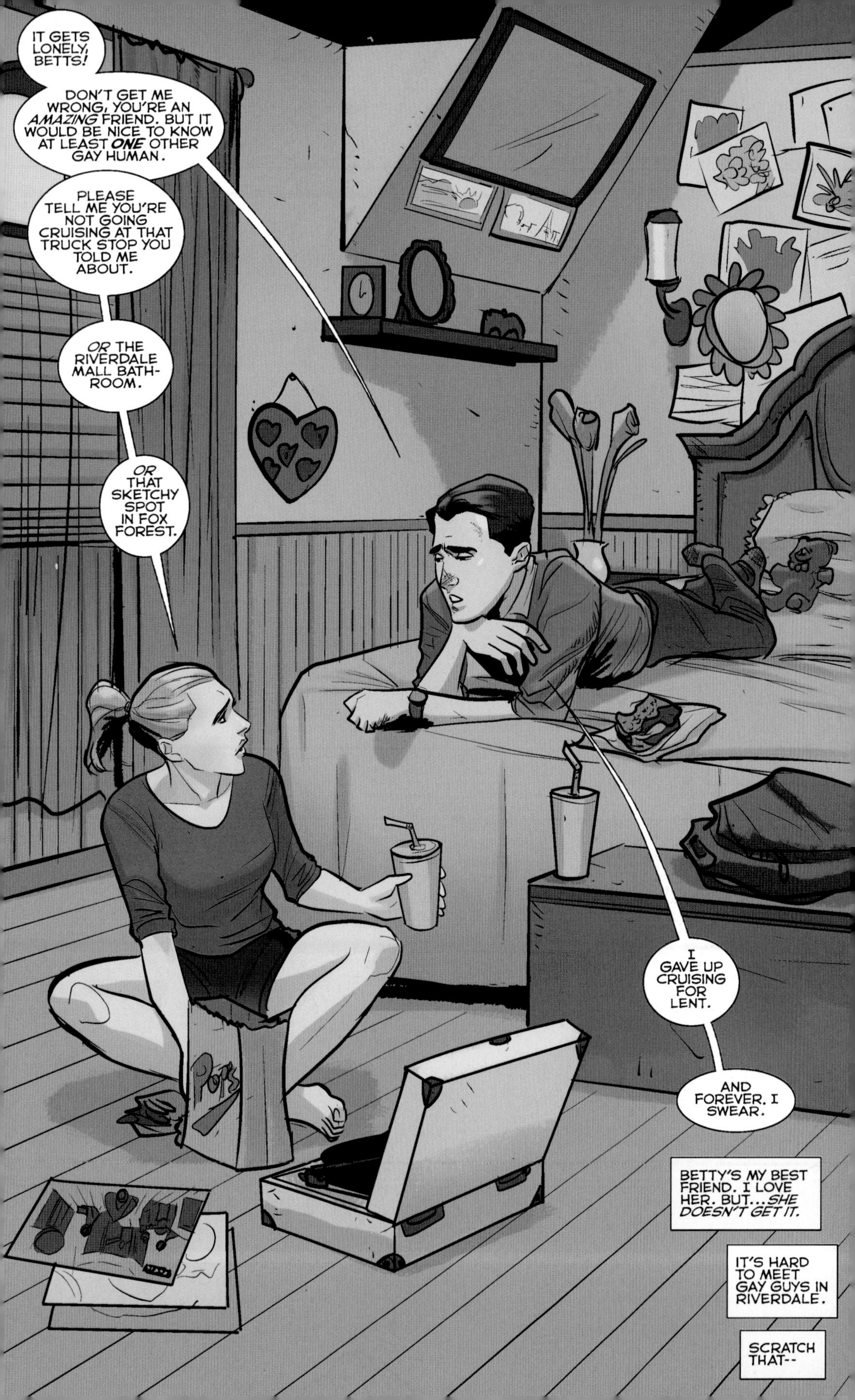
IT GETS LONELY, BETTS!
DON'T GET ME WRONG, YOU'RE AN *AMAZING* FRIEND. BUT IT WOULD BE NICE TO KNOW AT LEAST ***ONE*** OTHER GAY HUMAN.
PLEASE TELL ME YOU'RE NOT GOING CRUISING AT THAT TRUCK STOP YOU TOLD ME ABOUT.
OR THE RIVERDALE MALL BATH-ROOM.
OR THAT SKETCHY SPOT IN FOX FOREST.
I GAVE UP CRUISING FOR LENT.
AND FOREVER. I SWEAR.
BETTY'S MY BEST FRIEND. I LOVE HER. BUT...*SHE DOESN'T GET IT.*
IT'S HARD TO MEET GAY GUYS IN RIVERDALE.
SCRATCH THAT--

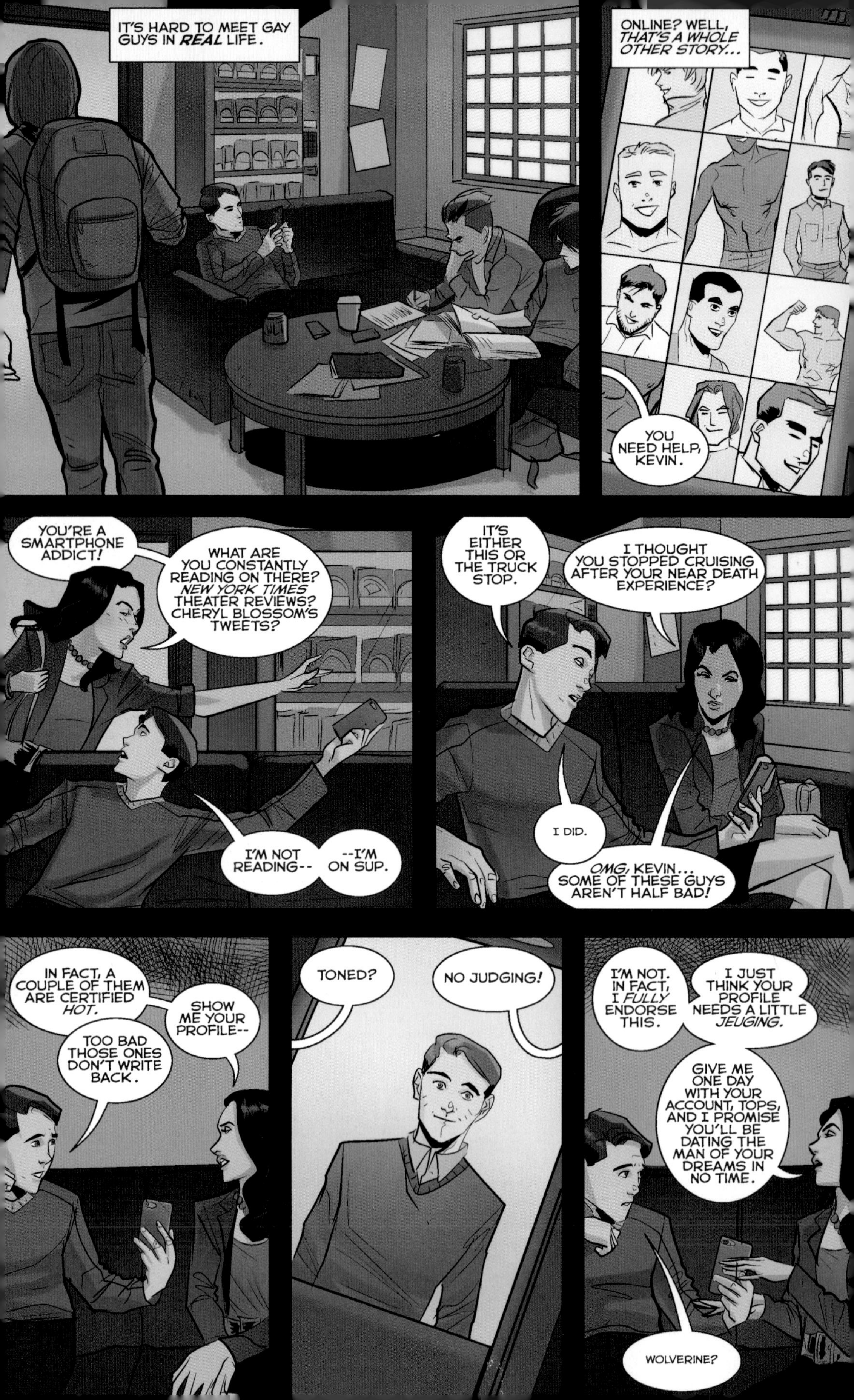
IT'S HARD TO MEET GAY GUYS IN *REAL* LIFE.
ONLINE? WELL, *THAT'S A WHOLE OTHER STORY...*
YOU NEED HELP, KEVIN.
YOU'RE A SMARTPHONE ADDICT!
WHAT ARE YOU CONSTANTLY READING ON THERE? *NEW YORK TIMES* THEATER REVIEWS? CHERYL BLOSSOM'S TWEETS?
I'M NOT READING--
--I'M ON SUP.
IT'S EITHER THIS OR THE TRUCK STOP.
I THOUGHT YOU STOPPED CRUISING AFTER YOUR NEAR DEATH EXPERIENCE?
I DID.
OMG, KEVIN... SOME OF THESE GUYS AREN'T HALF BAD!
IN FACT, A COUPLE OF THEM ARE CERTIFIED *HOT.*
TOO BAD THOSE ONES DON'T WRITE BACK.
SHOW ME YOUR PROFILE--
TONED?
NO JUDGING!
I'M NOT. IN FACT, I *FULLY* ENDORSE THIS.
I JUST THINK YOUR PROFILE NEEDS A LITTLE *JEUGING.*
GIVE ME ONE DAY WITH YOUR ACCOUNT, TOPS, AND I PROMISE YOU'LL BE DATING THE MAN OF YOUR DREAMS IN NO TIME.
WOLVERINE?

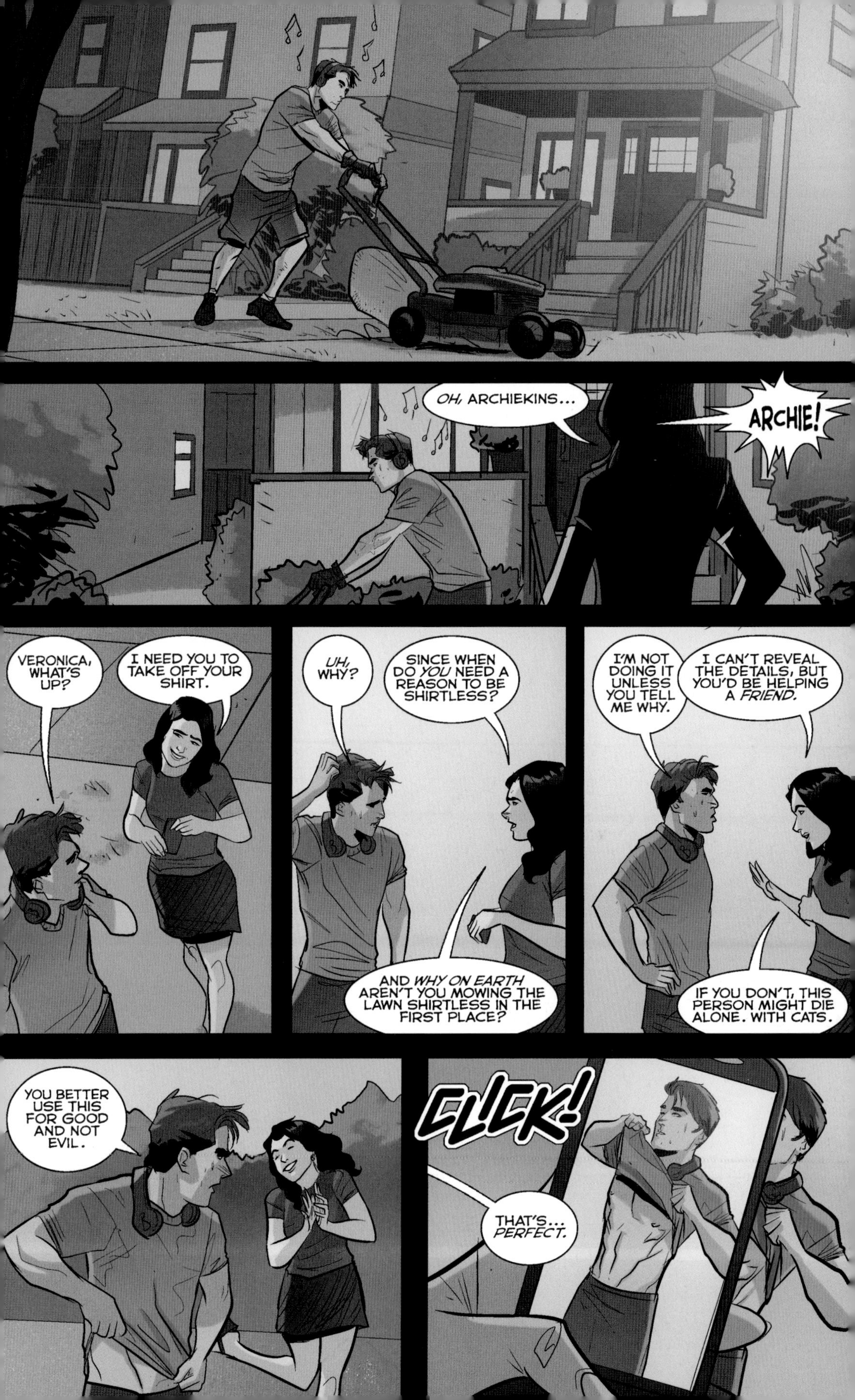

OH, ARCHIEKINS...
ARCHIE!
VERONICA, WHAT'S UP?
I NEED YOU TO TAKE OFF YOUR SHIRT.
UH, WHY?
SINCE WHEN DO YOU NEED A REASON TO BE SHIRTLESS?
AND WHY ON EARTH AREN'T YOU MOWING THE LAWN SHIRTLESS IN THE FIRST PLACE?
I'M NOT DOING IT UNLESS YOU TELL ME WHY.
I CAN'T REVEAL THE DETAILS, BUT YOU'D BE HELPING A FRIEND.
IF YOU DON'T, THIS PERSON MIGHT DIE ALONE. WITH CATS.
YOU BETTER USE THIS FOR GOOD AND NOT EVIL.
CLICK!
THAT'S... PERFECT.

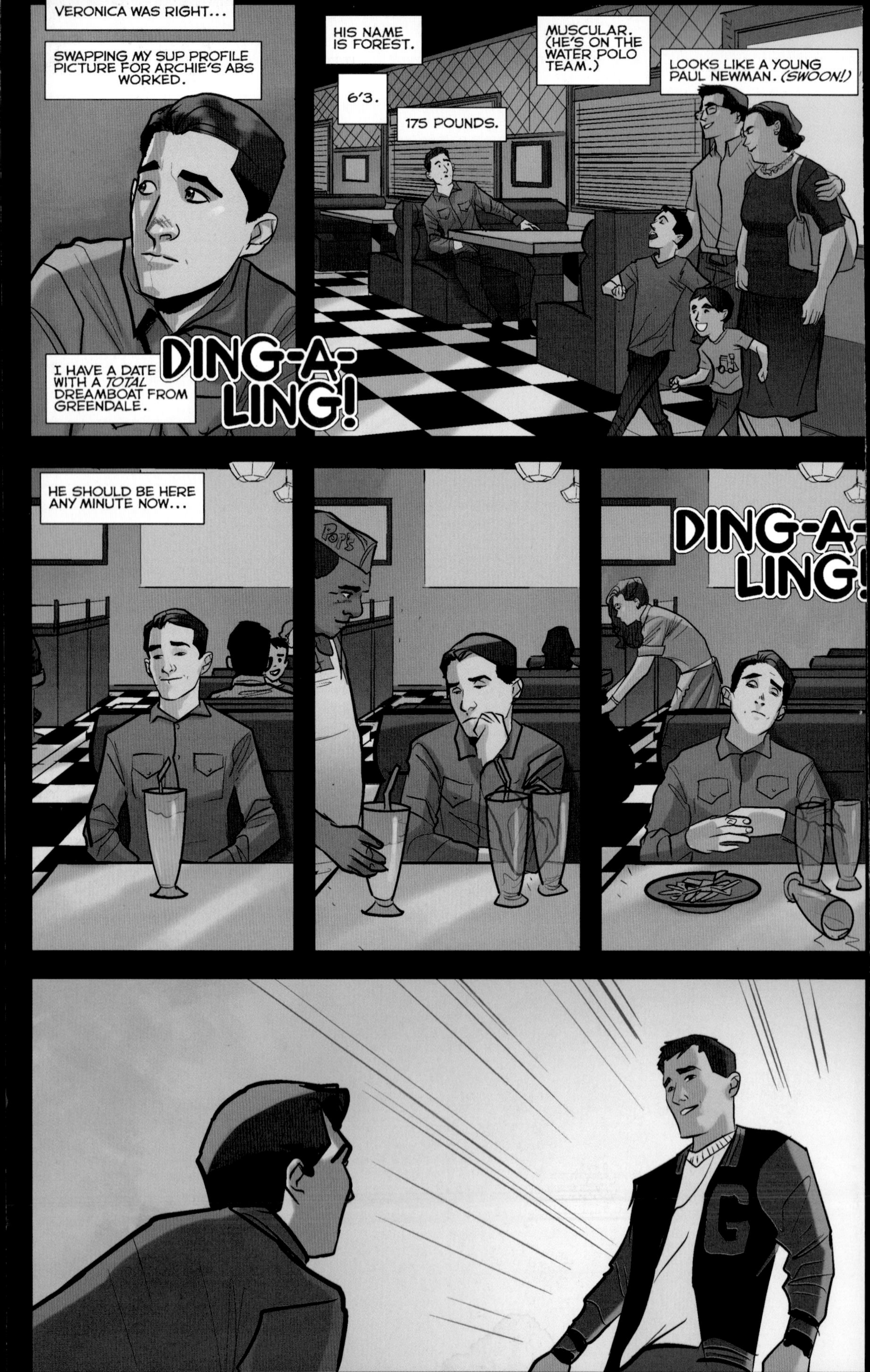
VERONICA WAS RIGHT...
SWAPPING MY SUP PROFILE PICTURE FOR ARCHIE'S ABS WORKED.
I HAVE A DATE WITH A *TOTAL* DREAMBOAT FROM GREENDALE.
DING-A-LING!
HIS NAME IS FOREST.
6'3.
175 POUNDS.
MUSCULAR. (HE'S ON THE WATER POLO TEAM.)
LOOKS LIKE A YOUNG PAUL NEWMAN. *(SWOON!)*
HE SHOULD BE HERE ANY MINUTE NOW...
POP'S
DING-A-LING!

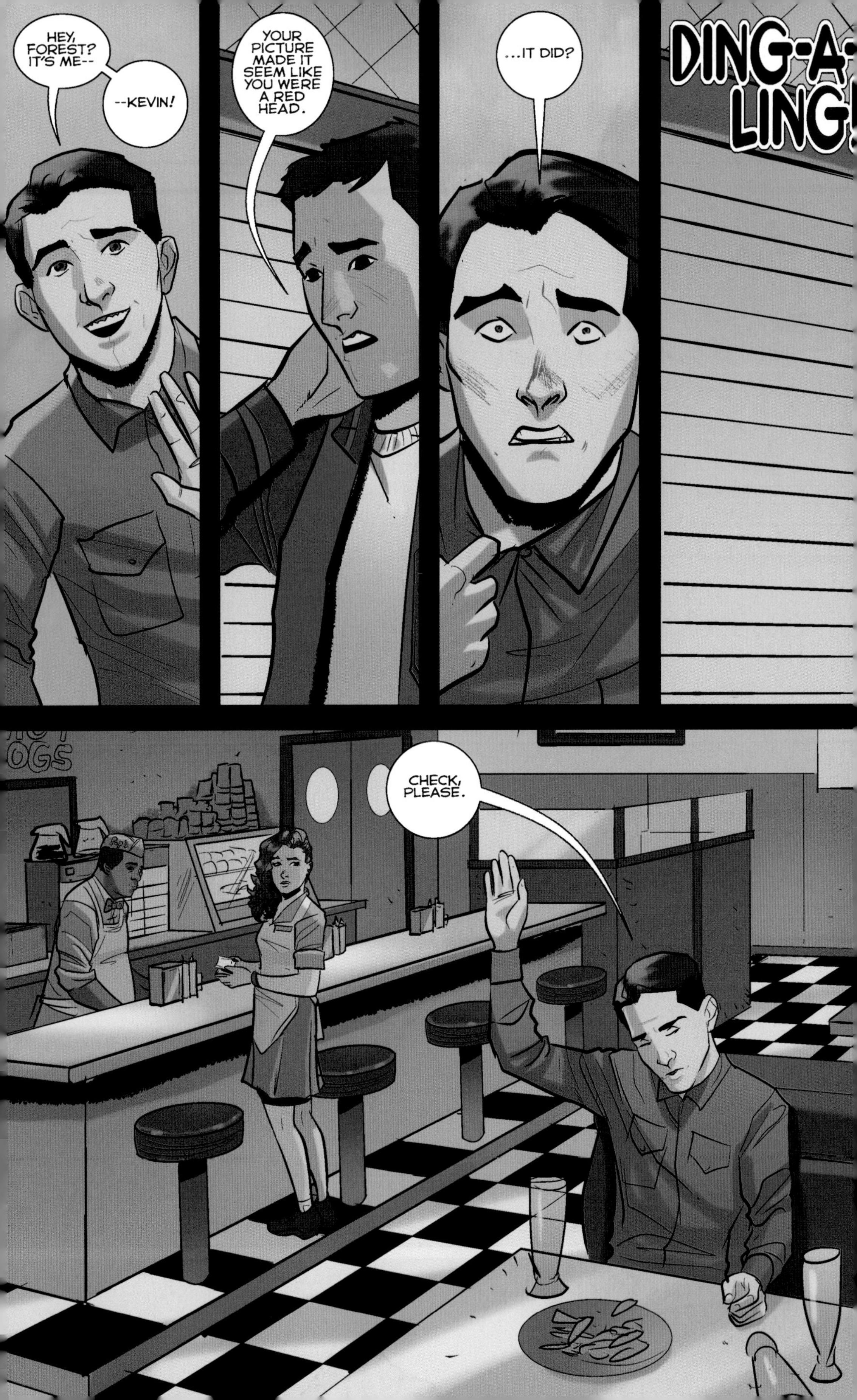
HEY, FOREST? IT'S ME--
--KEVIN!
YOUR PICTURE MADE IT SEEM LIKE YOU WERE A RED HEAD.
...IT DID?
DING-A-LING!
OGS
CHECK, PLEASE.

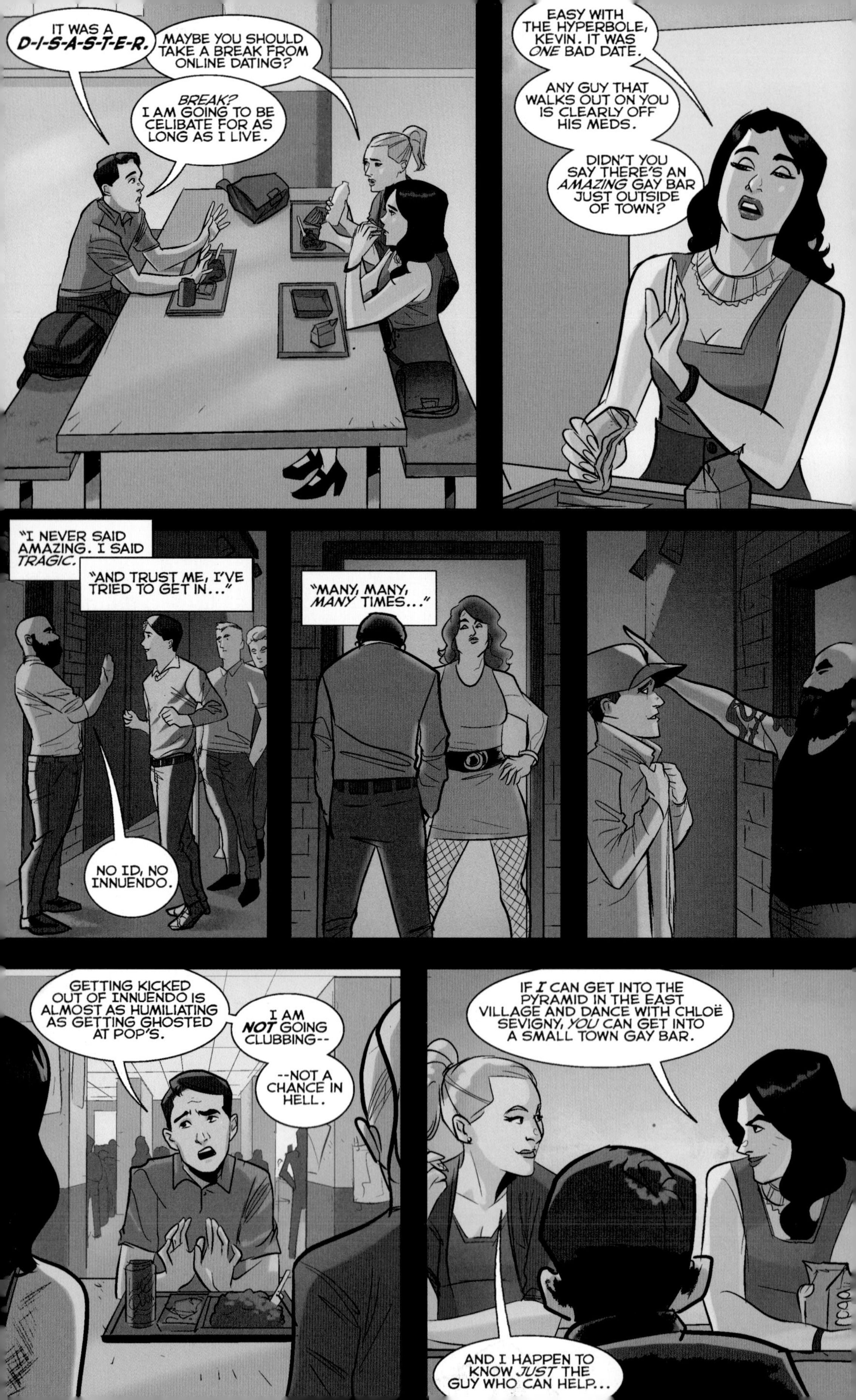

IT WAS A D-I-S-A-S-T-E-R.
MAYBE YOU SHOULD TAKE A BREAK FROM ONLINE DATING?
BREAK? I AM GOING TO BE CELIBATE FOR AS LONG AS I LIVE.
EASY WITH THE HYPERBOLE, KEVIN. IT WAS ONE BAD DATE.
ANY GUY THAT WALKS OUT ON YOU IS CLEARLY OFF HIS MEDS.
DIDN'T YOU SAY THERE'S AN AMAZING GAY BAR JUST OUTSIDE OF TOWN?
"I NEVER SAID AMAZING. I SAID TRAGIC.
"AND TRUST ME, I'VE TRIED TO GET IN..."
NO ID, NO INNUENDO.
"MANY, MANY, MANY TIMES..."
GETTING KICKED OUT OF INNUENDO IS ALMOST AS HUMILIATING AS GETTING GHOSTED AT POP'S.
I AM NOT GOING CLUBBING--
--NOT A CHANCE IN HELL.
IF I CAN GET INTO THE PYRAMID IN THE EAST VILLAGE AND DANCE WITH CHLOË SEVIGNY, YOU CAN GET INTO A SMALL TOWN GAY BAR.
AND I HAPPEN TO KNOW JUST THE GUY WHO CAN HELP...

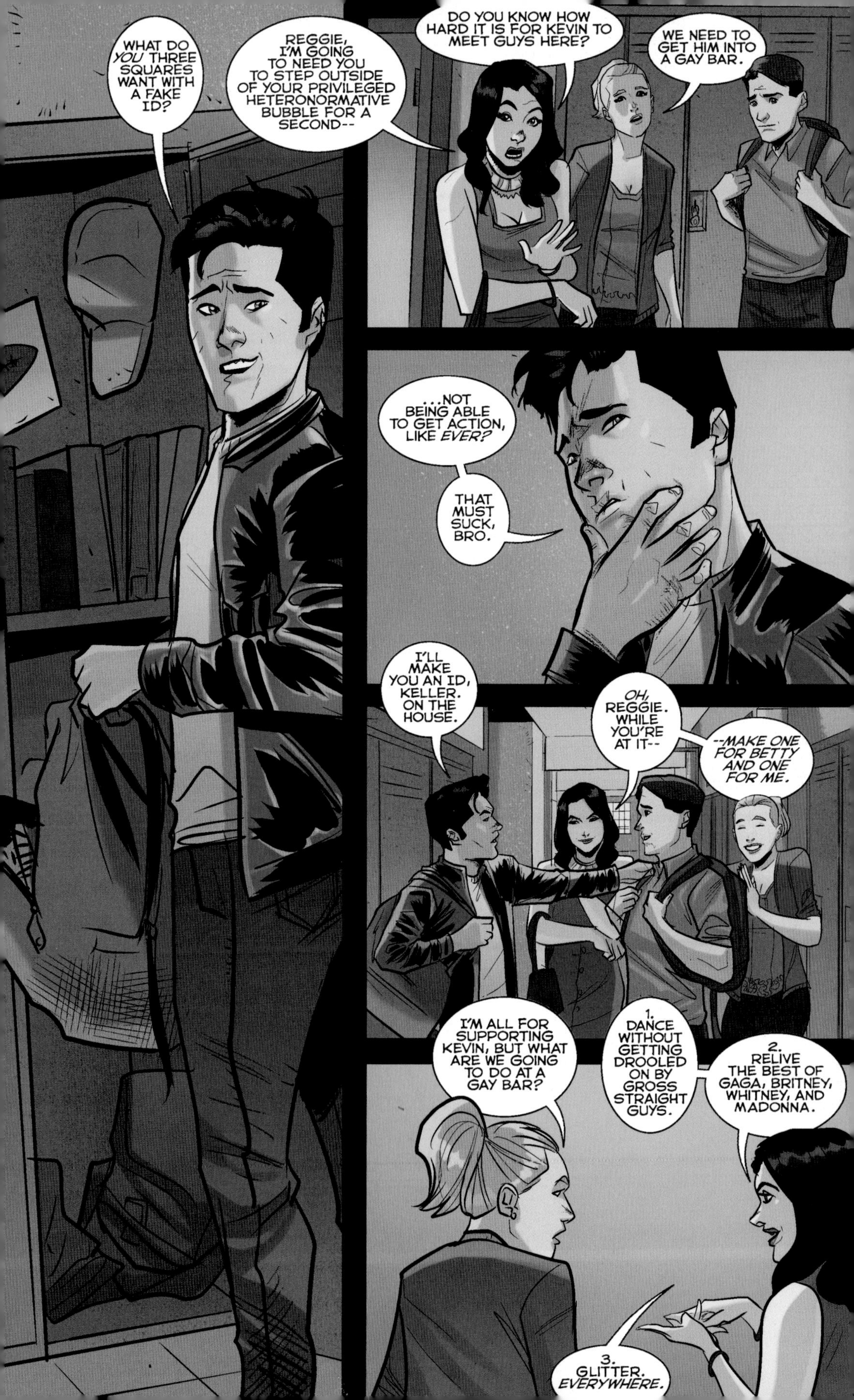
WHAT DO *YOU* THREE SQUARES WANT WITH A FAKE ID?
REGGIE, I'M GOING TO NEED YOU TO STEP OUTSIDE OF YOUR PRIVILEGED HETERONORMATIVE BUBBLE FOR A SECOND--
DO YOU KNOW HOW HARD IT IS FOR KEVIN TO MEET GUYS HERE?
WE NEED TO GET HIM INTO A GAY BAR.
...NOT BEING ABLE TO GET ACTION, LIKE *EVER?*
THAT MUST SUCK, BRO.
I'LL MAKE YOU AN ID, KELLER. ON THE HOUSE.
OH, REGGIE. WHILE YOU'RE AT IT--
--MAKE ONE FOR BETTY AND ONE FOR ME.
I'M ALL FOR SUPPORTING KEVIN, BUT WHAT ARE WE GOING TO DO AT A GAY BAR?
1. DANCE WITHOUT GETTING DROOLED ON BY GROSS STRAIGHT GUYS.
2. RELIVE THE BEST OF GAGA, BRITNEY, WHITNEY, AND MADONNA.
3. GLITTER. *EVERYWHERE.*

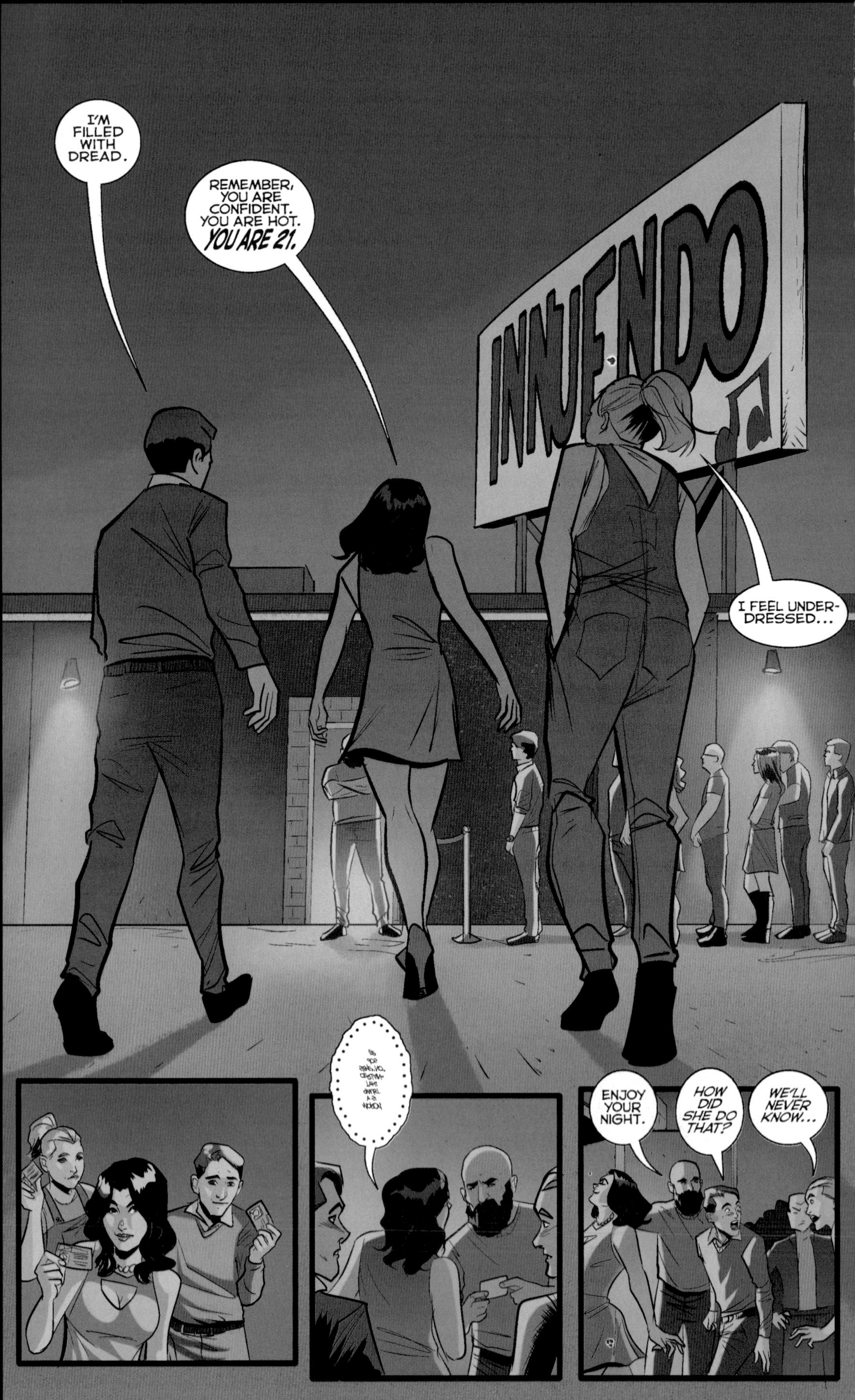
I'M FILLED WITH DREAD.
REMEMBER, YOU ARE CONFIDENT. YOU ARE HOT. YOU ARE 21.
INNUENDO
I FEEL UNDER-DRESSED...
ENJOY YOUR NIGHT.
HOW DID SHE DO THAT?
WE'LL NEVER KNOW...

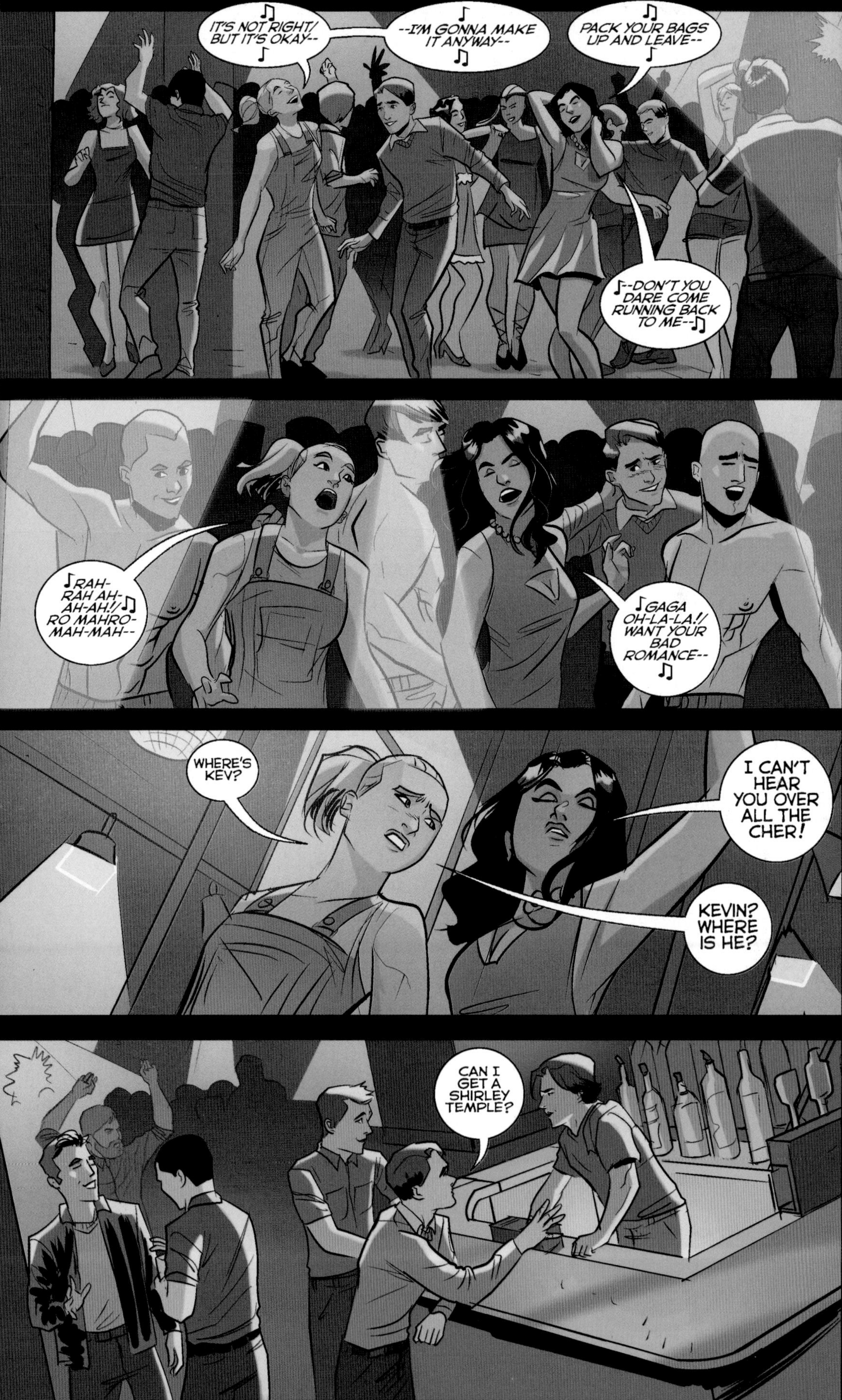
IT'S NOT RIGHT/ BUT IT'S OKAY--
--I'M GONNA MAKE IT ANYWAY--
PACK YOUR BAGS UP AND LEAVE--
--DON'T YOU DARE COME RUNNING BACK TO ME--
RAH-RAH AH-AH-AH!/ RO MAHRO-MAH-MAH--
GAGA OH-LA-LA!/ WANT YOUR BAD ROMANCE--
WHERE'S KEV?
I CAN'T HEAR YOU OVER ALL THE CHER!
KEVIN? WHERE IS HE?
CAN I GET A SHIRLEY TEMPLE?

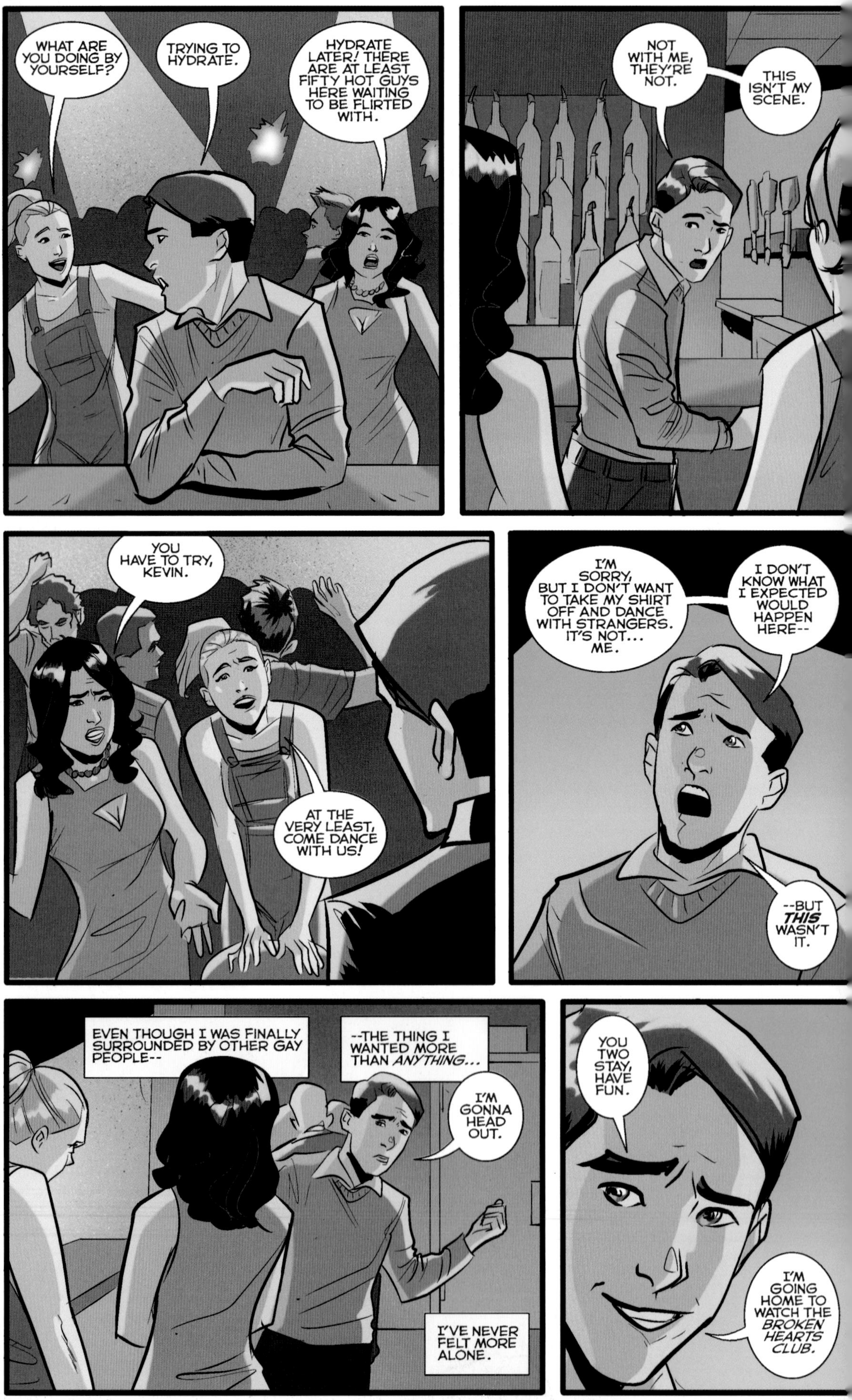
WHAT ARE YOU DOING BY YOURSELF?
TRYING TO HYDRATE.
HYDRATE LATER! THERE ARE AT LEAST FIFTY HOT GUYS HERE WAITING TO BE FLIRTED WITH.
NOT WITH ME, THEY'RE NOT.
THIS ISN'T MY SCENE.
YOU HAVE TO TRY, KEVIN.
AT THE VERY LEAST, COME DANCE WITH US!
I'M SORRY, BUT I DON'T WANT TO TAKE MY SHIRT OFF AND DANCE WITH STRANGERS. IT'S NOT... ME.
I DON'T KNOW WHAT I EXPECTED WOULD HAPPEN HERE--
--BUT *THIS* WASN'T IT.
EVEN THOUGH I WAS FINALLY SURROUNDED BY OTHER GAY PEOPLE--
--THE THING I WANTED MORE THAN *ANYTHING*...
I'M GONNA HEAD OUT.
I'VE NEVER FELT MORE ALONE.
YOU TWO STAY, HAVE FUN.
I'M GOING HOME TO WATCH THE *BROKEN HEARTS CLUB.*

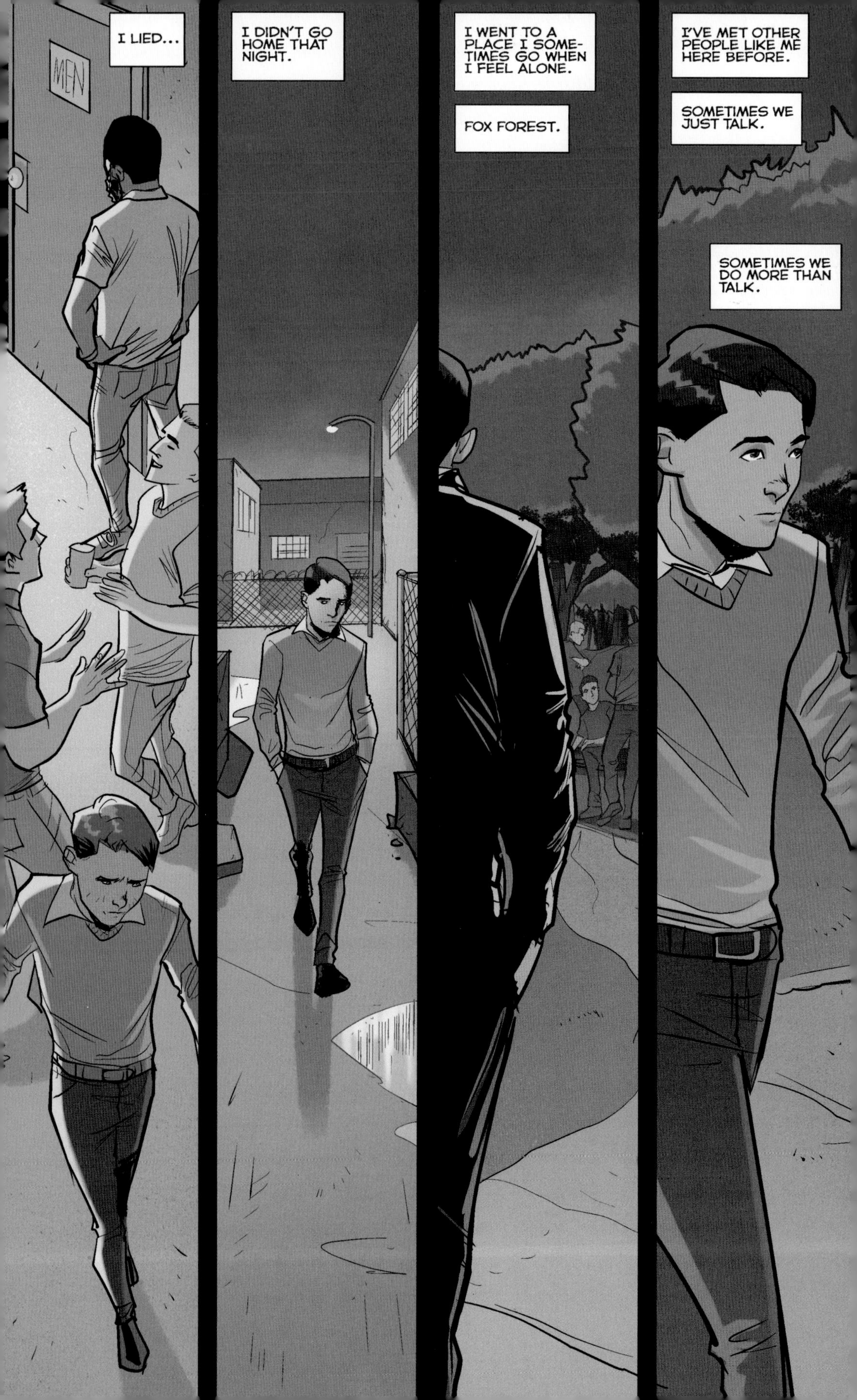
I LIED...
MEN
I DIDN'T GO HOME THAT NIGHT.
I WENT TO A PLACE I SOMETIMES GO WHEN I FEEL ALONE.
FOX FOREST.
I'VE MET OTHER PEOPLE LIKE ME HERE BEFORE.
SOMETIMES WE JUST TALK.
SOMETIMES WE DO MORE THAN TALK.

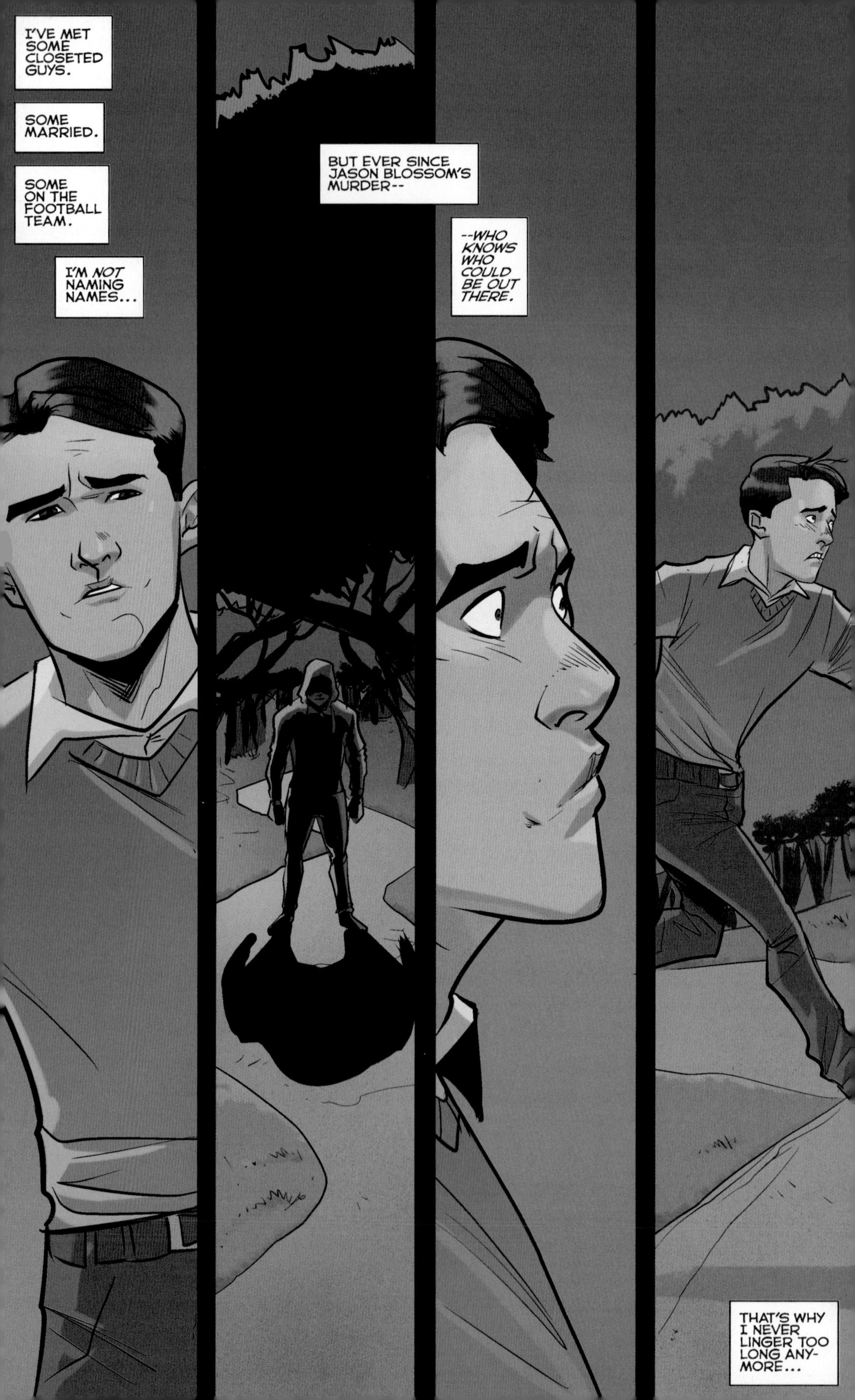
I'VE MET SOME CLOSETED GUYS.
SOME MARRIED.
SOME ON THE FOOTBALL TEAM.
I'M *NOT* NAMING NAMES...
BUT EVER SINCE JASON BLOSSOM'S MURDER--
--*WHO KNOWS WHO COULD BE OUT THERE.*
THAT'S WHY I NEVER LINGER TOO LONG ANY-MORE...

DINER

ISSUE FIVE

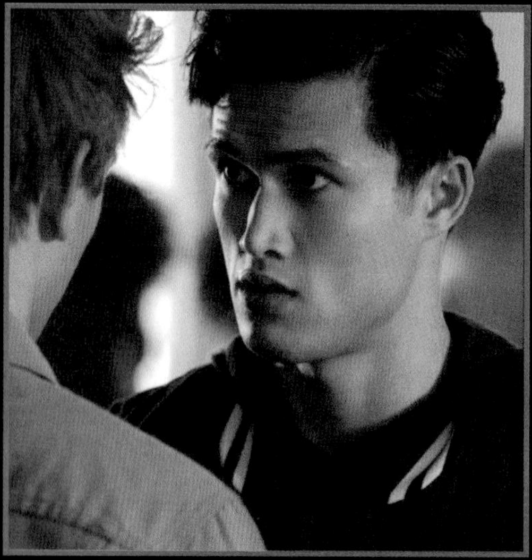

MANTLE THE MAGNIFICENT

WRITERS:
TESSA LEIGH WILLIAMS
AND **BRIAN E. PATERSON**

ART:
THOMAS PITILLI

COLORS:
ANDRE SZYMANOWICZ

LETTERS:
JANICE CHIANG

STARRING
REGGIE MANTLE

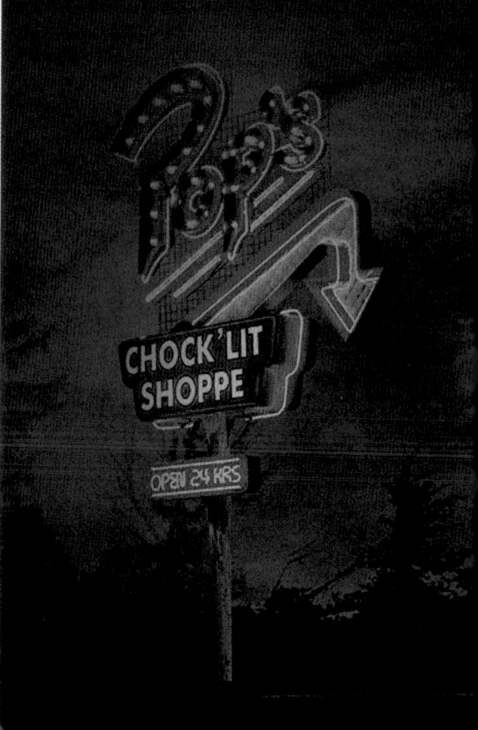
CHOCK'LIT SHOPPE
OPEN 24 HRS

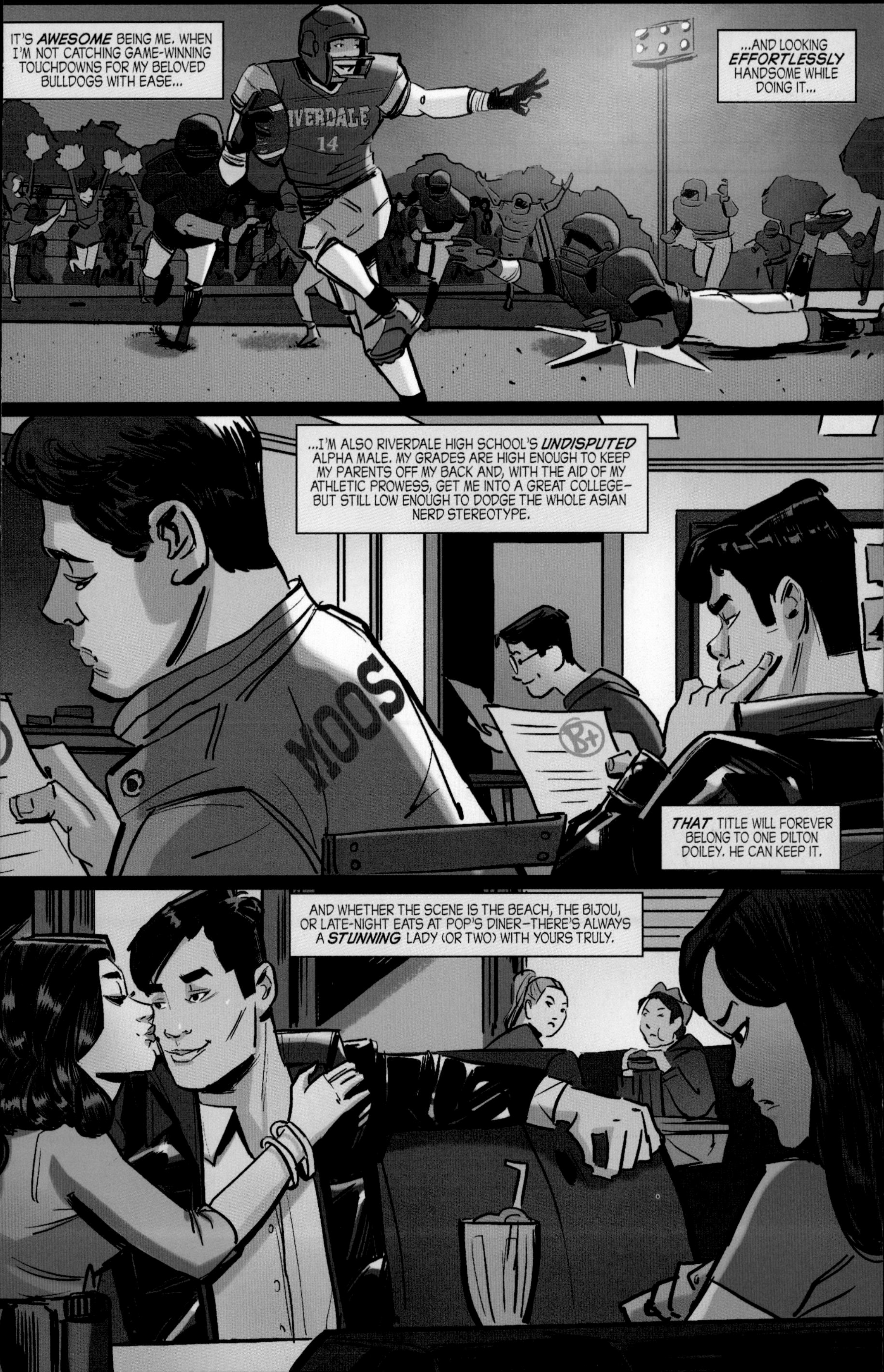
IT'S AWESOME BEING ME. WHEN I'M NOT CATCHING GAME-WINNING TOUCHDOWNS FOR MY BELOVED BULLDOGS WITH EASE...
RIVERDALE 14
...AND LOOKING EFFORTLESSLY HANDSOME WHILE DOING IT...
...I'M ALSO RIVERDALE HIGH SCHOOL'S UNDISPUTED ALPHA MALE. MY GRADES ARE HIGH ENOUGH TO KEEP MY PARENTS OFF MY BACK AND, WITH THE AID OF MY ATHLETIC PROWESS, GET ME INTO A GREAT COLLEGE–BUT STILL LOW ENOUGH TO DODGE THE WHOLE ASIAN NERD STEREOTYPE.
MOOS
B+
THAT TITLE WILL FOREVER BELONG TO ONE DILTON DOILEY. HE CAN KEEP IT.
AND WHETHER THE SCENE IS THE BEACH, THE BIJOU, OR LATE-NIGHT EATS AT POP'S DINER–THERE'S ALWAYS A STUNNING LADY (OR TWO) WITH YOURS TRULY.

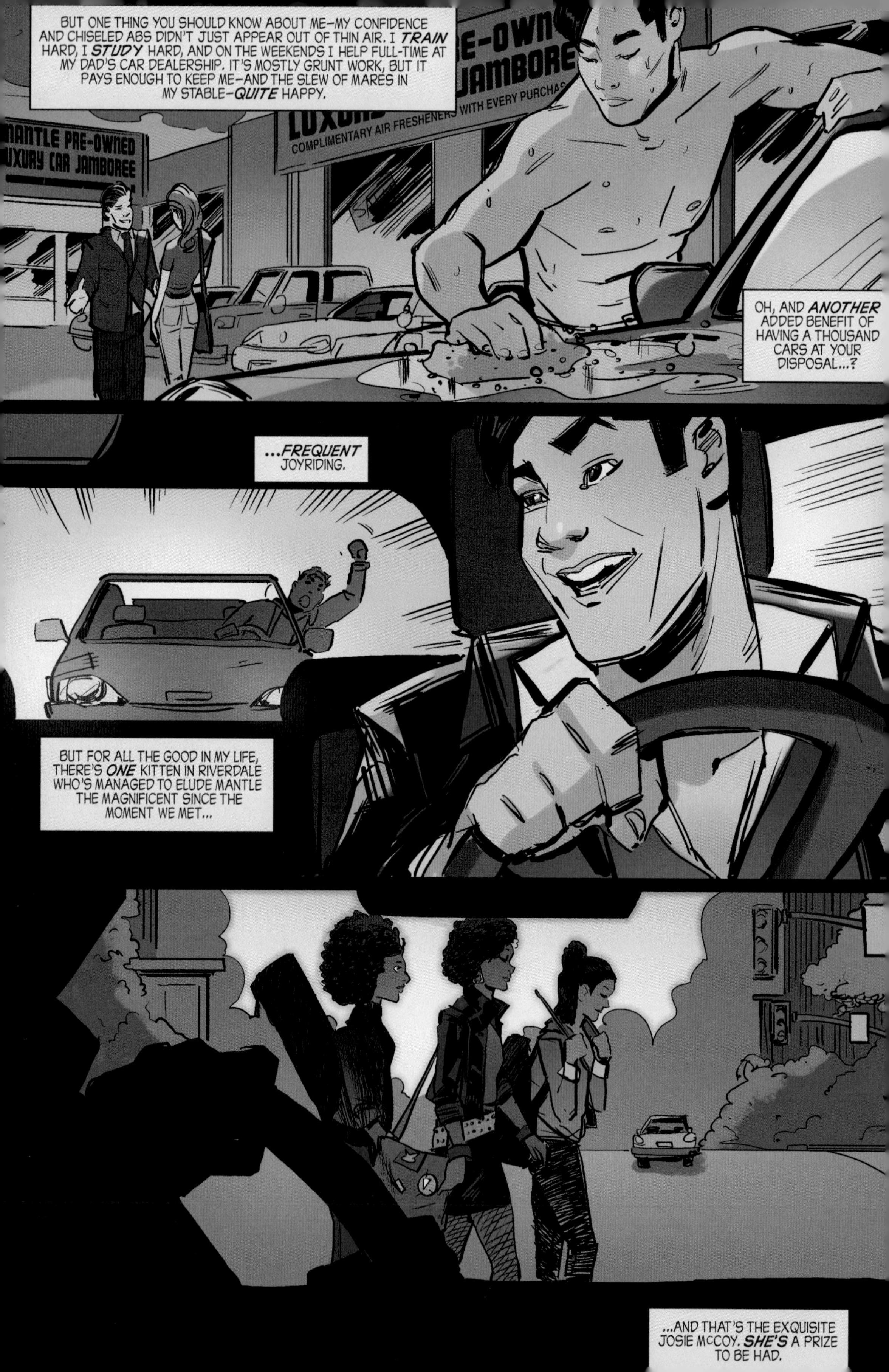
BUT ONE THING YOU SHOULD KNOW ABOUT ME—MY CONFIDENCE AND CHISELED ABS DIDN'T JUST APPEAR OUT OF THIN AIR. I TRAIN HARD, I STUDY HARD, AND ON THE WEEKENDS I HELP FULL-TIME AT MY DAD'S CAR DEALERSHIP. IT'S MOSTLY GRUNT WORK, BUT IT PAYS ENOUGH TO KEEP ME—AND THE SLEW OF MARES IN MY STABLE—QUITE HAPPY.
MANTLE PRE-OWNED LUXURY CAR JAMBOREE
COMPLIMENTARY AIR FRESHENERS WITH EVERY PURCHAS
OH, AND ANOTHER ADDED BENEFIT OF HAVING A THOUSAND CARS AT YOUR DISPOSAL...?
...FREQUENT JOYRIDING.
BUT FOR ALL THE GOOD IN MY LIFE, THERE'S ONE KITTEN IN RIVERDALE WHO'S MANAGED TO ELUDE MANTLE THE MAGNIFICENT SINCE THE MOMENT WE MET...
...AND THAT'S THE EXQUISITE JOSIE McCOY. SHE'S A PRIZE TO BE HAD.

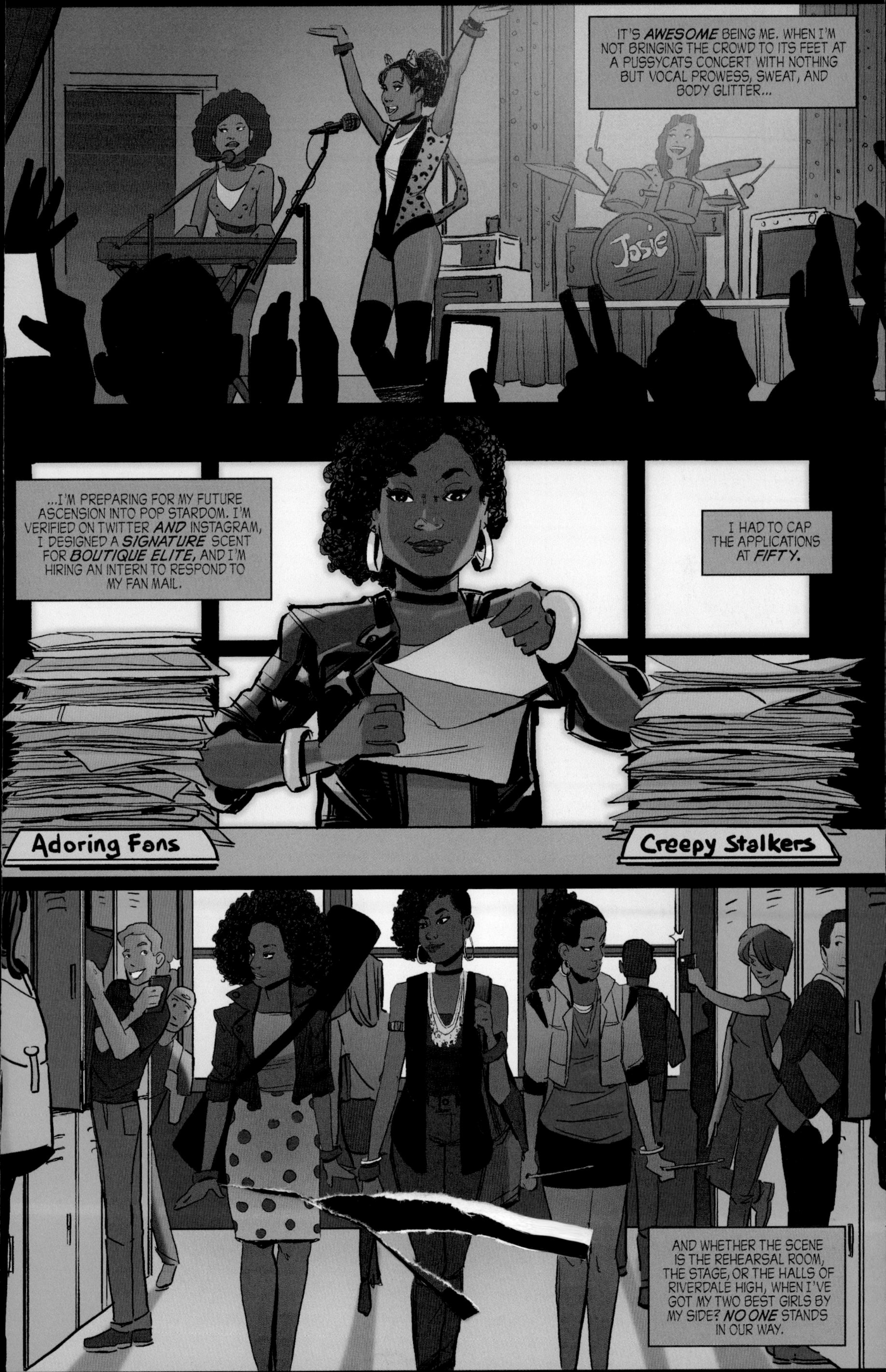
IT'S AWESOME BEING ME. WHEN I'M NOT BRINGING THE CROWD TO ITS FEET AT A PUSSYCATS CONCERT WITH NOTHING BUT VOCAL PROWESS, SWEAT, AND BODY GLITTER...
Josie
...I'M PREPARING FOR MY FUTURE ASCENSION INTO POP STARDOM. I'M VERIFIED ON TWITTER AND INSTAGRAM, I DESIGNED A SIGNATURE SCENT FOR BOUTIQUE ELITE, AND I'M HIRING AN INTERN TO RESPOND TO MY FAN MAIL.
I HAD TO CAP THE APPLICATIONS AT FIFTY.
Adoring Fans
Creepy Stalkers
AND WHETHER THE SCENE IS THE REHEARSAL ROOM, THE STAGE, OR THE HALLS OF RIVERDALE HIGH, WHEN I'VE GOT MY TWO BEST GIRLS BY MY SIDE? NO ONE STANDS IN OUR WAY.

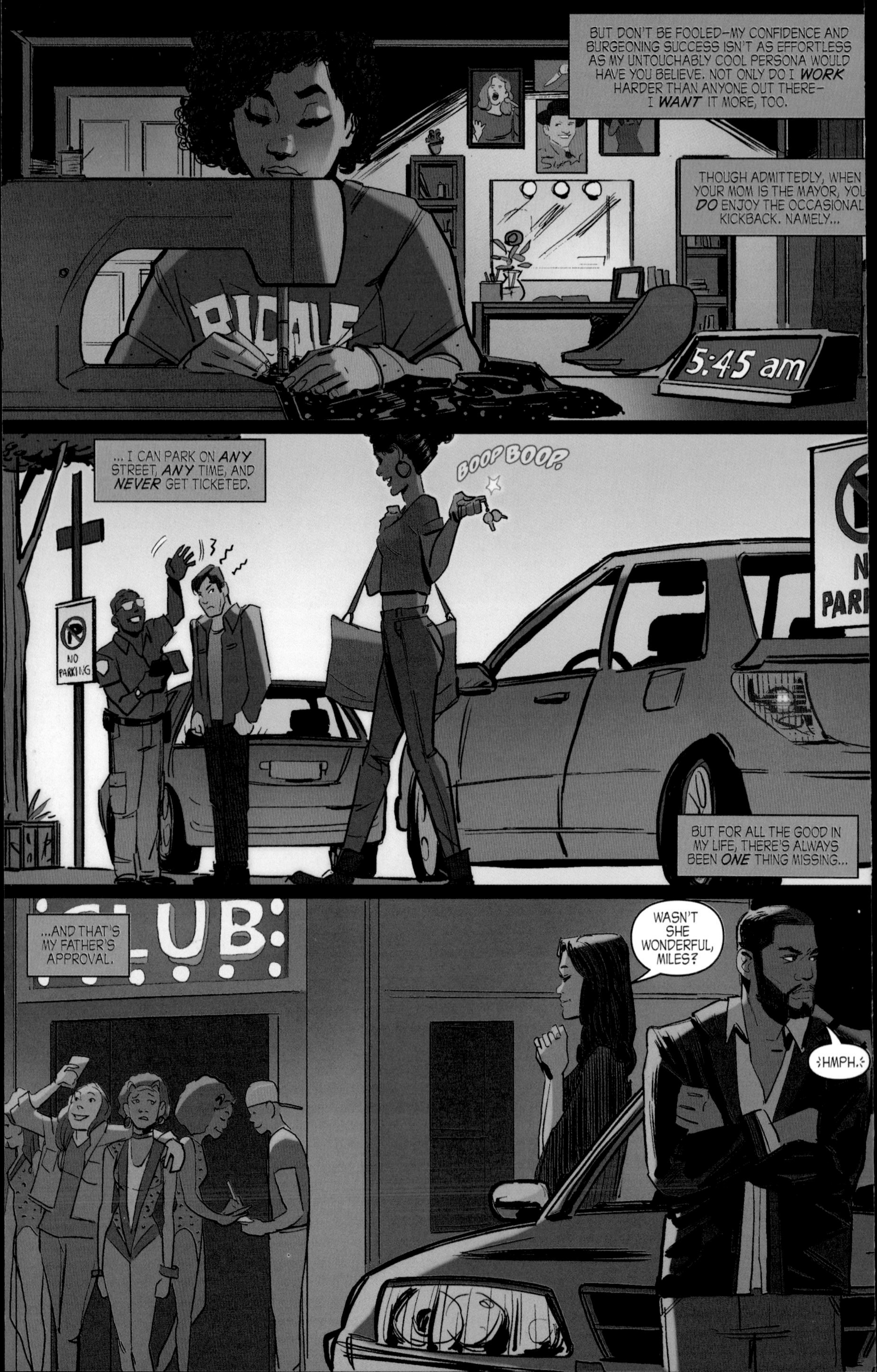
BUT DON'T BE FOOLED—MY CONFIDENCE AND BURGEONING SUCCESS ISN'T AS EFFORTLESS AS MY UNTOUCHABLY COOL PERSONA WOULD HAVE YOU BELIEVE. NOT ONLY DO I WORK HARDER THAN ANYONE OUT THERE— I WANT IT MORE, TOO.
THOUGH ADMITTEDLY, WHEN YOUR MOM IS THE MAYOR, YOU DO ENJOY THE OCCASIONAL KICKBACK. NAMELY...
5:45 am
... I CAN PARK ON ANY STREET, ANY TIME, AND NEVER GET TICKETED.
BOOP BOOP
NO PARKING
BUT FOR ALL THE GOOD IN MY LIFE, THERE'S ALWAYS BEEN ONE THING MISSING...
...AND THAT'S MY FATHER'S APPROVAL.
WASN'T SHE WONDERFUL, MILES?
HMPH.

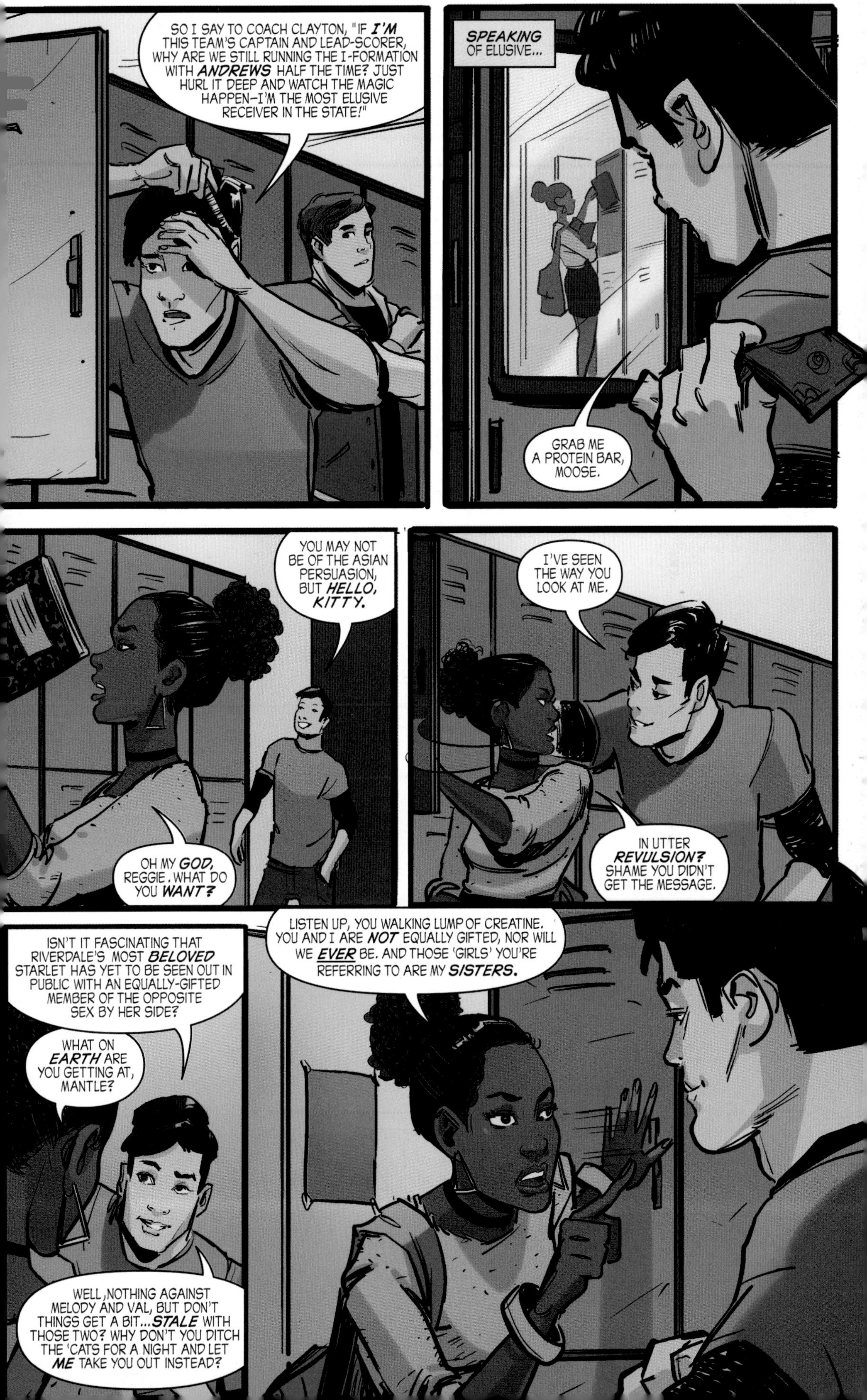
SO I SAY TO COACH CLAYTON, "IF I'M THIS TEAM'S CAPTAIN AND LEAD-SCORER, WHY ARE WE STILL RUNNING THE I-FORMATION WITH ANDREWS HALF THE TIME? JUST HURL IT DEEP AND WATCH THE MAGIC HAPPEN—I'M THE MOST ELUSIVE RECEIVER IN THE STATE!"
SPEAKING OF ELUSIVE...
GRAB ME A PROTEIN BAR, MOOSE.
YOU MAY NOT BE OF THE ASIAN PERSUASION, BUT HELLO, KITTY.
OH MY GOD, REGGIE. WHAT DO YOU WANT?
I'VE SEEN THE WAY YOU LOOK AT ME.
IN UTTER REVULSION? SHAME YOU DIDN'T GET THE MESSAGE.
ISN'T IT FASCINATING THAT RIVERDALE'S MOST BELOVED STARLET HAS YET TO BE SEEN OUT IN PUBLIC WITH AN EQUALLY-GIFTED MEMBER OF THE OPPOSITE SEX BY HER SIDE?
WHAT ON EARTH ARE YOU GETTING AT, MANTLE?
WELL, NOTHING AGAINST MELODY AND VAL, BUT DON'T THINGS GET A BIT...STALE WITH THOSE TWO? WHY DON'T YOU DITCH THE 'CATS FOR A NIGHT AND LET ME TAKE YOU OUT INSTEAD?
LISTEN UP, YOU WALKING LUMP OF CREATINE. YOU AND I ARE NOT EQUALLY GIFTED, NOR WILL WE EVER BE. AND THOSE 'GIRLS' YOU'RE REFERRING TO ARE MY SISTERS.

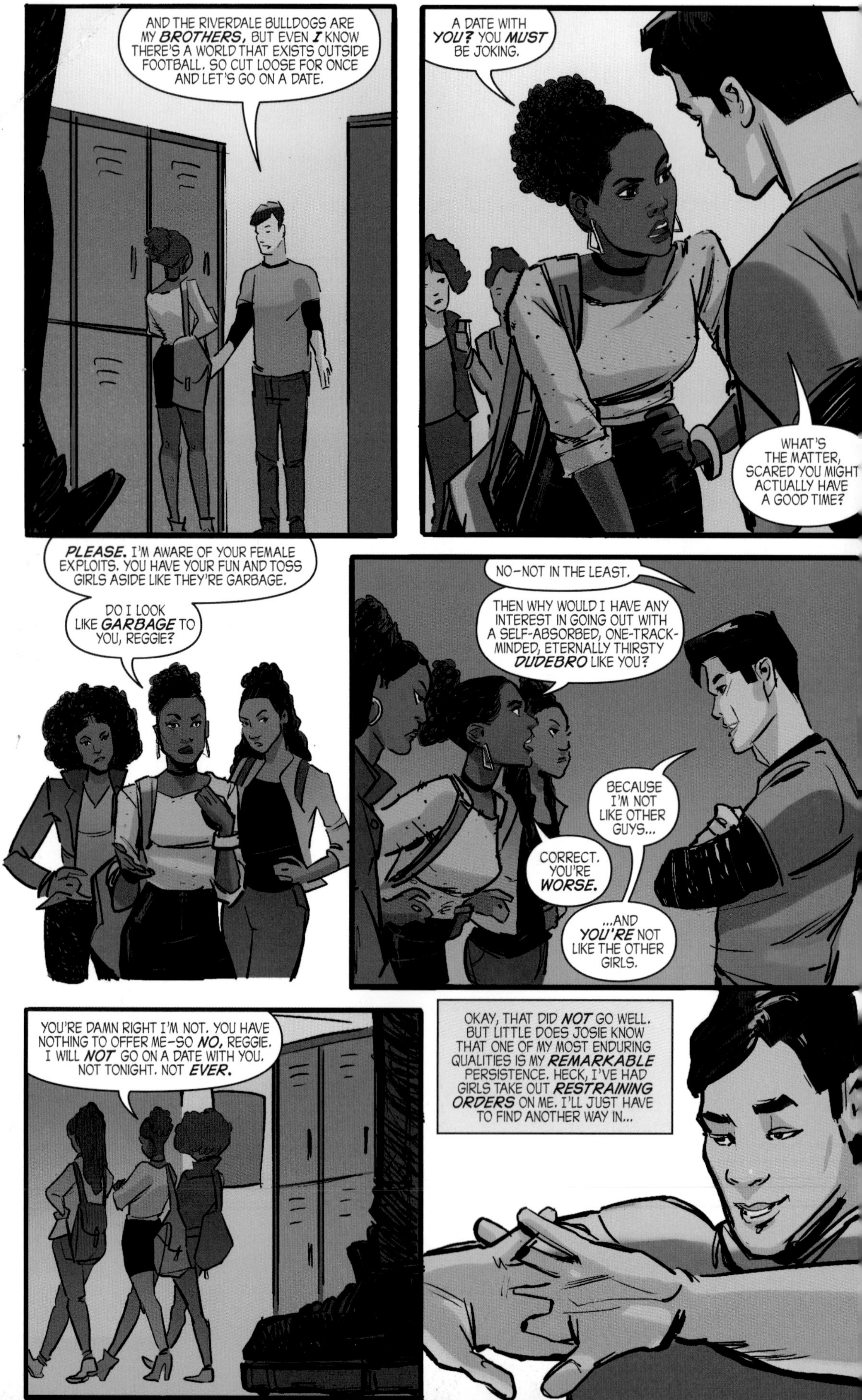
AND THE RIVERDALE BULLDOGS ARE MY BROTHERS, BUT EVEN I KNOW THERE'S A WORLD THAT EXISTS OUTSIDE FOOTBALL. SO CUT LOOSE FOR ONCE AND LET'S GO ON A DATE.
A DATE WITH YOU? YOU MUST BE JOKING.
WHAT'S THE MATTER, SCARED YOU MIGHT ACTUALLY HAVE A GOOD TIME?
PLEASE. I'M AWARE OF YOUR FEMALE EXPLOITS. YOU HAVE YOUR FUN AND TOSS GIRLS ASIDE LIKE THEY'RE GARBAGE.
DO I LOOK LIKE GARBAGE TO YOU, REGGIE?
NO—NOT IN THE LEAST.
THEN WHY WOULD I HAVE ANY INTEREST IN GOING OUT WITH A SELF-ABSORBED, ONE-TRACK-MINDED, ETERNALLY THIRSTY DUDEBRO LIKE YOU?
BECAUSE I'M NOT LIKE OTHER GUYS...
CORRECT. YOU'RE WORSE.
...AND YOU'RE NOT LIKE THE OTHER GIRLS.
YOU'RE DAMN RIGHT I'M NOT. YOU HAVE NOTHING TO OFFER ME—SO NO, REGGIE. I WILL NOT GO ON A DATE WITH YOU. NOT TONIGHT. NOT EVER.
OKAY, THAT DID NOT GO WELL. BUT LITTLE DOES JOSIE KNOW THAT ONE OF MY MOST ENDURING QUALITIES IS MY REMARKABLE PERSISTENCE. HECK, I'VE HAD GIRLS TAKE OUT RESTRAINING ORDERS ON ME. I'LL JUST HAVE TO FIND ANOTHER WAY IN...

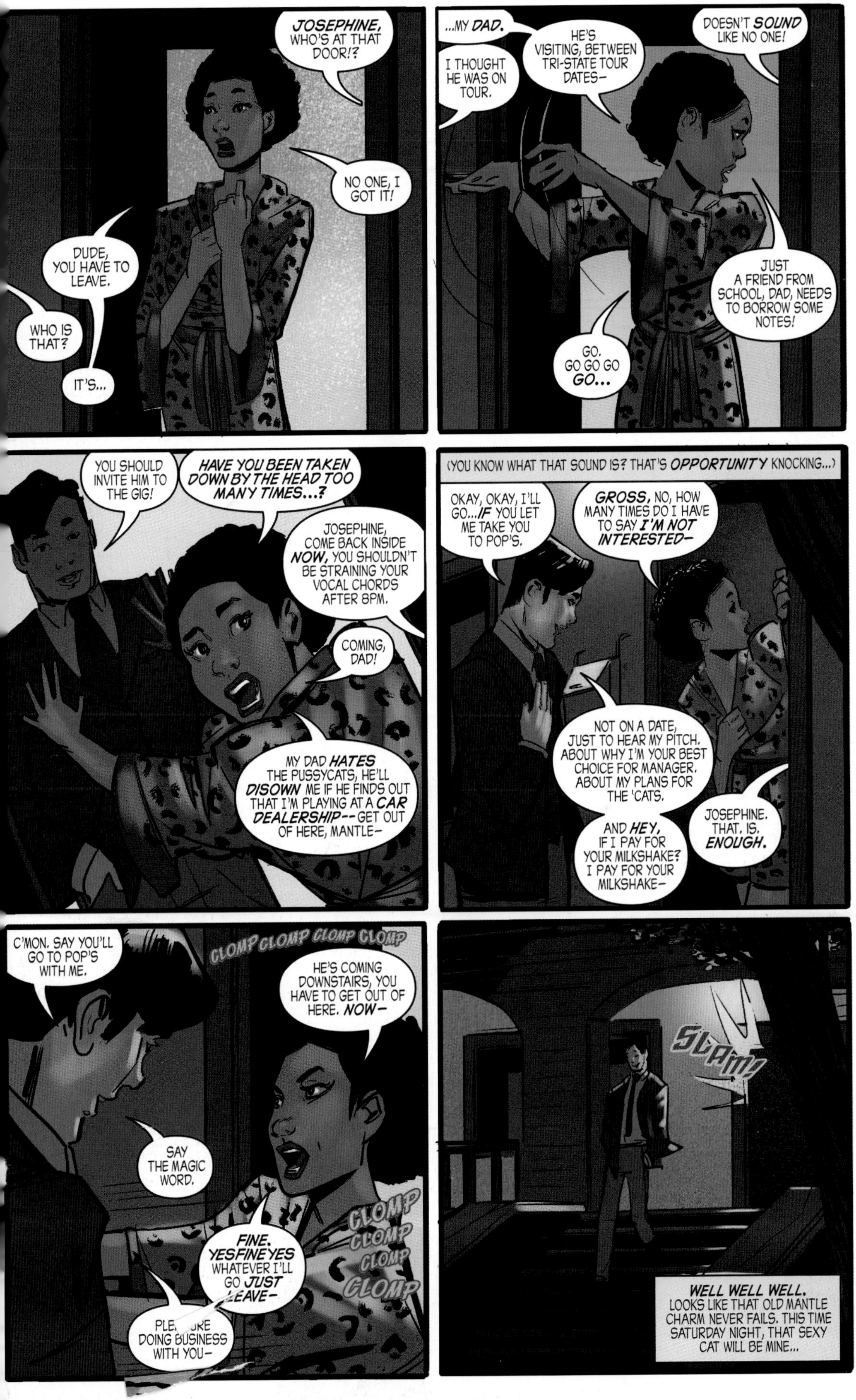
JOSEPHINE, WHO'S AT THAT DOOR!?
NO ONE, I GOT IT!
DUDE, YOU HAVE TO LEAVE.
WHO IS THAT?
IT'S...
...MY DAD.
I THOUGHT HE WAS ON TOUR.
HE'S VISITING, BETWEEN TRI-STATE TOUR DATES-
DOESN'T SOUND LIKE NO ONE!
JUST A FRIEND FROM SCHOOL, DAD, NEEDS TO BORROW SOME NOTES!
GO. GO GO GO GO...
YOU SHOULD INVITE HIM TO THE GIG!
HAVE YOU BEEN TAKEN DOWN BY THE HEAD TOO MANY TIMES...?
JOSEPHINE, COME BACK INSIDE NOW, YOU SHOULDN'T BE STRAINING YOUR VOCAL CHORDS AFTER 8PM.
COMING, DAD!
MY DAD HATES THE PUSSYCATS, HE'LL DISOWN ME IF HE FINDS OUT THAT I'M PLAYING AT A CAR DEALERSHIP--GET OUT OF HERE, MANTLE-
(YOU KNOW WHAT THAT SOUND IS? THAT'S OPPORTUNITY KNOCKING...)
OKAY, OKAY, I'LL GO...IF YOU LET ME TAKE YOU TO POP'S.
GROSS, NO, HOW MANY TIMES DO I HAVE TO SAY I'M NOT INTERESTED-
NOT ON A DATE, JUST TO HEAR MY PITCH. ABOUT WHY I'M YOUR BEST CHOICE FOR MANAGER. ABOUT MY PLANS FOR THE 'CATS.
AND HEY, IF I PAY FOR YOUR MILKSHAKE? I PAY FOR YOUR MILKSHAKE-
JOSEPHINE. THAT. IS. ENOUGH.
C'MON. SAY YOU'LL GO TO POP'S WITH ME.
CLOMP CLOMP CLOMP CLOMP
HE'S COMING DOWNSTAIRS, YOU HAVE TO GET OUT OF HERE. NOW-
SAY THE MAGIC WORD.
FINE. YESFINEYES WHATEVER I'LL GO JUST LEAVE-
CLOMP CLOMP CLOMP CLOMP
PLEASURE DOING BUSINESS WITH YOU-
SLAM!
WELL WELL WELL. LOOKS LIKE THAT OLD MANTLE CHARM NEVER FAILS. THIS TIME SATURDAY NIGHT, THAT SEXY CAT WILL BE MINE...

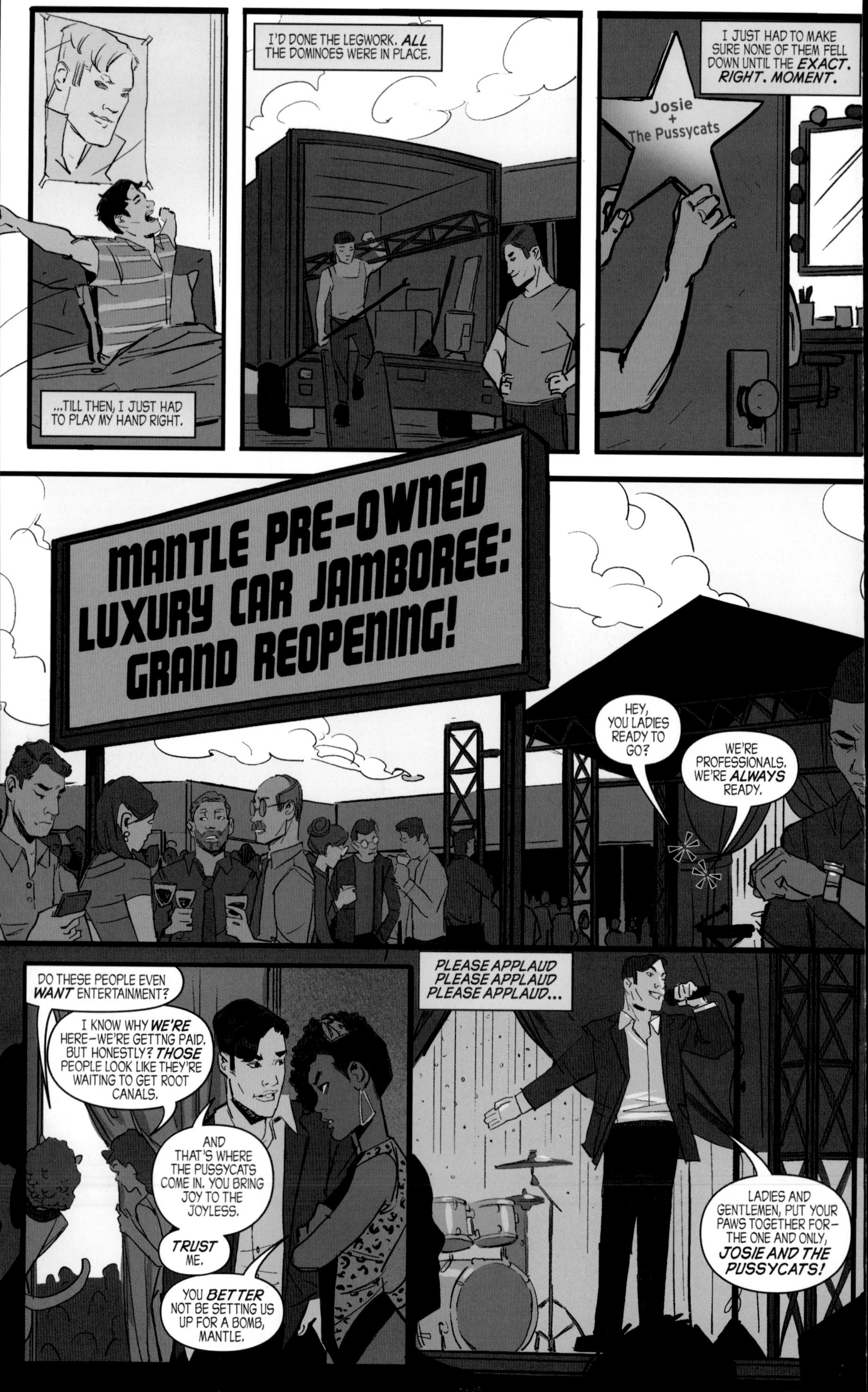
...TILL THEN, I JUST HAD TO PLAY MY HAND RIGHT.
I'D DONE THE LEGWORK. ALL THE DOMINOES WERE IN PLACE.
I JUST HAD TO MAKE SURE NONE OF THEM FELL DOWN UNTIL THE EXACT. RIGHT. MOMENT.
Josie + The Pussycats
MANTLE PRE-OWNED LUXURY CAR JAMBOREE: GRAND REOPENING!
HEY, YOU LADIES READY TO GO?
WE'RE PROFESSIONALS. WE'RE ALWAYS READY.
DO THESE PEOPLE EVEN WANT ENTERTAINMENT?
I KNOW WHY WE'RE HERE—WE'RE GETTNG PAID. BUT HONESTLY? THOSE PEOPLE LOOK LIKE THEY'RE WAITING TO GET ROOT CANALS.
AND THAT'S WHERE THE PUSSYCATS COME IN. YOU BRING JOY TO THE JOYLESS.
TRUST ME.
YOU BETTER NOT BE SETTING US UP FOR A BOMB, MANTLE.
PLEASE APPLAUD PLEASE APPLAUD PLEASE APPLAUD...
LADIES AND GENTLEMEN, PUT YOUR PAWS TOGETHER FOR—THE ONE AND ONLY, JOSIE AND THE PUSSYCATS!

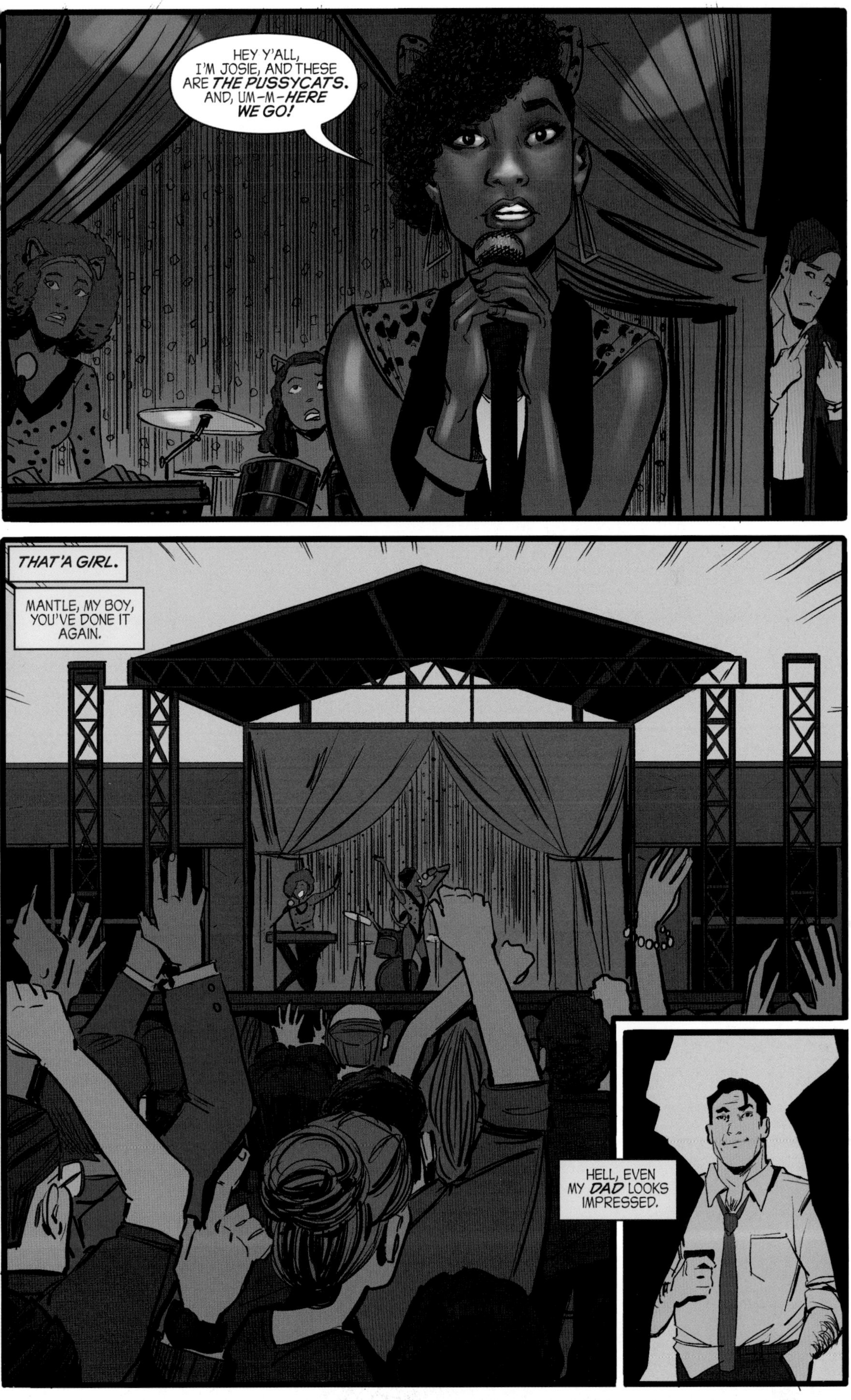
HEY Y'ALL, I'M JOSIE, AND THESE ARE THE PUSSYCATS. AND, UM-M-HERE WE GO!
THAT'A GIRL.
MANTLE, MY BOY, YOU'VE DONE IT AGAIN.
HELL, EVEN MY DAD LOOKS IMPRESSED.

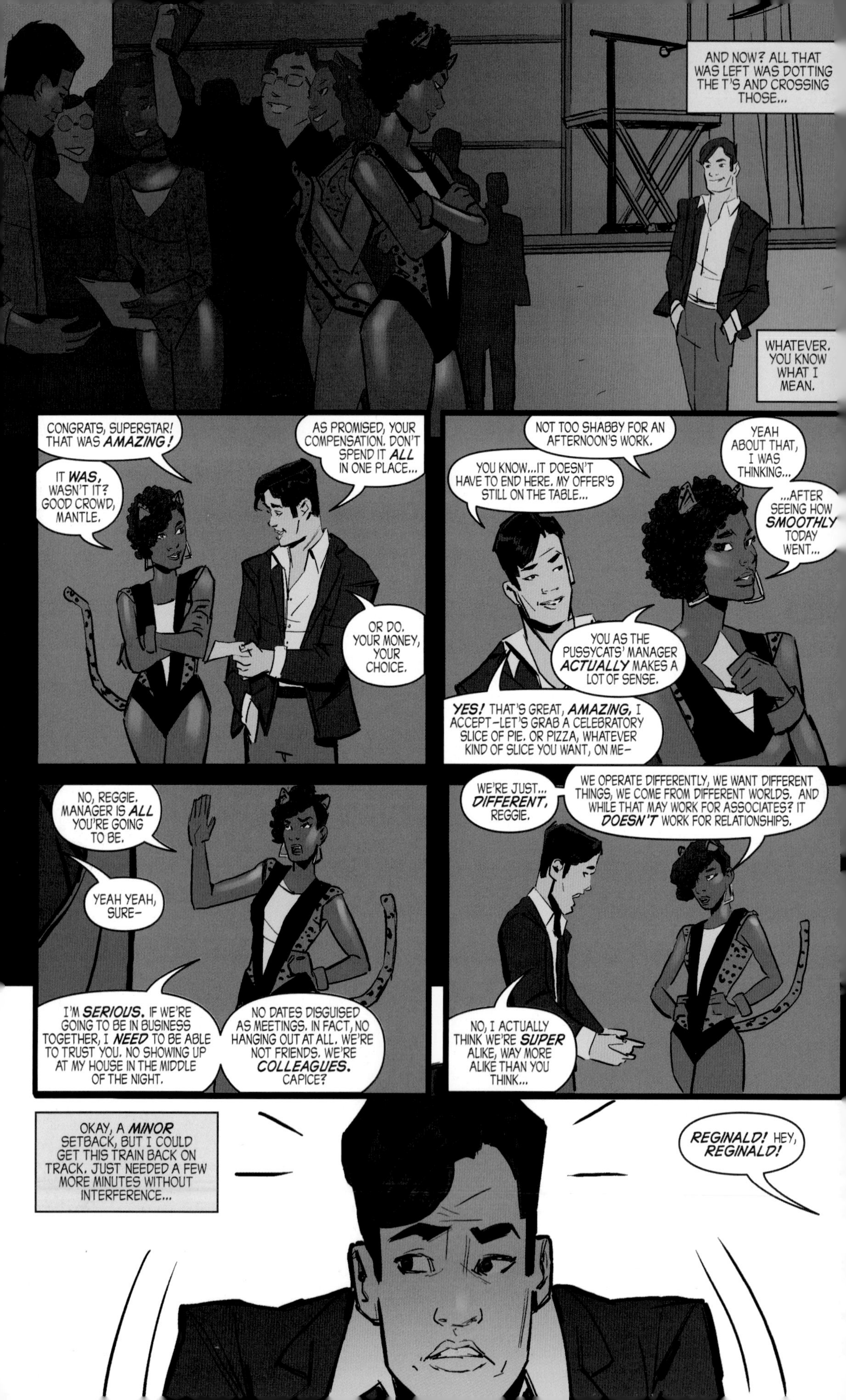
AND NOW? ALL THAT WAS LEFT WAS DOTTING THE T'S AND CROSSING THOSE...
WHATEVER. YOU KNOW WHAT I MEAN.
CONGRATS, SUPERSTAR! THAT WAS AMAZING!
AS PROMISED, YOUR COMPENSATION. DON'T SPEND IT ALL IN ONE PLACE...
IT WAS, WASN'T IT? GOOD CROWD, MANTLE.
OR DO. YOUR MONEY, YOUR CHOICE.
NOT TOO SHABBY FOR AN AFTERNOON'S WORK.
YOU KNOW...IT DOESN'T HAVE TO END HERE. MY OFFER'S STILL ON THE TABLE...
YEAH ABOUT THAT, I WAS THINKING...
...AFTER SEEING HOW SMOOTHLY TODAY WENT...
YOU AS THE PUSSYCATS' MANAGER ACTUALLY MAKES A LOT OF SENSE.
YES! THAT'S GREAT, AMAZING, I ACCEPT–LET'S GRAB A CELEBRATORY SLICE OF PIE. OR PIZZA, WHATEVER KIND OF SLICE YOU WANT, ON ME–
NO, REGGIE. MANAGER IS ALL YOU'RE GOING TO BE.
YEAH YEAH, SURE–
I'M SERIOUS. IF WE'RE GOING TO BE IN BUSINESS TOGETHER, I NEED TO BE ABLE TO TRUST YOU. NO SHOWING UP AT MY HOUSE IN THE MIDDLE OF THE NIGHT.
NO DATES DISGUISED AS MEETINGS. IN FACT, NO HANGING OUT AT ALL. WE'RE NOT FRIENDS. WE'RE COLLEAGUES. CAPICE?
WE'RE JUST... DIFFERENT, REGGIE.
WE OPERATE DIFFERENTLY, WE WANT DIFFERENT THINGS, WE COME FROM DIFFERENT WORLDS. AND WHILE THAT MAY WORK FOR ASSOCIATES? IT DOESN'T WORK FOR RELATIONSHIPS.
NO, I ACTUALLY THINK WE'RE SUPER ALIKE, WAY MORE ALIKE THAN YOU THINK...
OKAY, A MINOR SETBACK, BUT I COULD GET THIS TRAIN BACK ON TRACK. JUST NEEDED A FEW MORE MINUTES WITHOUT INTERFERENCE...
REGINALD! HEY, REGINALD!

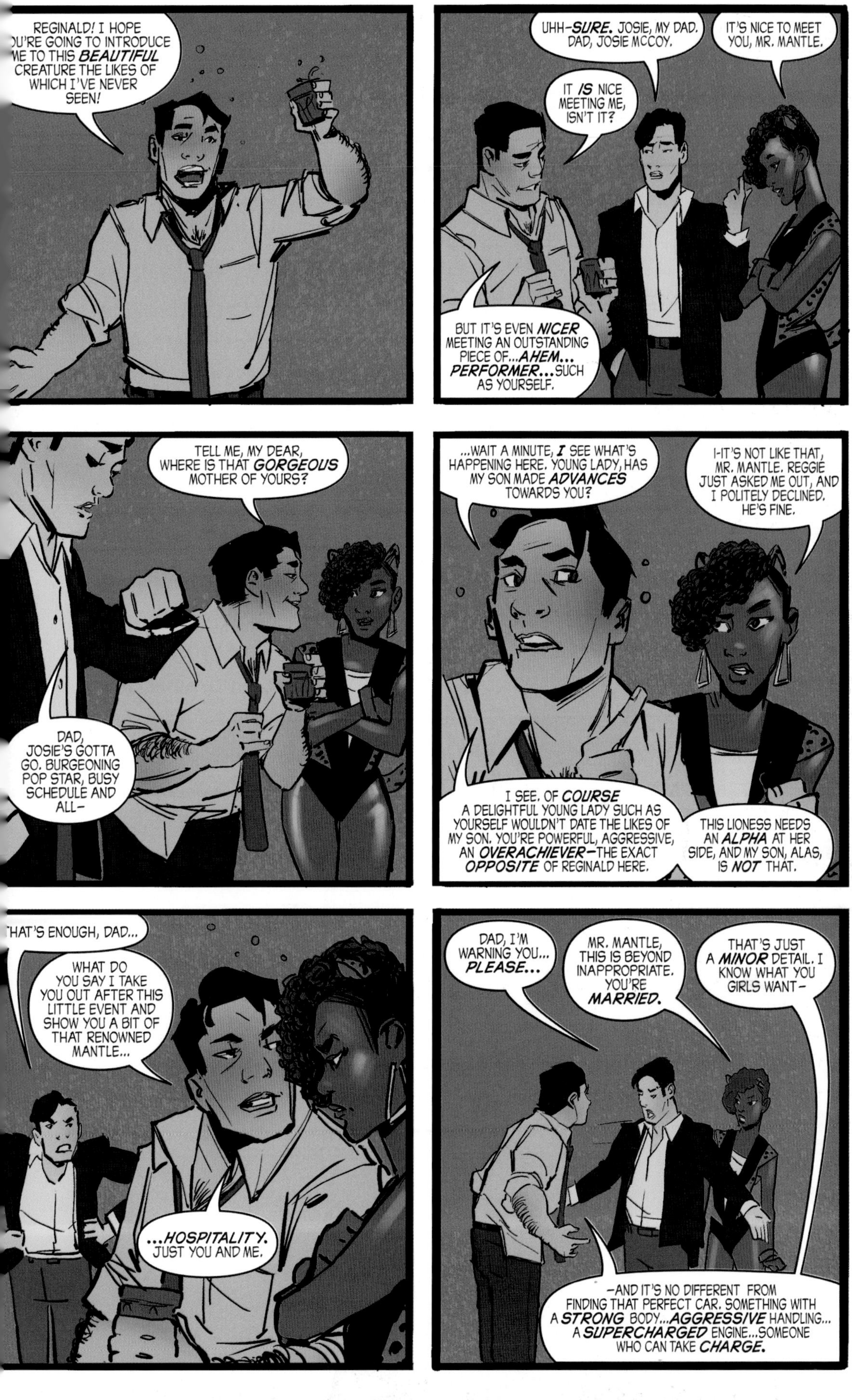
REGINALD! I HOPE OU'RE GOING TO INTRODUCE ME TO THIS *BEAUTIFUL* CREATURE THE LIKES OF WHICH I'VE NEVER SEEN!
UHH–*SURE.* JOSIE, MY DAD. DAD, JOSIE MCCOY.
IT'S NICE TO MEET YOU, MR. MANTLE.
IT *IS* NICE MEETING ME, ISN'T IT?
BUT IT'S EVEN *NICER* MEETING AN OUTSTANDING PIECE OF...*AHEM... PERFORMER...*SUCH AS YOURSELF.
TELL ME, MY DEAR, WHERE IS THAT *GORGEOUS* MOTHER OF YOURS?
DAD, JOSIE'S GOTTA GO. BURGEONING POP STAR, BUSY SCHEDULE AND ALL–
...WAIT A MINUTE, *I* SEE WHAT'S HAPPENING HERE. YOUNG LADY, HAS MY SON MADE *ADVANCES* TOWARDS YOU?
I-IT'S NOT LIKE THAT, MR. MANTLE. REGGIE JUST ASKED ME OUT, AND I POLITELY DECLINED. HE'S FINE.
I SEE. OF *COURSE* A DELIGHTFUL YOUNG LADY SUCH AS YOURSELF WOULDN'T DATE THE LIKES OF MY SON. YOU'RE POWERFUL, AGGRESSIVE, AN *OVERACHIEVER*–THE EXACT *OPPOSITE* OF REGINALD HERE.
THIS LIONESS NEEDS AN *ALPHA* AT HER SIDE, AND MY SON, ALAS, IS *NOT* THAT.
HAT'S ENOUGH, DAD...
WHAT DO YOU SAY I TAKE YOU OUT AFTER THIS LITTLE EVENT AND SHOW YOU A BIT OF THAT RENOWNED MANTLE...
...HOSPITALITY. JUST YOU AND ME.
DAD, I'M WARNING YOU... *PLEASE...*
MR. MANTLE, THIS IS BEYOND INAPPROPRIATE. YOU'RE *MARRIED.*
THAT'S JUST A *MINOR* DETAIL. I KNOW WHAT YOU GIRLS WANT–
–AND IT'S NO DIFFERENT FROM FINDING THAT PERFECT CAR. SOMETHING WITH A *STRONG* BODY...*AGGRESSIVE* HANDLING... A *SUPERCHARGED* ENGINE...SOMEONE WHO CAN TAKE *CHARGE.*

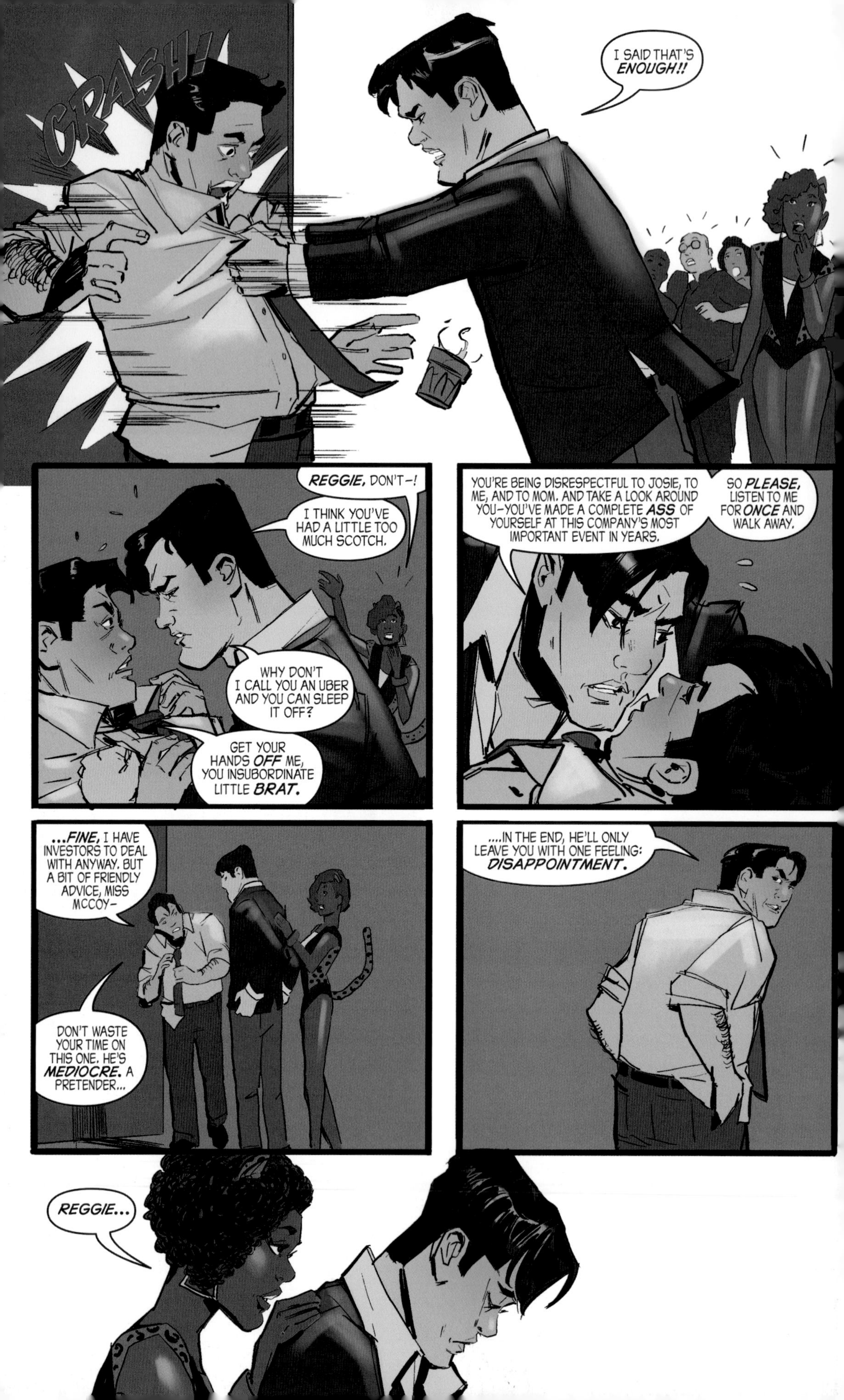

CRASH!!
I SAID THAT'S ENOUGH!!
REGGIE, DON'T–!
I THINK YOU'VE HAD A LITTLE TOO MUCH SCOTCH.
WHY DON'T I CALL YOU AN UBER AND YOU CAN SLEEP IT OFF?
GET YOUR HANDS OFF ME, YOU INSUBORDINATE LITTLE BRAT.
YOU'RE BEING DISRESPECTFUL TO JOSIE, TO ME, AND TO MOM. AND TAKE A LOOK AROUND YOU–YOU'VE MADE A COMPLETE ASS OF YOURSELF AT THIS COMPANY'S MOST IMPORTANT EVENT IN YEARS.
SO PLEASE, LISTEN TO ME FOR ONCE AND WALK AWAY.
...FINE, I HAVE INVESTORS TO DEAL WITH ANYWAY. BUT A BIT OF FRIENDLY ADVICE, MISS MCCOY–
DON'T WASTE YOUR TIME ON THIS ONE. HE'S MEDIOCRE. A PRETENDER...
....IN THE END, HE'LL ONLY LEAVE YOU WITH ONE FEELING: DISAPPOINTMENT.
REGGIE...

DINER

ISSUE SIX

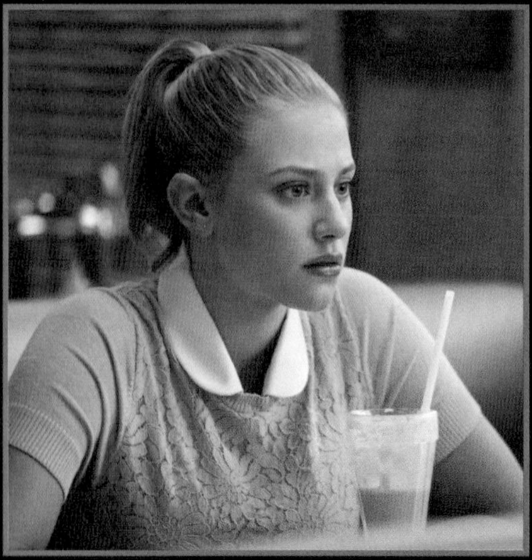

CHOCK'LIT SHOPPE OF HORRORS

WRITERS:
ROSS MAXWELL
AND **WILL EWING**

ART:
JOE EISMA

COLORS:
ANDRE SZYMANOWICZ

LETTERS:
JOHN WORKMAN

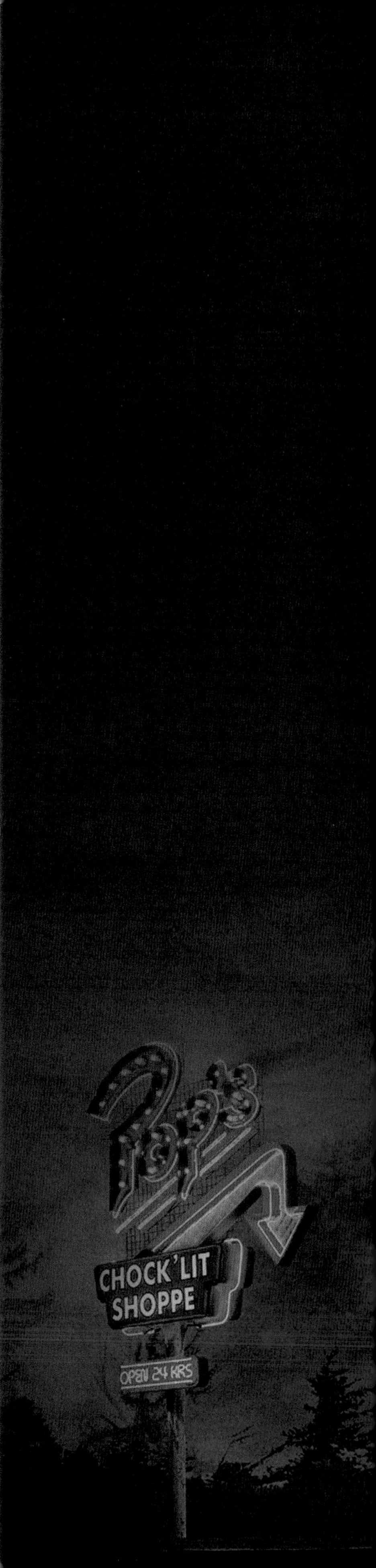
CHOCK'LIT SHOPPE
OPEN 24 HRS

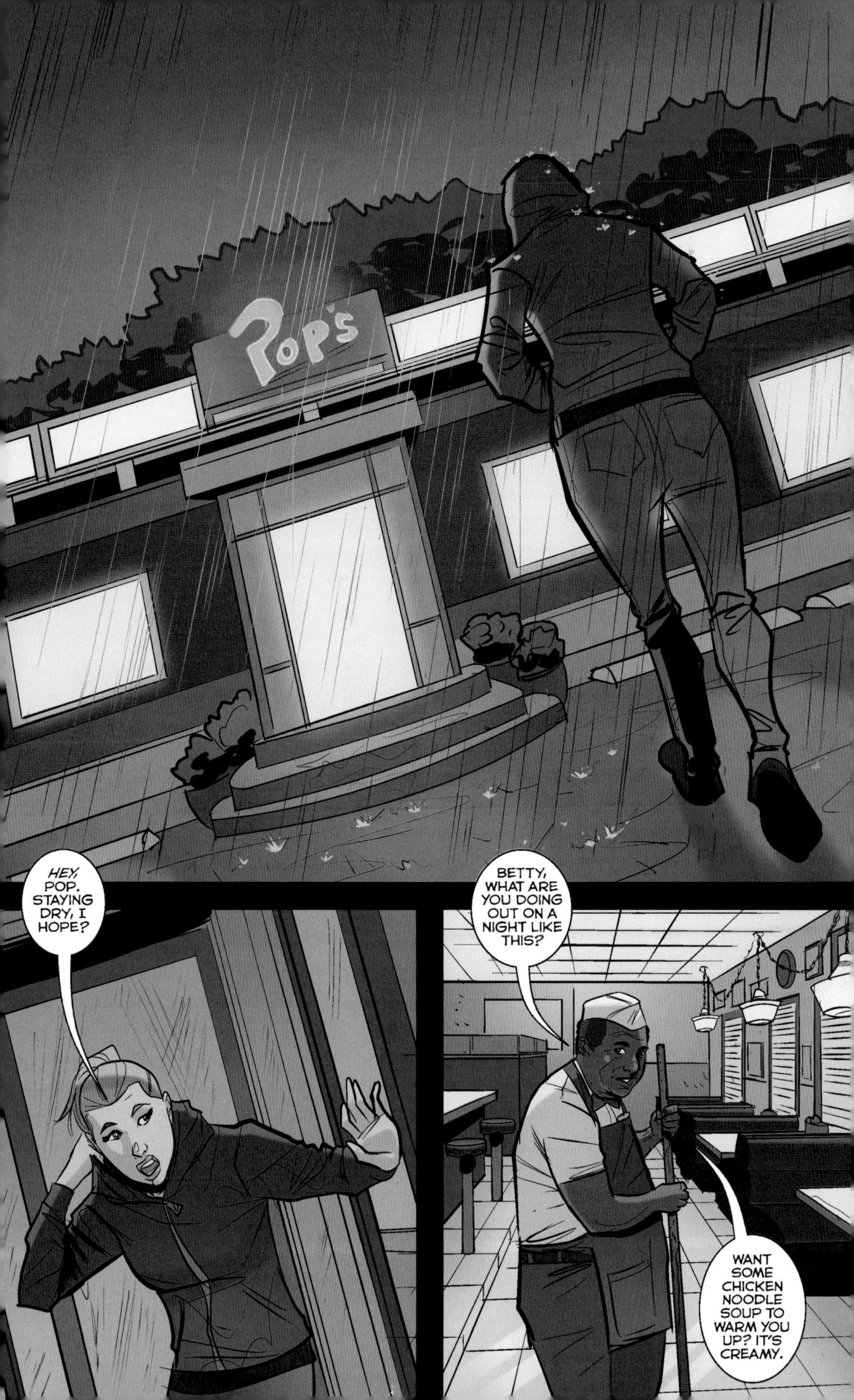
POP'S
HEY, POP. STAYING DRY, I HOPE?
BETTY, WHAT ARE YOU DOING OUT ON A NIGHT LIKE THIS?
WANT SOME CHICKEN NOODLE SOUP TO WARM YOU UP? IT'S CREAMY.

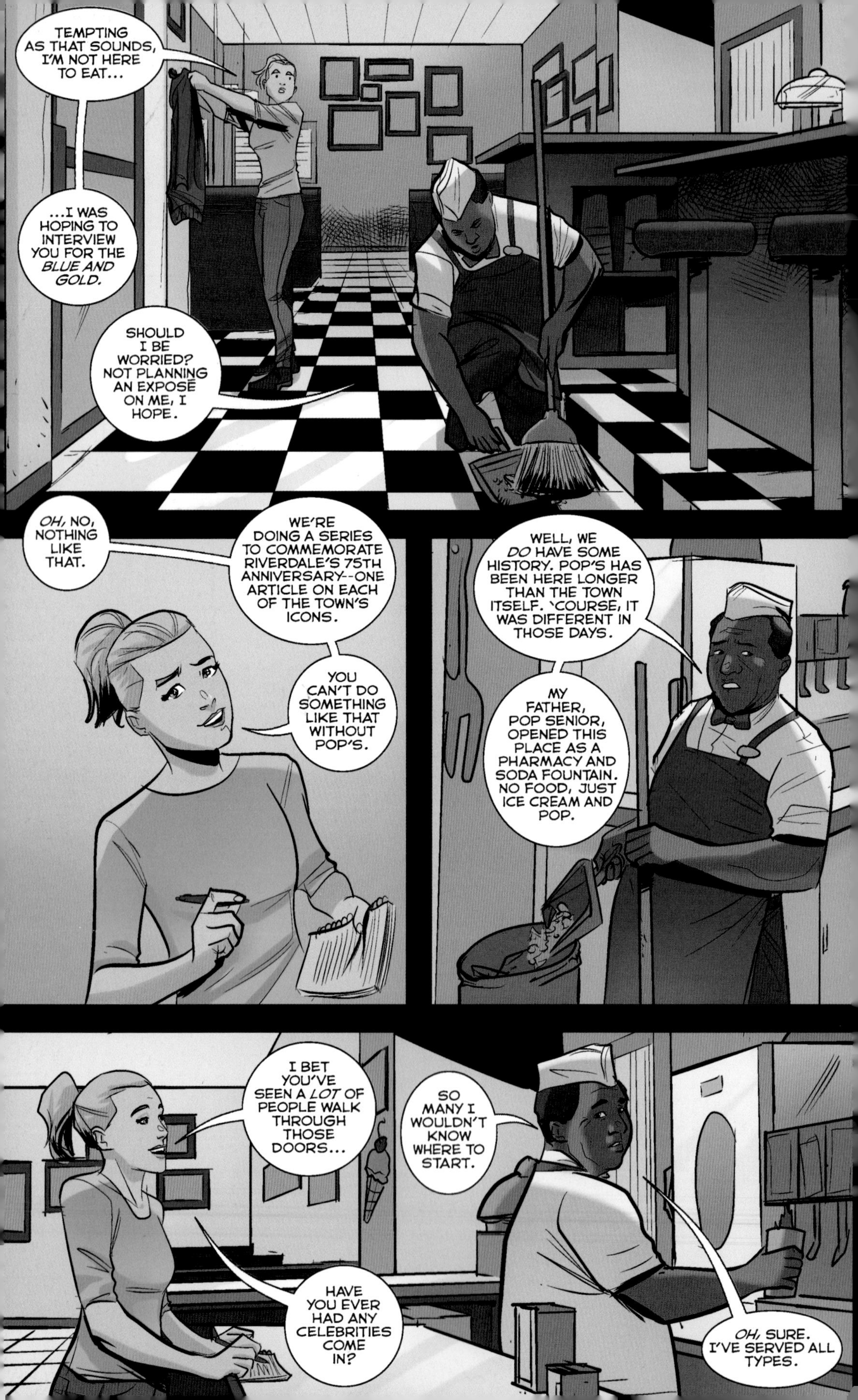
TEMPTING AS THAT SOUNDS, I'M NOT HERE TO EAT...
...I WAS HOPING TO INTERVIEW YOU FOR THE *BLUE AND GOLD.*
SHOULD I BE WORRIED? NOT PLANNING AN EXPOSÉ ON ME, I HOPE.
OH, NO, NOTHING LIKE THAT.
WE'RE DOING A SERIES TO COMMEMORATE RIVERDALE'S 75TH ANNIVERSARY--ONE ARTICLE ON EACH OF THE TOWN'S ICONS.
YOU CAN'T DO SOMETHING LIKE THAT WITHOUT POP'S.
WELL, WE *DO* HAVE SOME HISTORY. POP'S HAS BEEN HERE LONGER THAN THE TOWN ITSELF. 'COURSE, IT WAS DIFFERENT IN THOSE DAYS.
MY FATHER, POP SENIOR, OPENED THIS PLACE AS A PHARMACY AND SODA FOUNTAIN. NO FOOD, JUST ICE CREAM AND POP.
I BET YOU'VE SEEN A *LOT* OF PEOPLE WALK THROUGH THOSE DOORS...
SO MANY I WOULDN'T KNOW WHERE TO START.
HAVE YOU EVER HAD ANY CELEBRITIES COME IN?
OH, SURE. I'VE SERVED ALL TYPES.

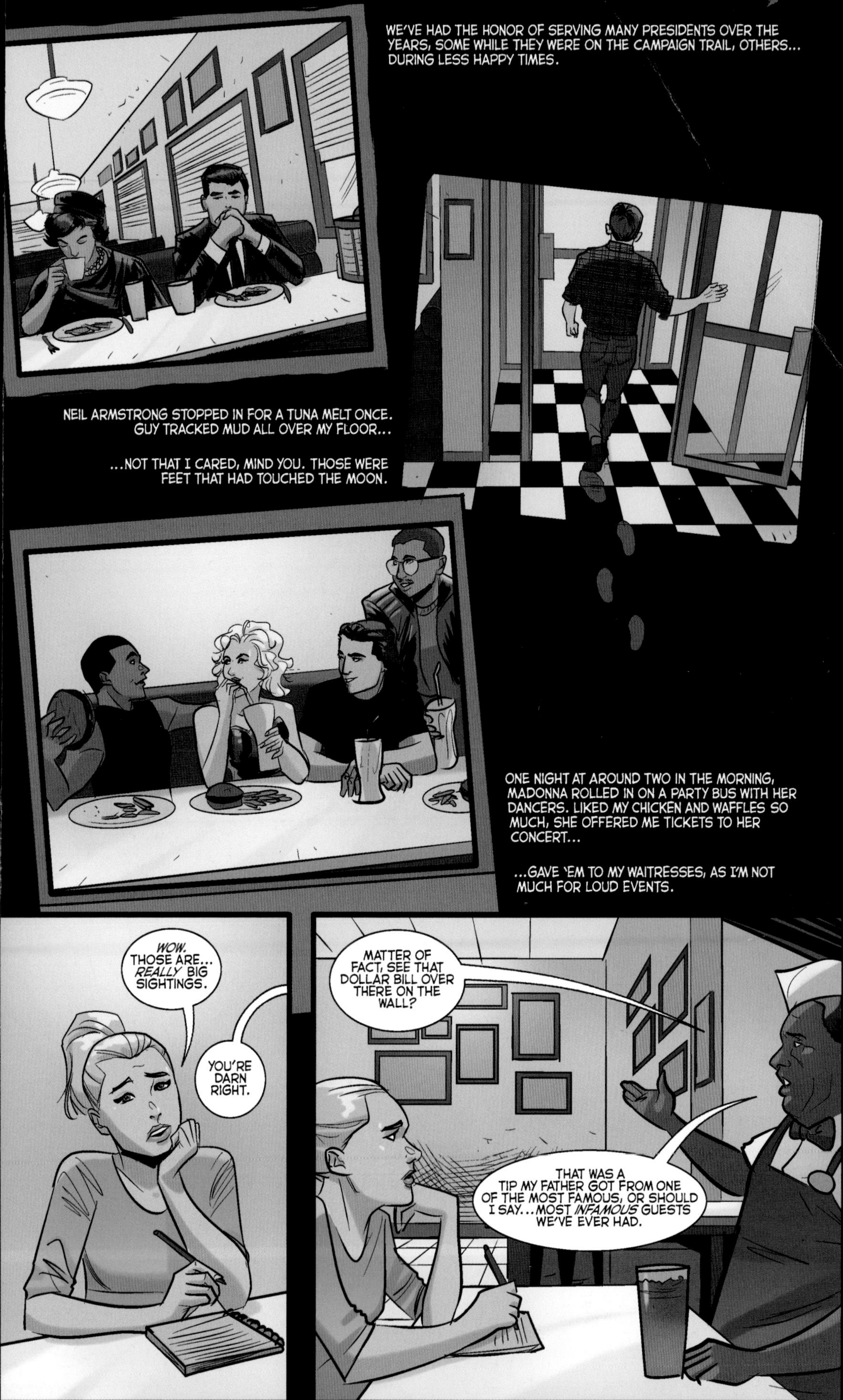
WE'VE HAD THE HONOR OF SERVING MANY PRESIDENTS OVER THE YEARS, SOME WHILE THEY WERE ON THE CAMPAIGN TRAIL, OTHERS... DURING LESS HAPPY TIMES.
NEIL ARMSTRONG STOPPED IN FOR A TUNA MELT ONCE. GUY TRACKED MUD ALL OVER MY FLOOR...
...NOT THAT I CARED, MIND YOU. THOSE WERE FEET THAT HAD TOUCHED THE MOON.
ONE NIGHT AT AROUND TWO IN THE MORNING, MADONNA ROLLED IN ON A PARTY BUS WITH HER DANCERS. LIKED MY CHICKEN AND WAFFLES SO MUCH, SHE OFFERED ME TICKETS TO HER CONCERT...
...GAVE 'EM TO MY WAITRESSES, AS I'M NOT MUCH FOR LOUD EVENTS.
WOW. THOSE ARE... *REALLY* BIG SIGHTINGS.
YOU'RE DARN RIGHT.
MATTER OF FACT, SEE THAT DOLLAR BILL OVER THERE ON THE WALL?
THAT WAS A TIP MY FATHER GOT FROM ONE OF THE MOST FAMOUS, OR SHOULD I SAY... MOST *INFAMOUS* GUESTS WE'VE EVER HAD.

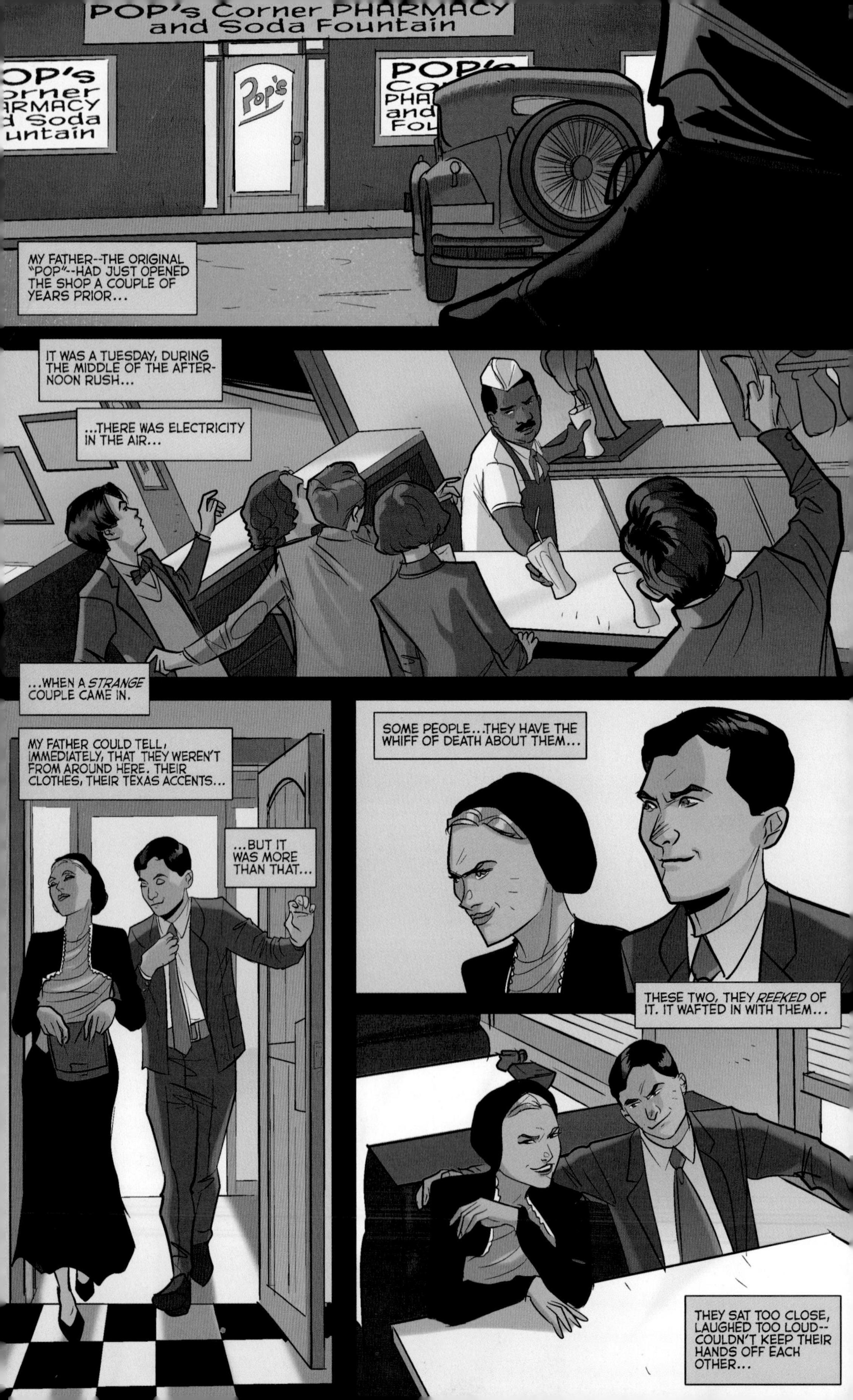
POP's Corner PHARMACY and Soda Fountain
Pop's
MY FATHER--THE ORIGINAL "POP"--HAD JUST OPENED THE SHOP A COUPLE OF YEARS PRIOR...
IT WAS A TUESDAY, DURING THE MIDDLE OF THE AFTER-NOON RUSH...
...THERE WAS ELECTRICITY IN THE AIR...
...WHEN A *STRANGE* COUPLE CAME IN.
MY FATHER COULD TELL, IMMEDIATELY, THAT THEY WEREN'T FROM AROUND HERE. THEIR CLOTHES, THEIR TEXAS ACCENTS...
...BUT IT WAS MORE THAN THAT...
SOME PEOPLE...THEY HAVE THE WHIFF OF DEATH ABOUT THEM...
THESE TWO, THEY *REEKED* OF IT. IT WAFTED IN WITH THEM...
THEY SAT TOO CLOSE, LAUGHED TOO LOUD--COULDN'T KEEP THEIR HANDS OFF EACH OTHER...

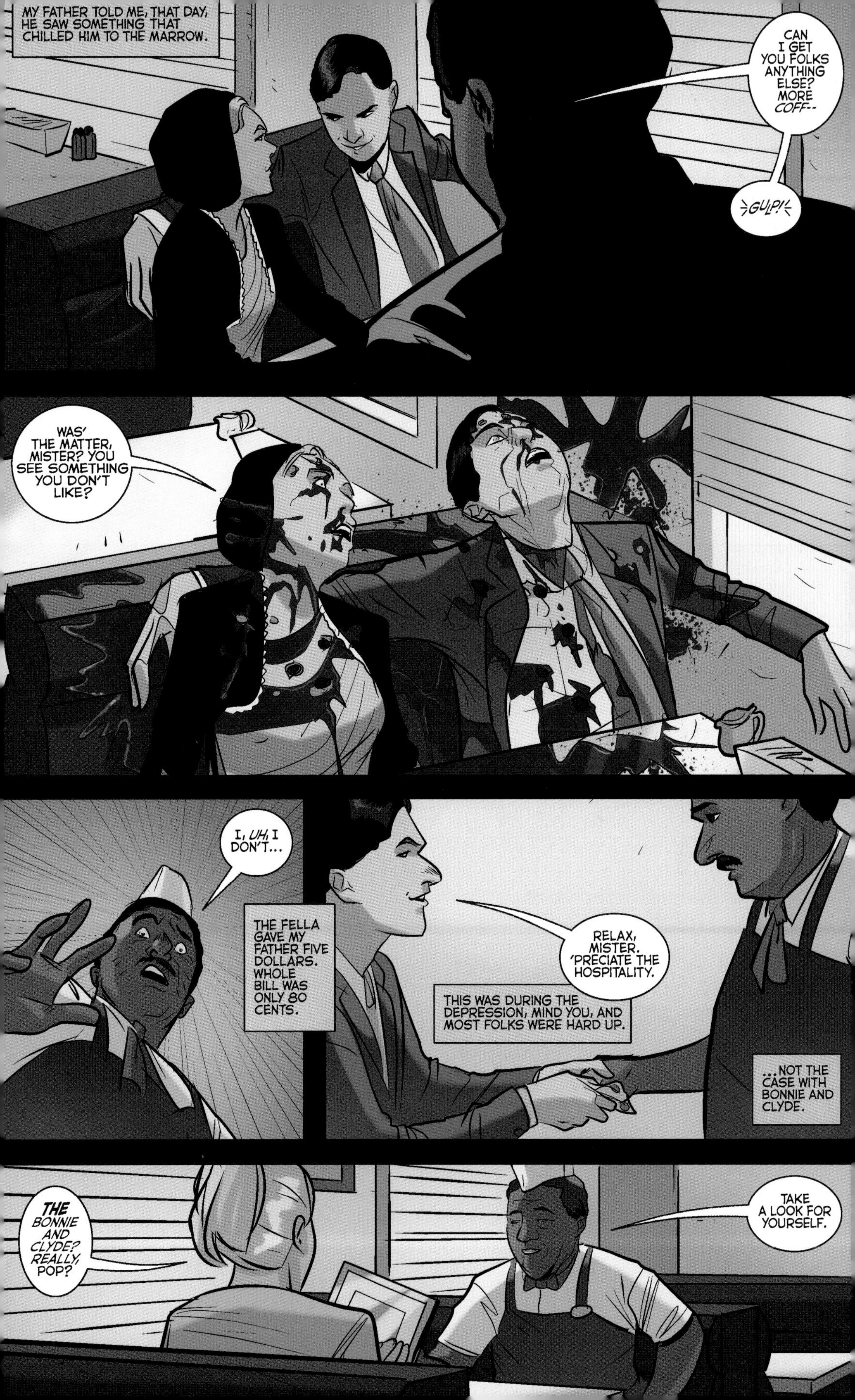
MY FATHER TOLD ME, THAT DAY, HE SAW SOMETHING THAT CHILLED HIM TO THE MARROW.
CAN I GET YOU FOLKS ANYTHING ELSE? MORE *COFF--*
GULP!
WAS' THE MATTER, MISTER? YOU SEE SOMETHING YOU DON'T LIKE?
I, *UH*, I DON'T...
THE FELLA GAVE MY FATHER FIVE DOLLARS. WHOLE BILL WAS ONLY 80 CENTS.
RELAX, MISTER. 'PRECIATE THE HOSPITALITY.
THIS WAS DURING THE DEPRESSION, MIND YOU, AND MOST FOLKS WERE HARD UP.
...NOT THE CASE WITH BONNIE AND CLYDE.
THE BONNIE AND CLYDE? REALLY, POP?
TAKE A LOOK FOR YOURSELF.

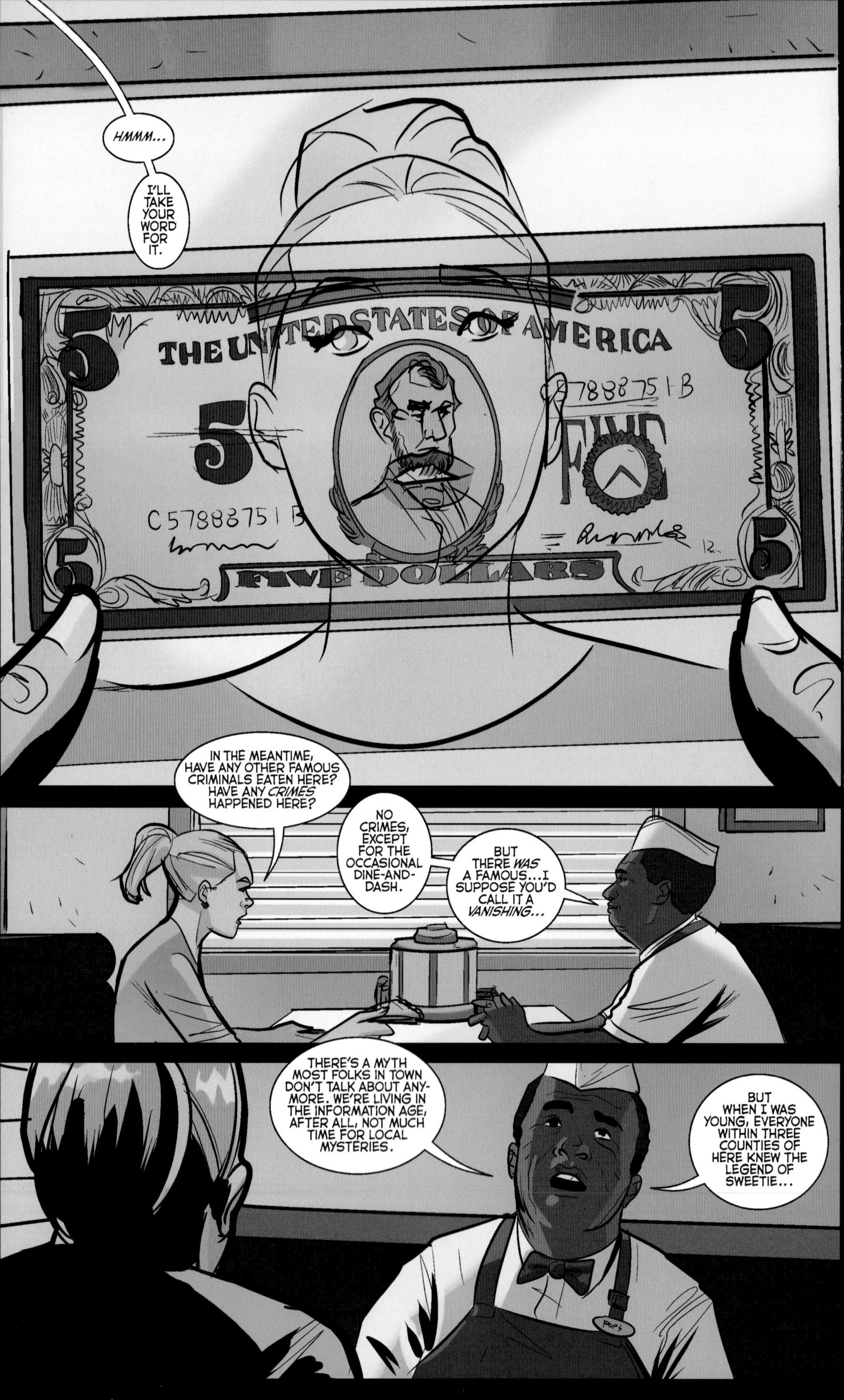

HMMM...
I'LL TAKE YOUR WORD FOR IT.
C57888751B
IN THE MEANTIME, HAVE ANY OTHER FAMOUS CRIMINALS EATEN HERE? HAVE ANY *CRIMES* HAPPENED HERE?
NO CRIMES, EXCEPT FOR THE OCCASIONAL DINE-AND-DASH.
BUT THERE *WAS* A FAMOUS...I SUPPOSE YOU'D CALL IT A *VANISHING*...
THERE'S A MYTH MOST FOLKS IN TOWN DON'T TALK ABOUT ANY-MORE. WE'RE LIVING IN THE INFORMATION AGE, AFTER ALL, NOT MUCH TIME FOR LOCAL MYSTERIES.
BUT WHEN I WAS YOUNG, EVERYONE WITHIN THREE COUNTIES OF HERE KNEW THE LEGEND OF SWEETIE...

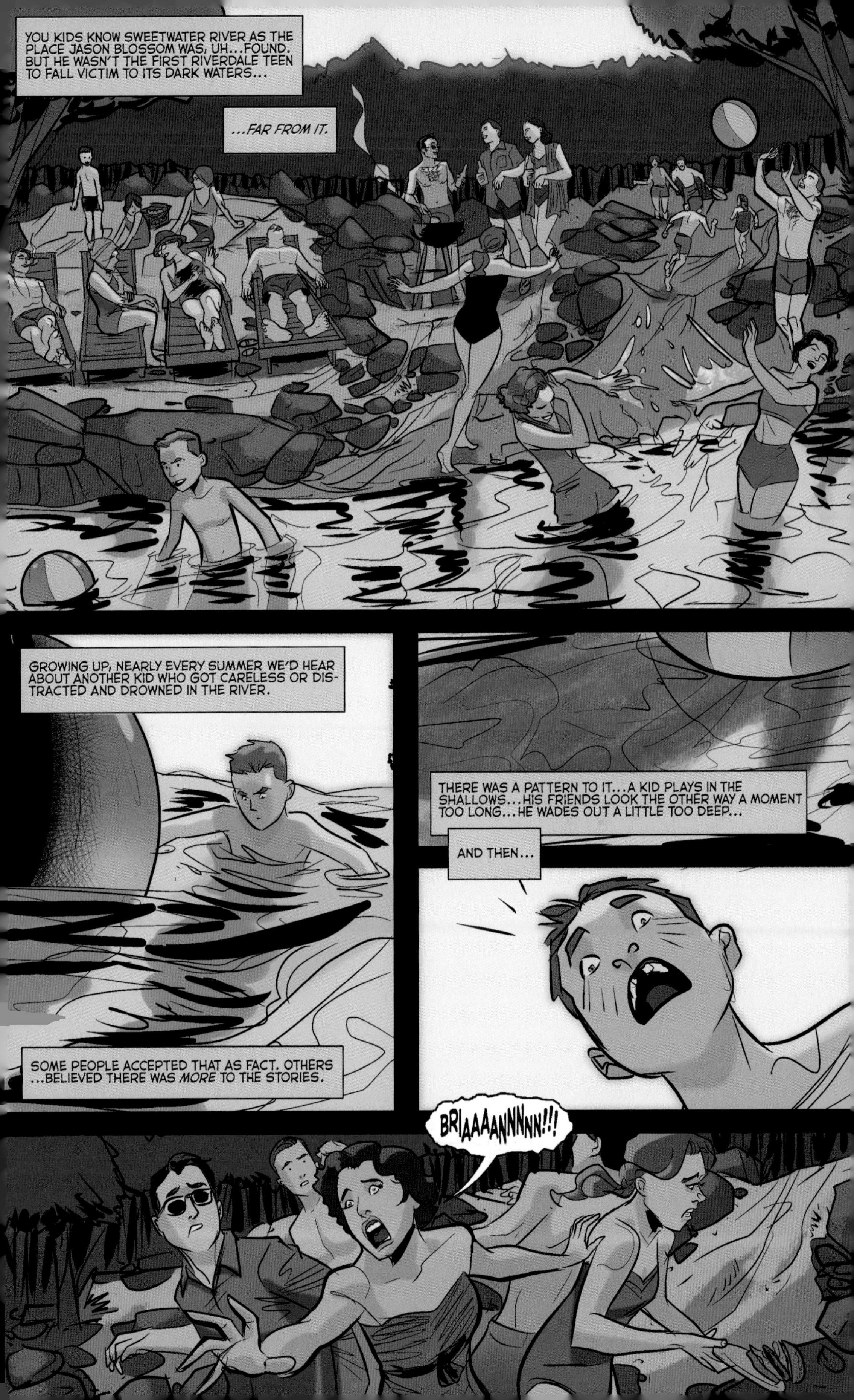
YOU KIDS KNOW SWEETWATER RIVER AS THE PLACE JASON BLOSSOM WAS, UH...FOUND. BUT HE WASN'T THE FIRST RIVERDALE TEEN TO FALL VICTIM TO ITS DARK WATERS...
...FAR FROM IT.
GROWING UP, NEARLY EVERY SUMMER WE'D HEAR ABOUT ANOTHER KID WHO GOT CARELESS OR DISTRACTED AND DROWNED IN THE RIVER.
SOME PEOPLE ACCEPTED THAT AS FACT. OTHERS ...BELIEVED THERE WAS *MORE* TO THE STORIES.
THERE WAS A PATTERN TO IT...A KID PLAYS IN THE SHALLOWS...HIS FRIENDS LOOK THE OTHER WAY A MOMENT TOO LONG...HE WADES OUT A LITTLE TOO DEEP...
AND THEN...
BRIAAAANNNNN!!!

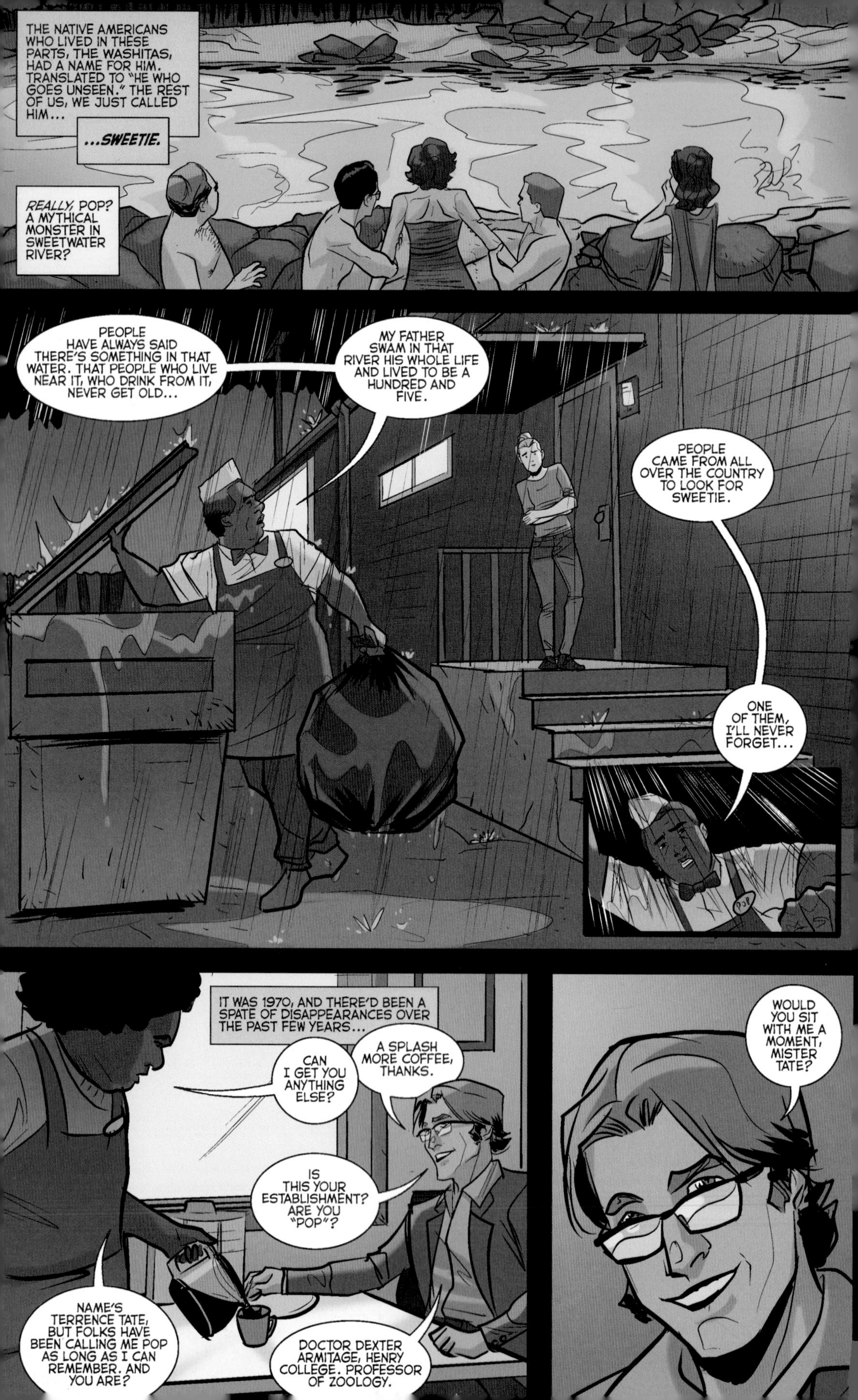
THE NATIVE AMERICANS WHO LIVED IN THESE PARTS, THE WASHITAS, HAD A NAME FOR HIM. TRANSLATED TO "HE WHO GOES UNSEEN." THE REST OF US, WE JUST CALLED HIM...
...SWEETIE.
REALLY, POP? A MYTHICAL MONSTER IN SWEETWATER RIVER?
PEOPLE HAVE ALWAYS SAID THERE'S SOMETHING IN THAT WATER. THAT PEOPLE WHO LIVE NEAR IT, WHO DRINK FROM IT, NEVER GET OLD...
MY FATHER SWAM IN THAT RIVER HIS WHOLE LIFE AND LIVED TO BE A HUNDRED AND FIVE.
PEOPLE CAME FROM ALL OVER THE COUNTRY TO LOOK FOR SWEETIE.
ONE OF THEM, I'LL NEVER FORGET...
POP
IT WAS 1970, AND THERE'D BEEN A SPATE OF DISAPPEARANCES OVER THE PAST FEW YEARS...
CAN I GET YOU ANYTHING ELSE?
A SPLASH MORE COFFEE, THANKS.
IS THIS YOUR ESTABLISHMENT? ARE YOU "POP"?
NAME'S TERRENCE TATE, BUT FOLKS HAVE BEEN CALLING ME POP AS LONG AS I CAN REMEMBER. AND YOU ARE?
DOCTOR DEXTER ARMITAGE, HENRY COLLEGE. PROFESSOR OF ZOOLOGY.
WOULD YOU SIT WITH ME A MOMENT, MISTER TATE?

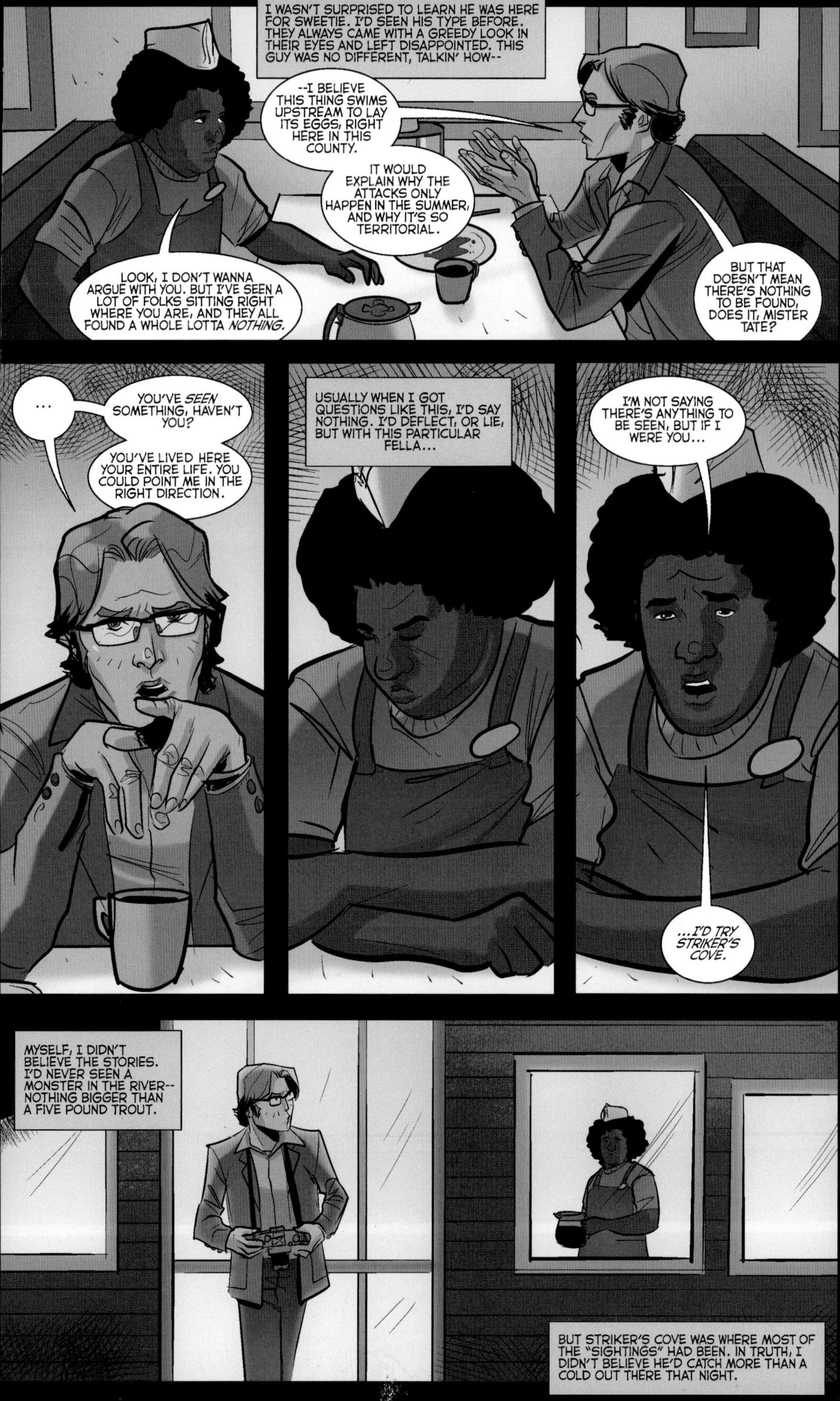
I WASN'T SURPRISED TO LEARN HE WAS HERE FOR SWEETIE. I'D SEEN HIS TYPE BEFORE. THEY ALWAYS CAME WITH A GREEDY LOOK IN THEIR EYES AND LEFT DISAPPOINTED. THIS GUY WAS NO DIFFERENT, TALKIN' HOW--
--I BELIEVE THIS THING SWIMS UPSTREAM TO LAY ITS EGGS, RIGHT HERE IN THIS COUNTY.
IT WOULD EXPLAIN WHY THE ATTACKS ONLY HAPPEN IN THE SUMMER, AND WHY IT'S SO TERRITORIAL.
LOOK, I DON'T WANNA ARGUE WITH YOU. BUT I'VE SEEN A LOT OF FOLKS SITTING RIGHT WHERE YOU ARE, AND THEY ALL FOUND A WHOLE LOTTA *NOTHING.*
BUT THAT DOESN'T MEAN THERE'S NOTHING TO BE FOUND, DOES IT, MISTER TATE?
...
YOU'VE *SEEN* SOMETHING, HAVEN'T YOU?
YOU'VE LIVED HERE YOUR ENTIRE LIFE. YOU COULD POINT ME IN THE RIGHT DIRECTION.
USUALLY WHEN I GOT QUESTIONS LIKE THIS, I'D SAY NOTHING. I'D DEFLECT, OR LIE, BUT WITH THIS PARTICULAR FELLA...
I'M NOT SAYING THERE'S ANYTHING TO BE SEEN, BUT IF I WERE YOU...
...I'D TRY STRIKER'S COVE.
MYSELF, I DIDN'T BELIEVE THE STORIES. I'D NEVER SEEN A MONSTER IN THE RIVER-- NOTHING BIGGER THAN A FIVE POUND TROUT.
BUT STRIKER'S COVE WAS WHERE MOST OF THE "SIGHTINGS" HAD BEEN. IN TRUTH, I DIDN'T BELIEVE HE'D CATCH MORE THAN A COLD OUT THERE THAT NIGHT.

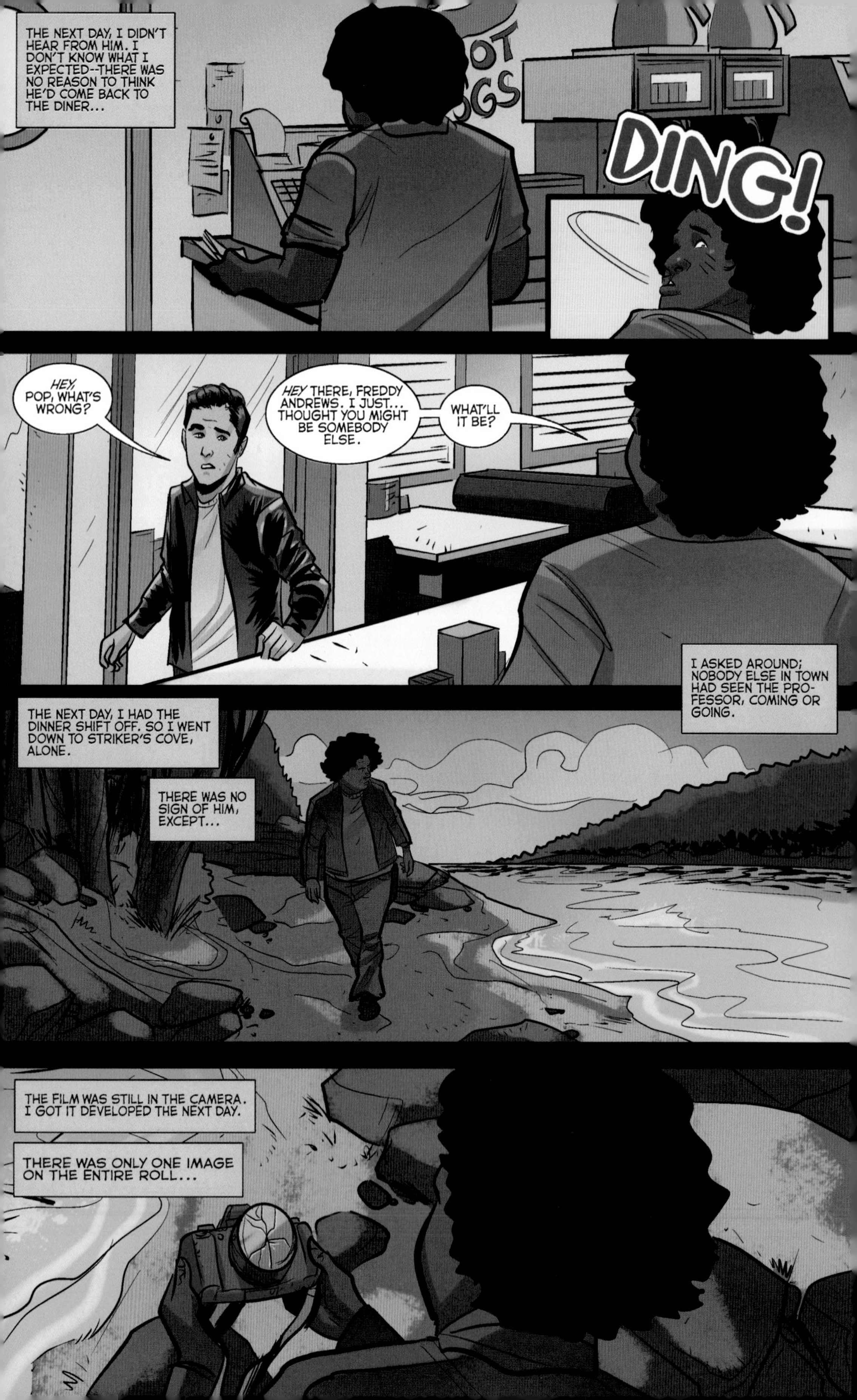
THE NEXT DAY, I DIDN'T HEAR FROM HIM. I DON'T KNOW WHAT I EXPECTED--THERE WAS NO REASON TO THINK HE'D COME BACK TO THE DINER...
DING!
HEY, POP, WHAT'S WRONG?
HEY THERE, FREDDY ANDREWS. I JUST... THOUGHT YOU MIGHT BE SOMEBODY ELSE.
WHAT'LL IT BE?
I ASKED AROUND; NOBODY ELSE IN TOWN HAD SEEN THE PROFESSOR, COMING OR GOING.
THE NEXT DAY, I HAD THE DINNER SHIFT OFF. SO I WENT DOWN TO STRIKER'S COVE, ALONE.
THERE WAS NO SIGN OF HIM, EXCEPT...
THE FILM WAS STILL IN THE CAMERA. I GOT IT DEVELOPED THE NEXT DAY.
THERE WAS ONLY ONE IMAGE ON THE ENTIRE ROLL...

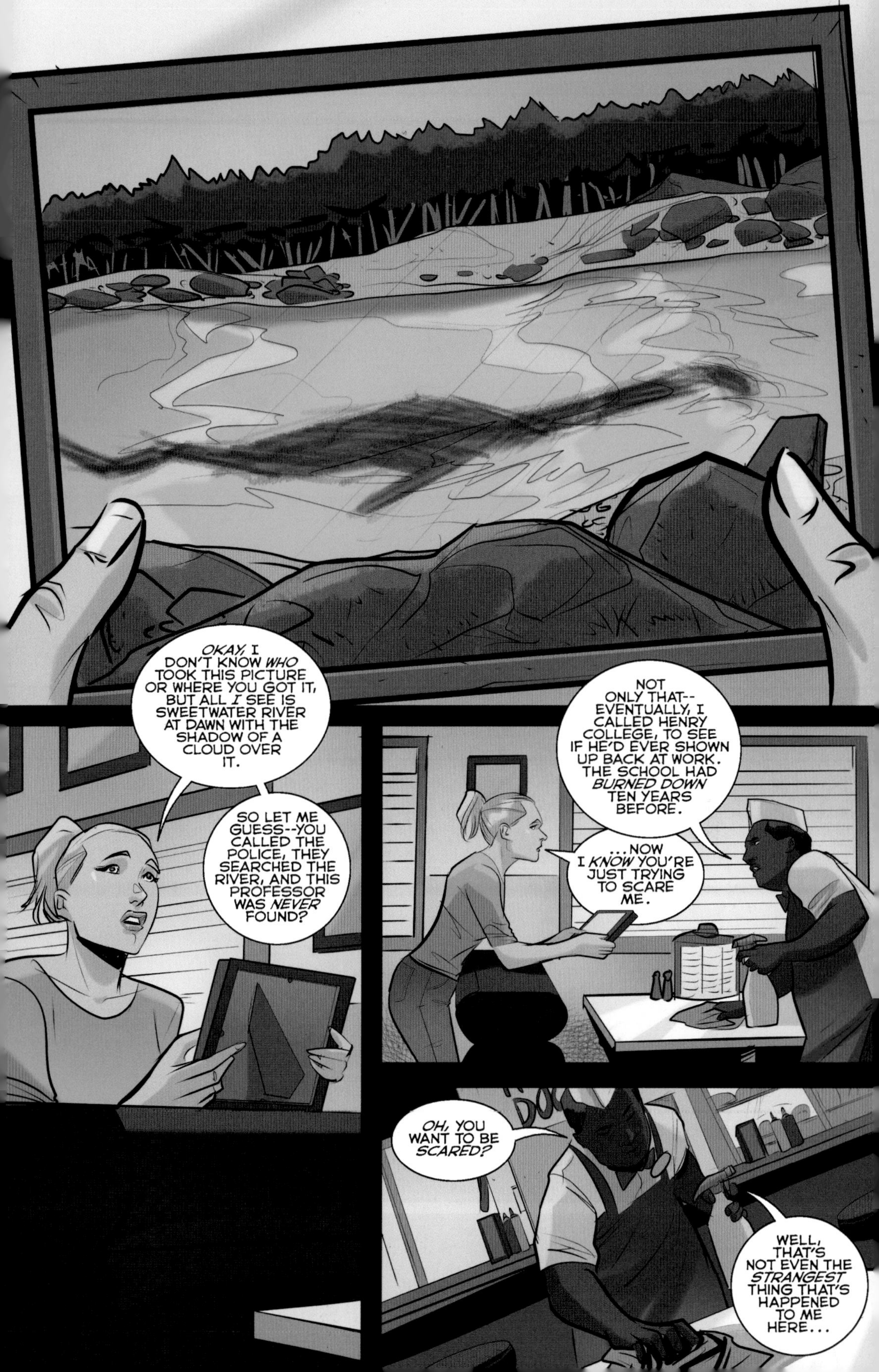
OKAY, I DON'T KNOW WHO TOOK THIS PICTURE OR WHERE YOU GOT IT, BUT ALL I SEE IS SWEETWATER RIVER AT DAWN WITH THE SHADOW OF A CLOUD OVER IT.
SO LET ME GUESS--YOU CALLED THE POLICE, THEY SEARCHED THE RIVER, AND THIS PROFESSOR WAS NEVER FOUND?
NOT ONLY THAT--EVENTUALLY, I CALLED HENRY COLLEGE, TO SEE IF HE'D EVER SHOWN UP BACK AT WORK. THE SCHOOL HAD BURNED DOWN TEN YEARS BEFORE.
...NOW I KNOW YOU'RE JUST TRYING TO SCARE ME.
OH, YOU WANT TO BE SCARED?
WELL, THAT'S NOT EVEN THE STRANGEST THING THAT'S HAPPENED TO ME HERE...

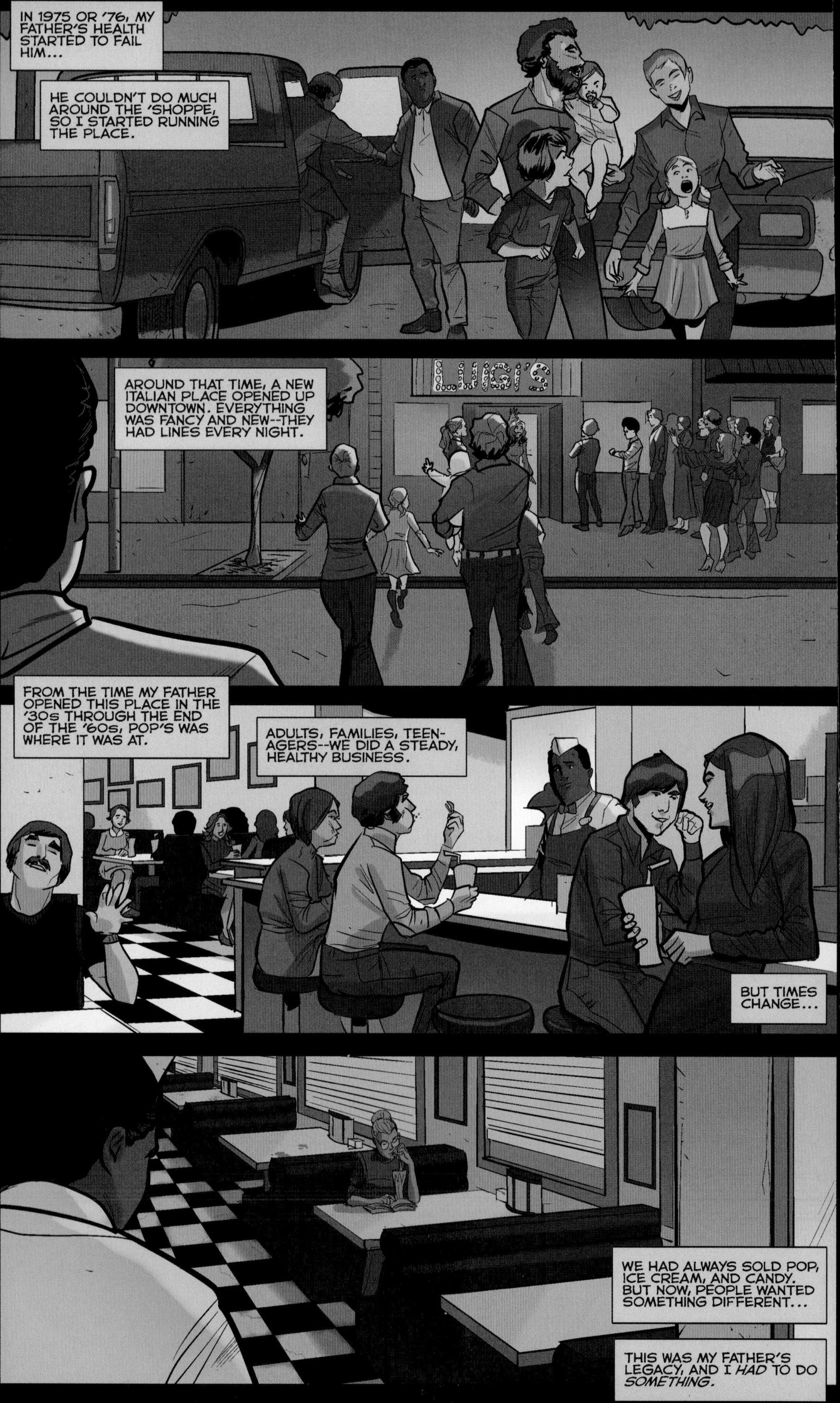

IN 1975 OR '76, MY FATHER'S HEALTH STARTED TO FAIL HIM...
HE COULDN'T DO MUCH AROUND THE 'SHOPPE, SO I STARTED RUNNING THE PLACE.
AROUND THAT TIME, A NEW ITALIAN PLACE OPENED UP DOWNTOWN. EVERYTHING WAS FANCY AND NEW--THEY HAD LINES EVERY NIGHT.
LUIGI'S
FROM THE TIME MY FATHER OPENED THIS PLACE IN THE '30s THROUGH THE END OF THE '60s, POP'S WAS WHERE IT WAS AT.
ADULTS, FAMILIES, TEEN-AGERS--WE DID A STEADY, HEALTHY BUSINESS.
BUT TIMES CHANGE...
WE HAD ALWAYS SOLD POP, ICE CREAM, AND CANDY. BUT NOW, PEOPLE WANTED SOMETHING DIFFERENT...
THIS WAS MY FATHER'S LEGACY, AND I *HAD* TO DO *SOMETHING*.

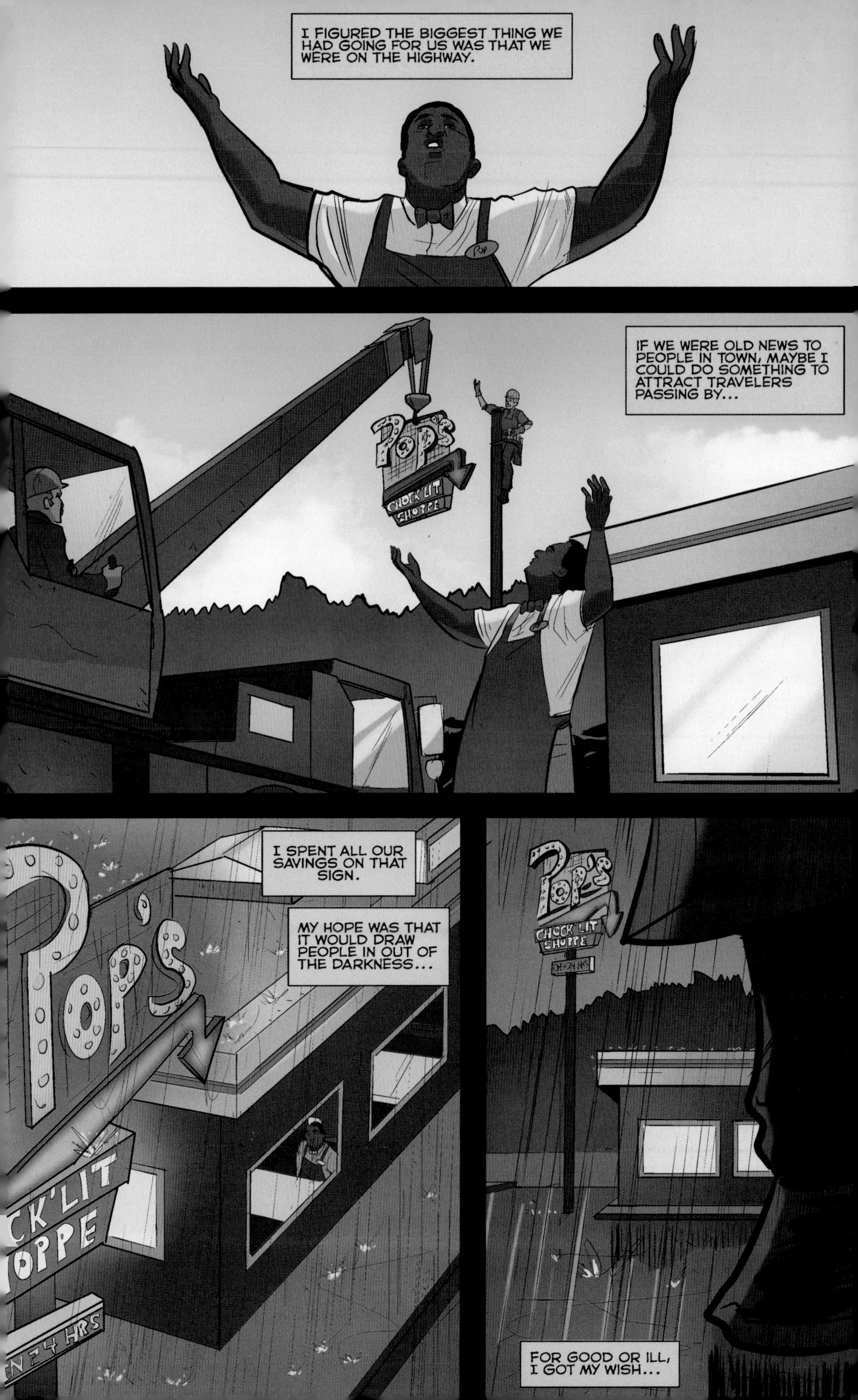
I FIGURED THE BIGGEST THING WE HAD GOING FOR US WAS THAT WE WERE ON THE HIGHWAY.
IF WE WERE OLD NEWS TO PEOPLE IN TOWN, MAYBE I COULD DO SOMETHING TO ATTRACT TRAVELERS PASSING BY...
POP'S
CHOCK'LIT SHOPPE
I SPENT ALL OUR SAVINGS ON THAT SIGN.
MY HOPE WAS THAT IT WOULD DRAW PEOPLE IN OUT OF THE DARKNESS...
POP'S
CK'LIT
OPPE
N 24 HRS
POP'S
CHOCK'LIT SHOPPE
FOR GOOD OR ILL, I GOT MY WISH...

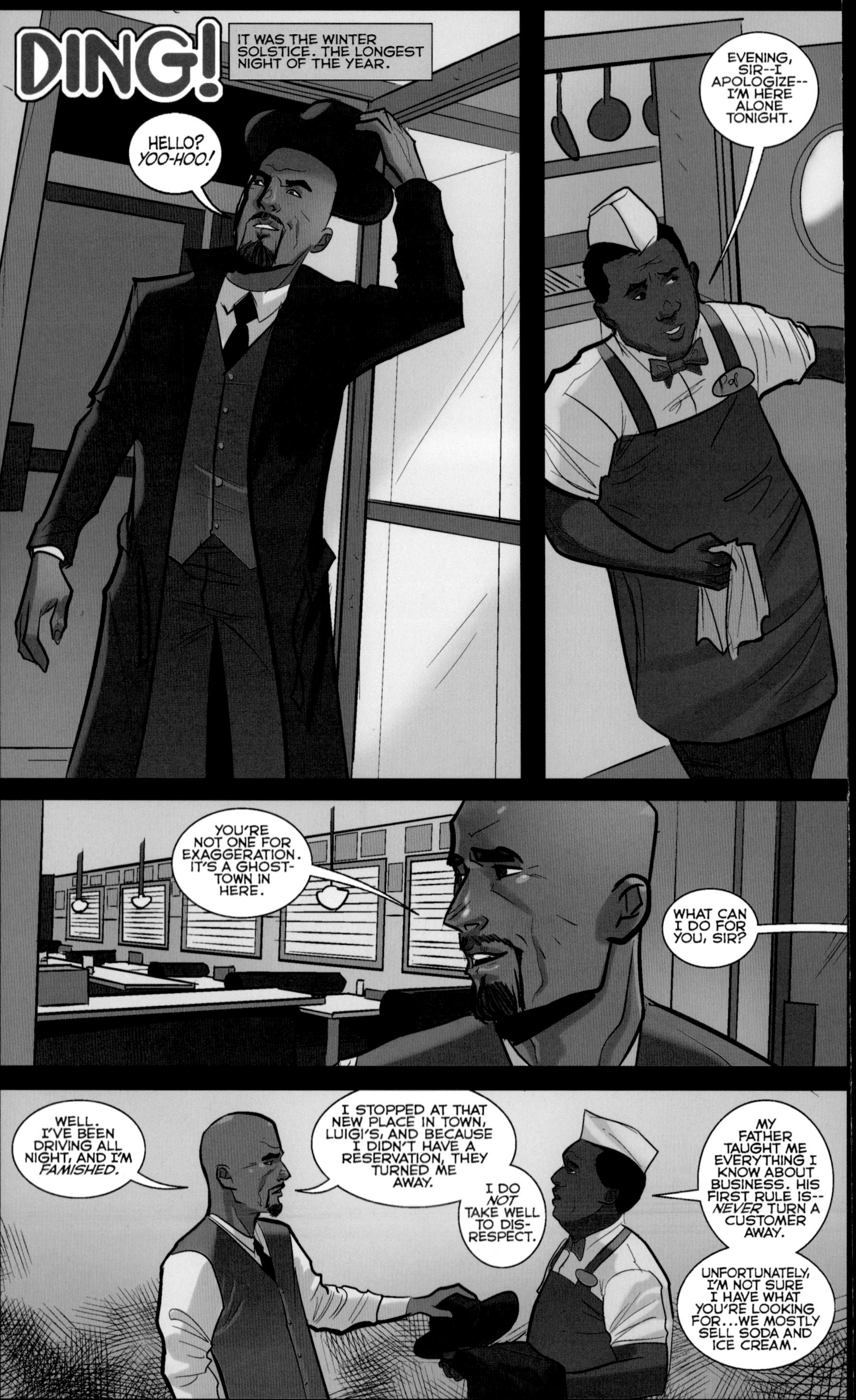
DING!
IT WAS THE WINTER SOLSTICE. THE LONGEST NIGHT OF THE YEAR.
HELLO? *YOO-HOO!*
EVENING, SIR--I APOLOGIZE--I'M HERE ALONE TONIGHT.
YOU'RE NOT ONE FOR EXAGGERATION. IT'S A GHOST-TOWN IN HERE.
WHAT CAN I DO FOR YOU, SIR?
WELL. I'VE BEEN DRIVING ALL NIGHT, AND I'M *FAMISHED.*
I STOPPED AT THAT NEW PLACE IN TOWN, LUIGI'S, AND BECAUSE I DIDN'T HAVE A RESERVATION, THEY TURNED ME AWAY.
I DO *NOT* TAKE WELL TO DIS-RESPECT.
MY FATHER TAUGHT ME EVERYTHING I KNOW ABOUT BUSINESS. HIS FIRST RULE IS--*NEVER* TURN A CUSTOMER AWAY.
UNFORTUNATELY, I'M NOT SURE I HAVE WHAT YOU'RE LOOKING FOR...WE MOSTLY SELL SODA AND ICE CREAM.

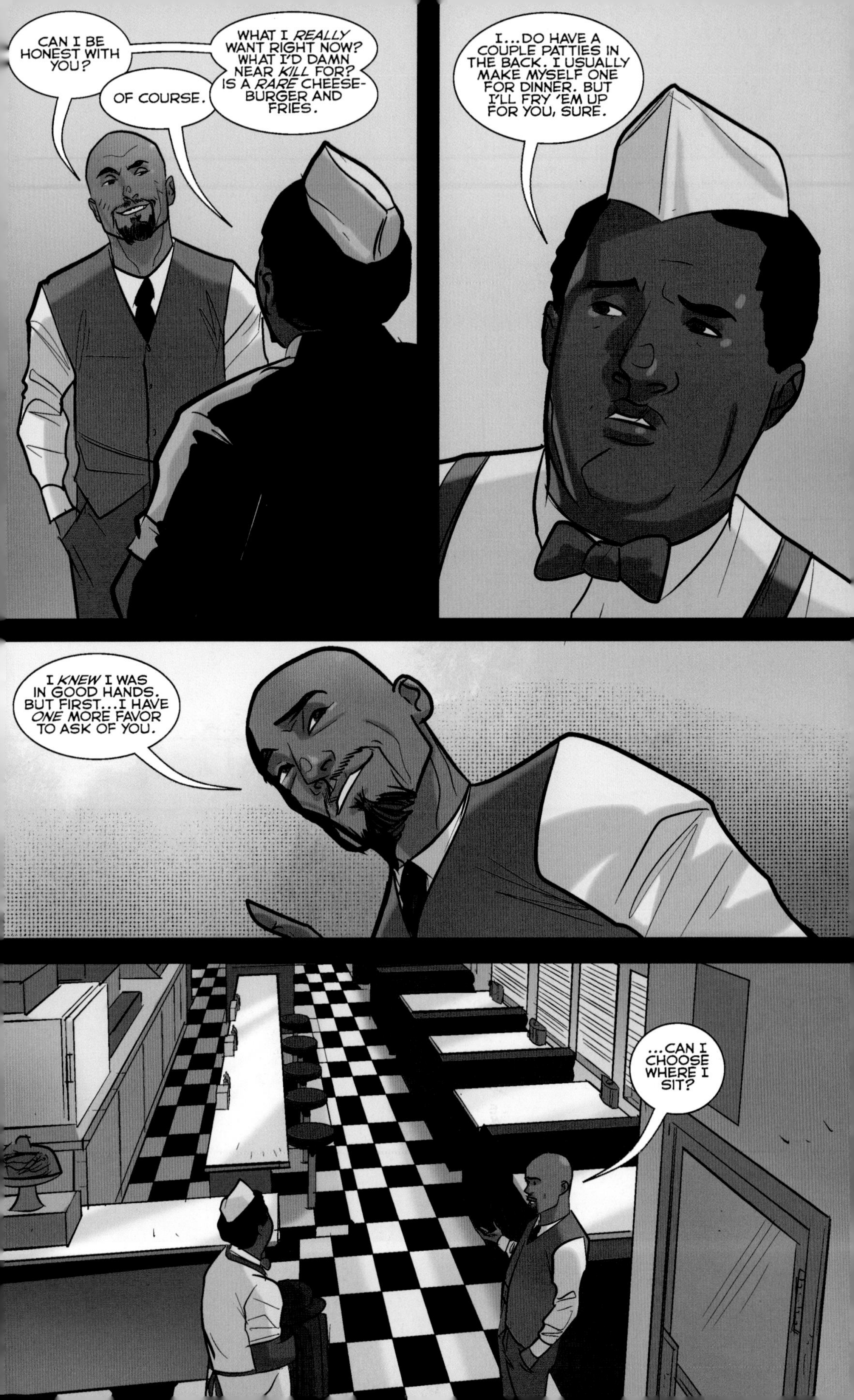
CAN I BE HONEST WITH YOU?
OF COURSE.
WHAT I *REALLY* WANT RIGHT NOW? WHAT I'D DAMN NEAR *KILL* FOR? IS A *RARE* CHEESE-BURGER AND FRIES.
I...DO HAVE A COUPLE PATTIES IN THE BACK. I USUALLY MAKE MYSELF ONE FOR DINNER. BUT I'LL FRY 'EM UP FOR YOU, SURE.
I *KNEW* I WAS IN GOOD HANDS. BUT FIRST...I HAVE *ONE* MORE FAVOR TO ASK OF YOU.
...CAN I CHOOSE WHERE I SIT?

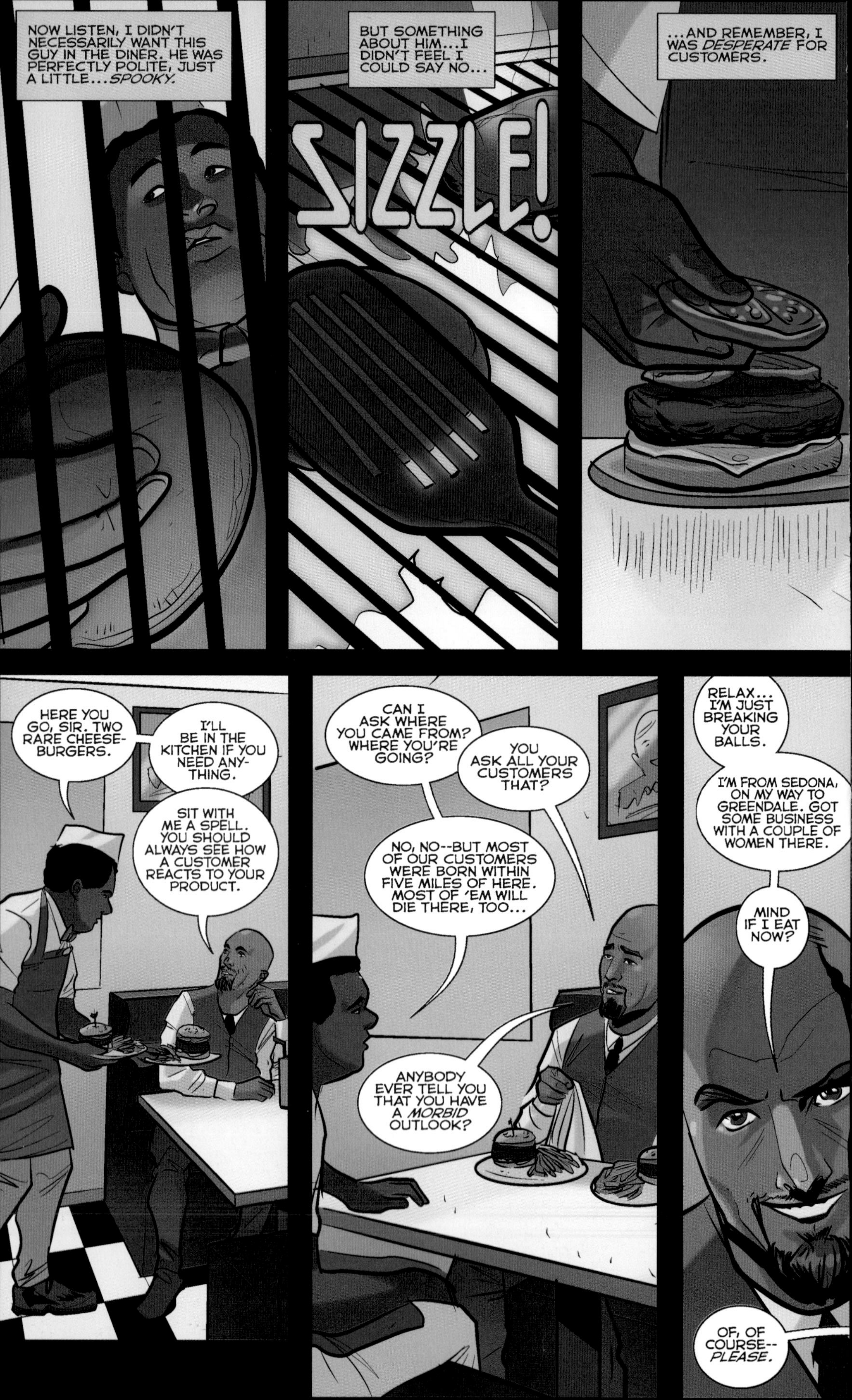
NOW LISTEN, I DIDN'T NECESSARILY WANT THIS GUY IN THE DINER. HE WAS PERFECTLY POLITE, JUST A LITTLE...*SPOOKY.*
BUT SOMETHING ABOUT HIM...I DIDN'T FEEL I COULD SAY NO...
SIZZLE!
...AND REMEMBER, I WAS *DESPERATE* FOR CUSTOMERS.
HERE YOU GO, SIR. TWO RARE CHEESE-BURGERS.
I'LL BE IN THE KITCHEN IF YOU NEED ANY-THING.
SIT WITH ME A SPELL. YOU SHOULD ALWAYS SEE HOW A CUSTOMER REACTS TO YOUR PRODUCT.
CAN I ASK WHERE YOU CAME FROM? WHERE YOU'RE GOING?
YOU ASK ALL YOUR CUSTOMERS THAT?
NO, NO--BUT MOST OF OUR CUSTOMERS WERE BORN WITHIN FIVE MILES OF HERE. MOST OF 'EM WILL DIE THERE, TOO...
ANYBODY EVER TELL YOU THAT YOU HAVE A *MORBID* OUTLOOK?
RELAX... I'M JUST BREAKING YOUR BALLS.
I'M FROM SEDONA, ON MY WAY TO GREENDALE. GOT SOME BUSINESS WITH A COUPLE OF WOMEN THERE.
MIND IF I EAT NOW?
OF, OF COURSE-- *PLEASE.*

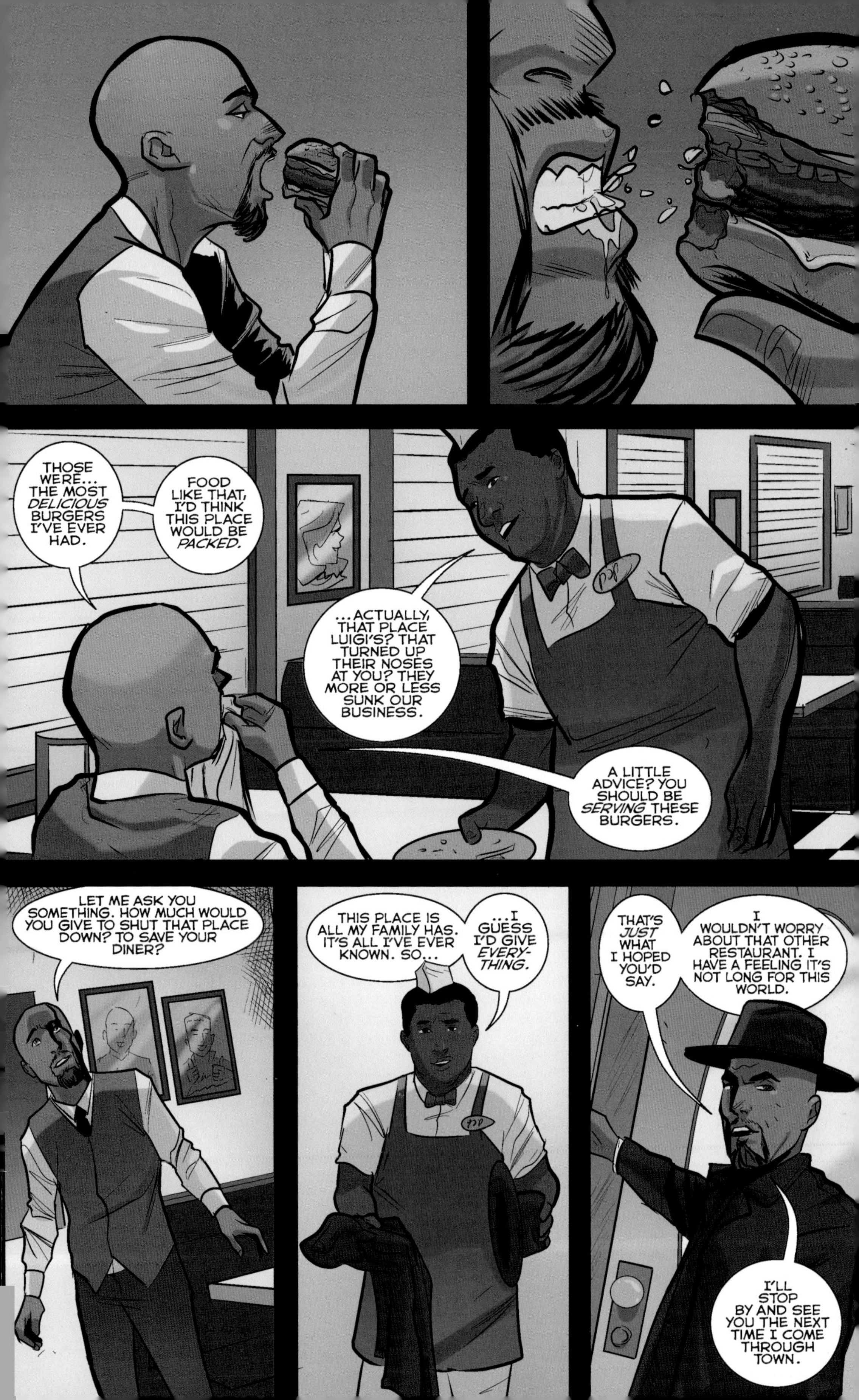
THOSE WERE... THE MOST *DELICIOUS* BURGERS I'VE EVER HAD.
FOOD LIKE THAT, I'D THINK THIS PLACE WOULD BE *PACKED*.
...ACTUALLY, THAT PLACE LUIGI'S? THAT TURNED UP THEIR NOSES AT YOU? THEY MORE OR LESS SUNK OUR BUSINESS.
A LITTLE ADVICE? YOU SHOULD BE *SERVING* THESE BURGERS.
LET ME ASK YOU SOMETHING. HOW MUCH WOULD YOU GIVE TO SHUT THAT PLACE DOWN? TO SAVE YOUR DINER?
THIS PLACE IS ALL MY FAMILY HAS. IT'S ALL I'VE EVER KNOWN. SO...
...I GUESS I'D GIVE *EVERY-THING.*
THAT'S *JUST* WHAT I HOPED YOU'D SAY.
I WOULDN'T WORRY ABOUT THAT OTHER RESTAURANT. I HAVE A FEELING IT'S NOT LONG FOR THIS WORLD.
I'LL STOP BY AND SEE YOU THE NEXT TIME I COME THROUGH TOWN.

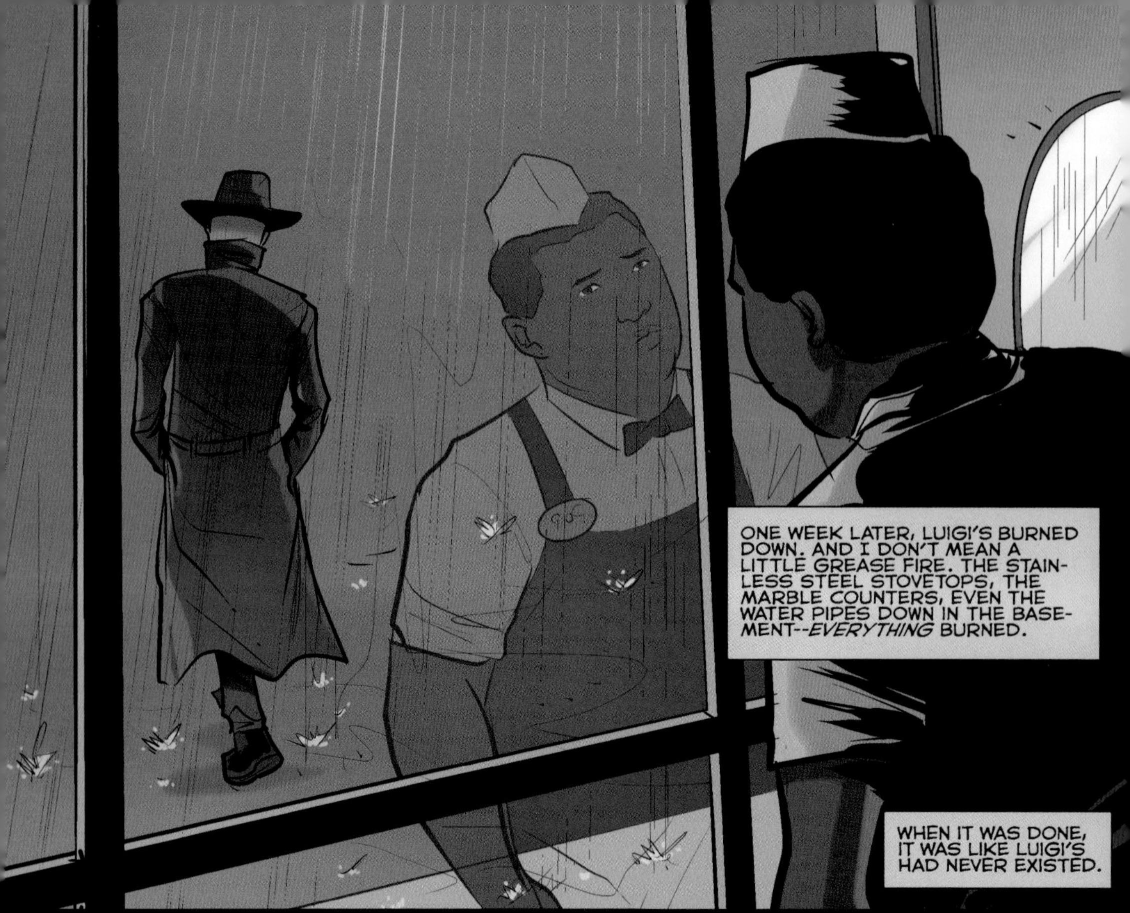
ONE WEEK LATER, LUIGI'S BURNED DOWN. AND I DON'T MEAN A LITTLE GREASE FIRE. THE STAINLESS STEEL STOVETOPS, THE MARBLE COUNTERS, EVEN THE WATER PIPES DOWN IN THE BASEMENT--*EVERYTHING* BURNED.
WHEN IT WAS DONE, IT WAS LIKE LUIGI'S HAD NEVER EXISTED.

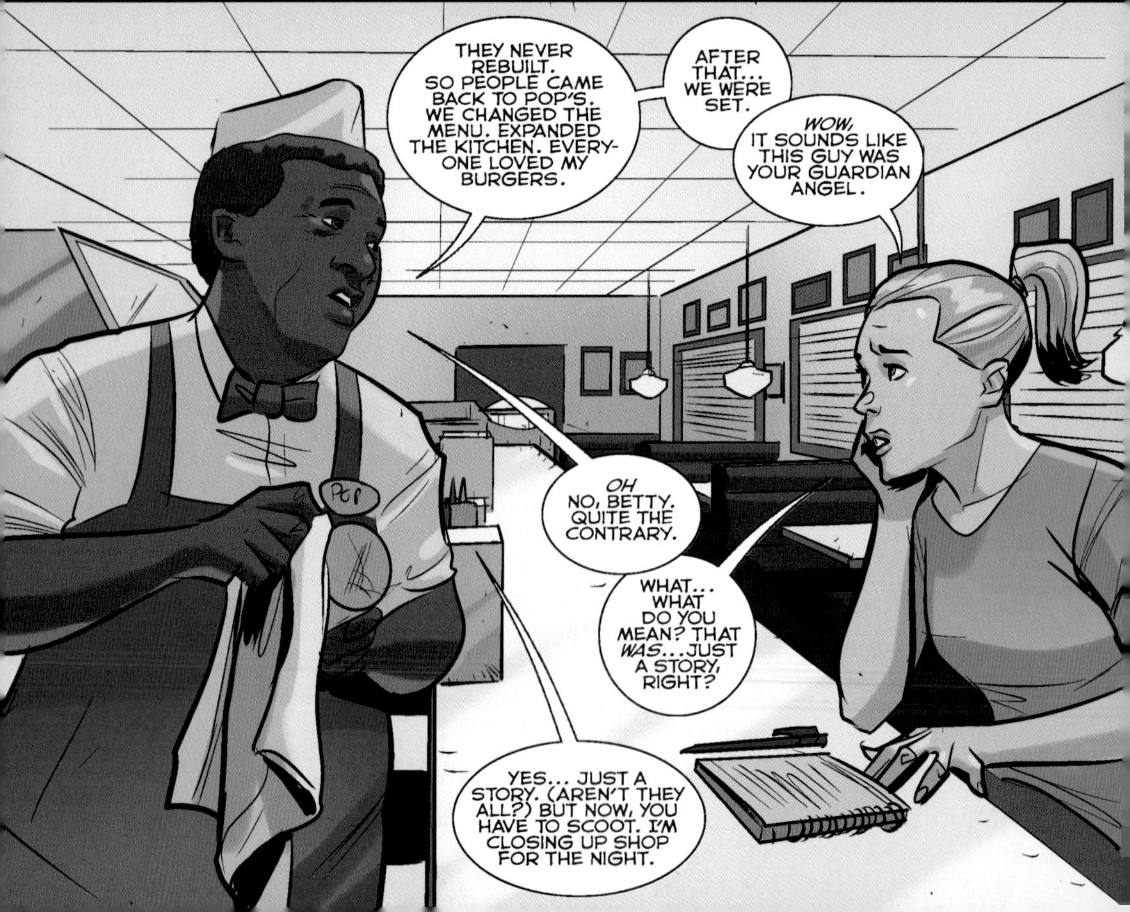
THEY NEVER REBUILT. SO PEOPLE CAME BACK TO POP'S. WE CHANGED THE MENU. EXPANDED THE KITCHEN. EVERYONE LOVED MY BURGERS.
AFTER THAT... WE WERE SET.
WOW, IT SOUNDS LIKE THIS GUY WAS YOUR GUARDIAN ANGEL.
OH NO, BETTY. QUITE THE CONTRARY.
WHAT... WHAT DO YOU MEAN? THAT *WAS*... JUST A STORY, RIGHT?
YES... JUST A STORY. (AREN'T THEY ALL?) BUT NOW, YOU HAVE TO SCOOT. I'M CLOSING UP SHOP FOR THE NIGHT.

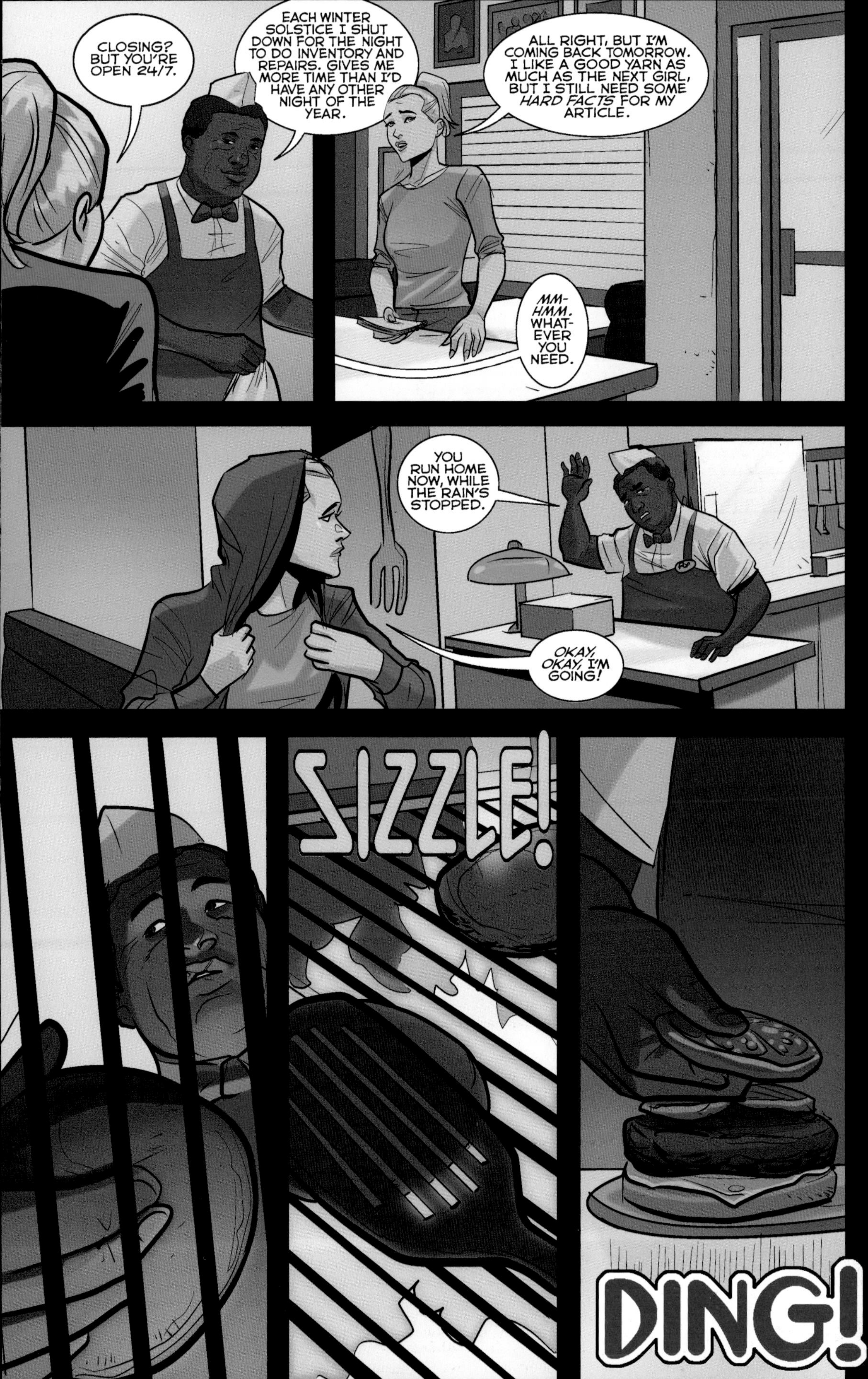

CLOSING? BUT YOU'RE OPEN 24/7.
EACH WINTER SOLSTICE I SHUT DOWN FOR THE NIGHT TO DO INVENTORY AND REPAIRS. GIVES ME MORE TIME THAN I'D HAVE ANY OTHER NIGHT OF THE YEAR.
ALL RIGHT, BUT I'M COMING BACK TOMORROW. I LIKE A GOOD YARN AS MUCH AS THE NEXT GIRL, BUT I STILL NEED SOME *HARD FACTS* FOR MY ARTICLE.
MM-HMM. WHAT-EVER YOU NEED.
YOU RUN HOME NOW, WHILE THE RAIN'S STOPPED.
OKAY, OKAY, I'M GOING!
SIZZLE!
DING!

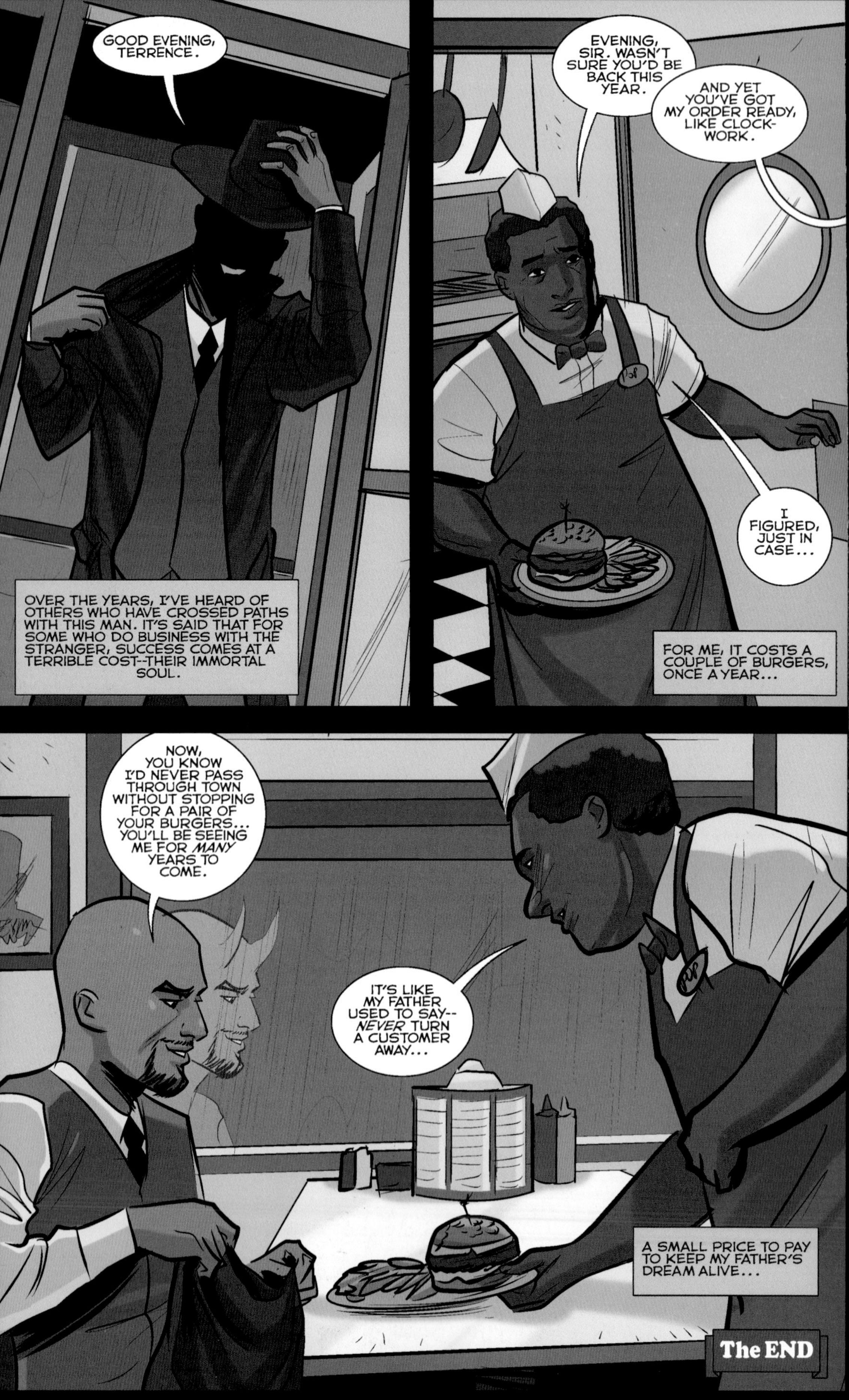

GOOD EVENING, TERRENCE.
OVER THE YEARS, I'VE HEARD OF OTHERS WHO HAVE CROSSED PATHS WITH THIS MAN. IT'S SAID THAT FOR SOME WHO DO BUSINESS WITH THE STRANGER, SUCCESS COMES AT A TERRIBLE COST--THEIR IMMORTAL SOUL.
EVENING, SIR. WASN'T SURE YOU'D BE BACK THIS YEAR.
AND YET YOU'VE GOT MY ORDER READY, LIKE CLOCK-WORK.
I FIGURED, JUST IN CASE...
FOR ME, IT COSTS A COUPLE OF BURGERS, ONCE A YEAR...
NOW, YOU KNOW I'D NEVER PASS THROUGH TOWN WITHOUT STOPPING FOR A PAIR OF YOUR BURGERS... YOU'LL BE SEEING ME FOR *MANY* YEARS TO COME.
IT'S LIKE MY FATHER USED TO SAY-- *NEVER* TURN A CUSTOMER AWAY...
A SMALL PRICE TO PAY TO KEEP MY FATHER'S DREAM ALIVE...
The END

DINER

ISSUE SEVEN

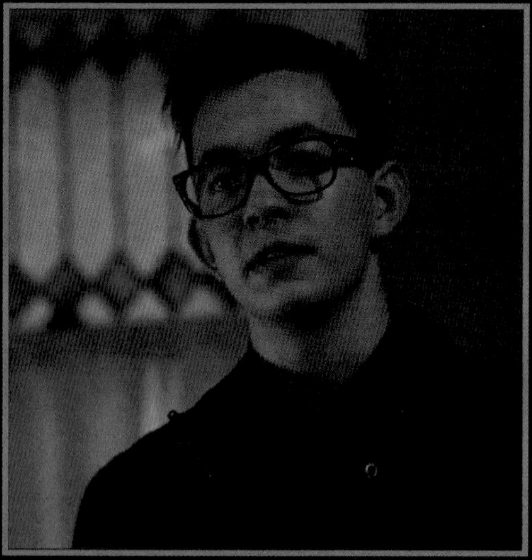

APOCALYPSE NOW!

WRITERS:
AARON ALLEN
AND **WILL EWING**

ART:
THOMAS PITILLI

COLORS:
ANDRE SZYMANOWICZ

LETTERS:
JANICE CHIANG

STARRING
DILTON DOILEY

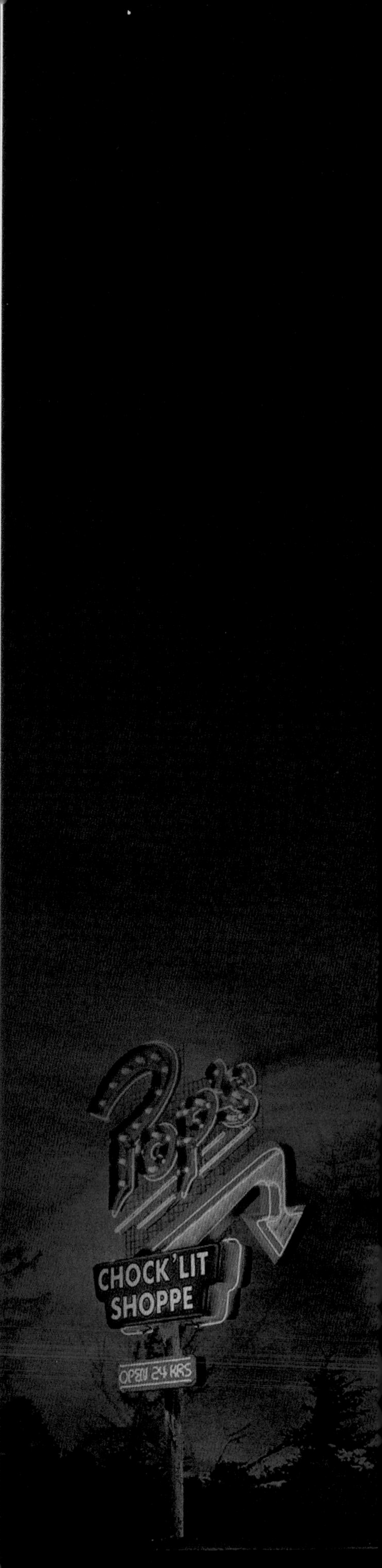
Pop's
CHOCK'LIT SHOPPE
OPEN 24 HRS

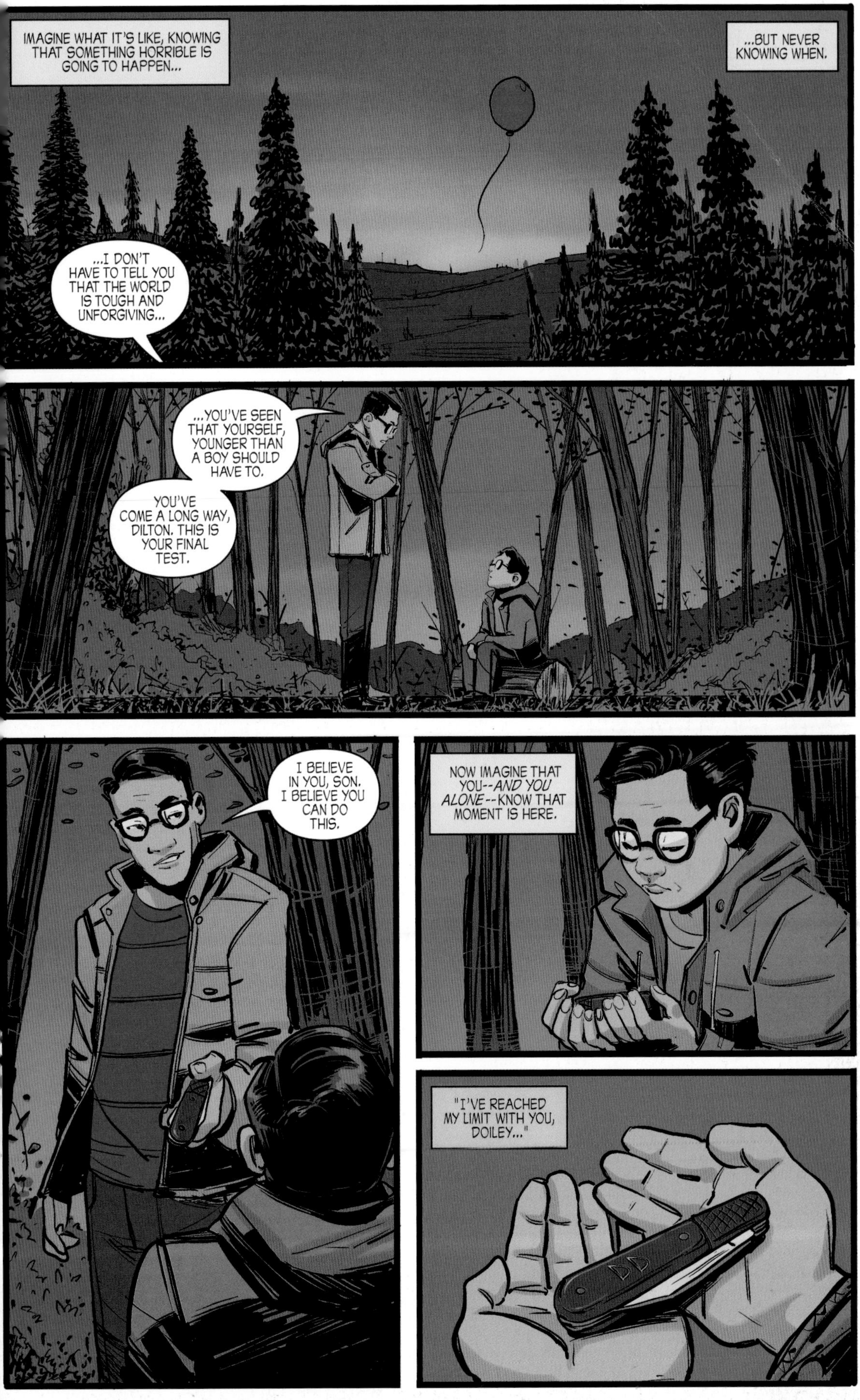
IMAGINE WHAT IT'S LIKE, KNOWING THAT SOMETHING HORRIBLE IS GOING TO HAPPEN...
...BUT NEVER KNOWING WHEN.
...I DON'T HAVE TO TELL YOU THAT THE WORLD IS TOUGH AND UNFORGIVING...
...YOU'VE SEEN THAT YOURSELF, YOUNGER THAN A BOY SHOULD HAVE TO.
YOU'VE COME A LONG WAY, DILTON. THIS IS YOUR FINAL TEST.
I BELIEVE IN YOU, SON. I BELIEVE YOU CAN DO THIS.
NOW IMAGINE THAT YOU--*AND YOU ALONE*--KNOW THAT MOMENT IS HERE.
"I'VE REACHED MY LIMIT WITH YOU, DOILEY..."

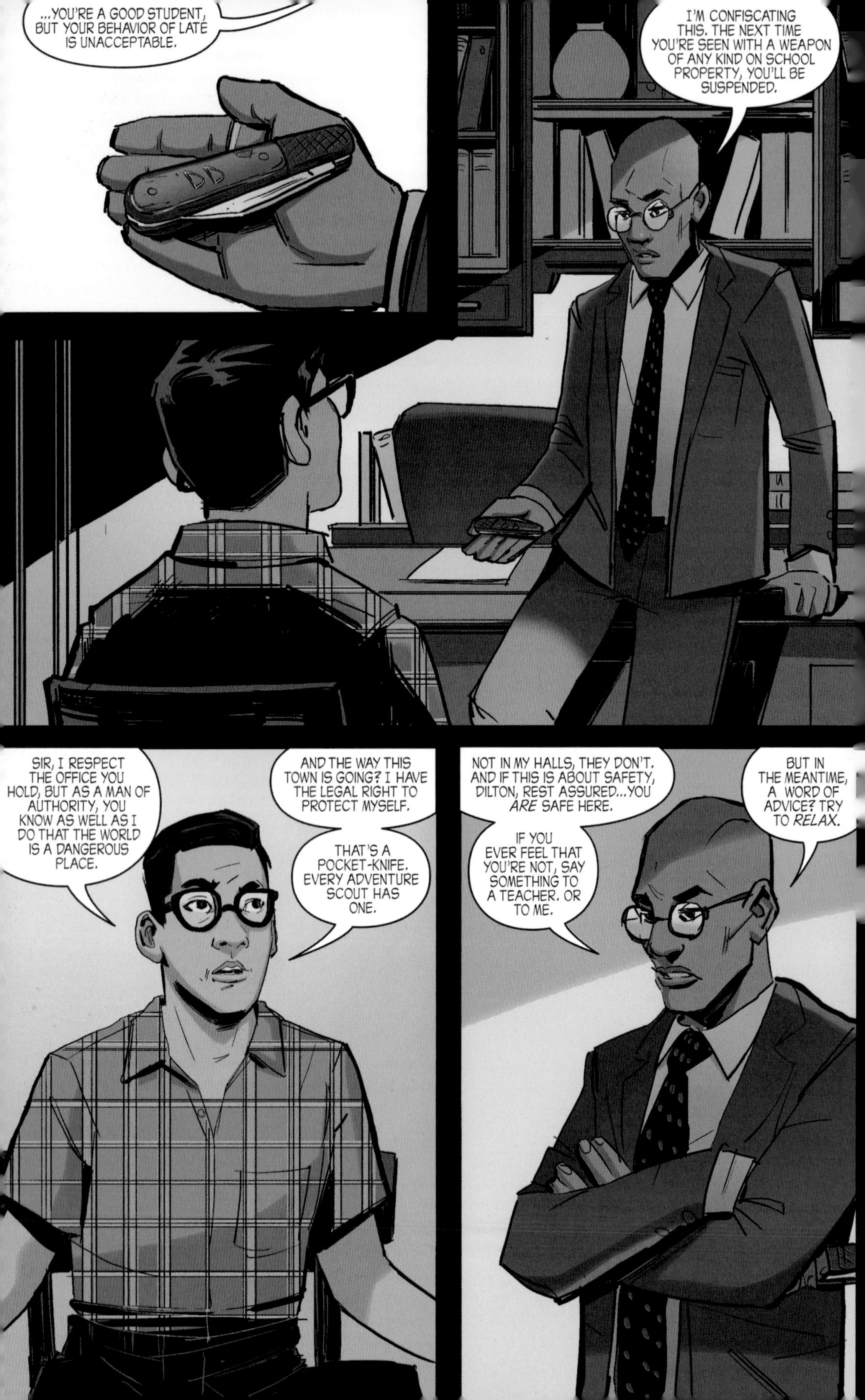
...YOU'RE A GOOD STUDENT, BUT YOUR BEHAVIOR OF LATE IS UNACCEPTABLE.
I'M CONFISCATING THIS. THE NEXT TIME YOU'RE SEEN WITH A WEAPON OF ANY KIND ON SCHOOL PROPERTY, YOU'LL BE SUSPENDED.
SIR, I RESPECT THE OFFICE YOU HOLD, BUT AS A MAN OF AUTHORITY, YOU KNOW AS WELL AS I DO THAT THE WORLD IS A DANGEROUS PLACE.
AND THE WAY THIS TOWN IS GOING? I HAVE THE LEGAL RIGHT TO PROTECT MYSELF.
THAT'S A POCKET-KNIFE. EVERY ADVENTURE SCOUT HAS ONE.
NOT IN MY HALLS, THEY DON'T. AND IF THIS IS ABOUT SAFETY, DILTON, REST ASSURED...YOU *ARE* SAFE HERE.
IF YOU EVER FEEL THAT YOU'RE NOT, SAY SOMETHING TO A TEACHER. OR TO ME.
BUT IN THE MEANTIME, A WORD OF ADVICE? TRY TO *RELAX*.

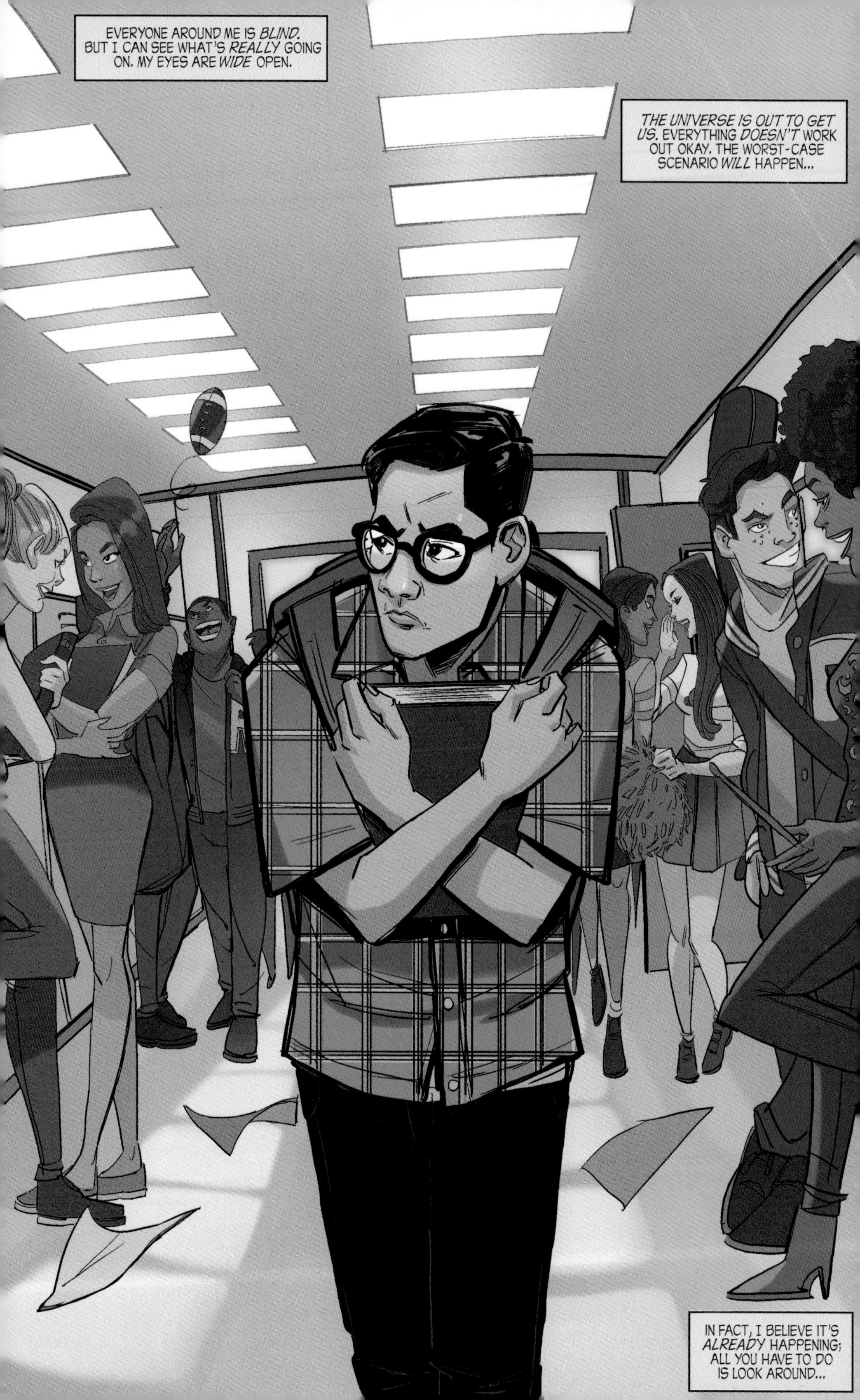
EVERYONE AROUND ME IS *BLIND*. BUT I CAN SEE WHAT'S *REALLY* GOING ON. MY EYES ARE *WIDE* OPEN.
THE UNIVERSE IS OUT TO GET US. EVERYTHING *DOESN'T* WORK OUT OKAY. THE WORST-CASE SCENARIO *WILL* HAPPEN...
IN FACT, I BELIEVE IT'S *ALREADY* HAPPENING; ALL YOU HAVE TO DO IS LOOK AROUND...

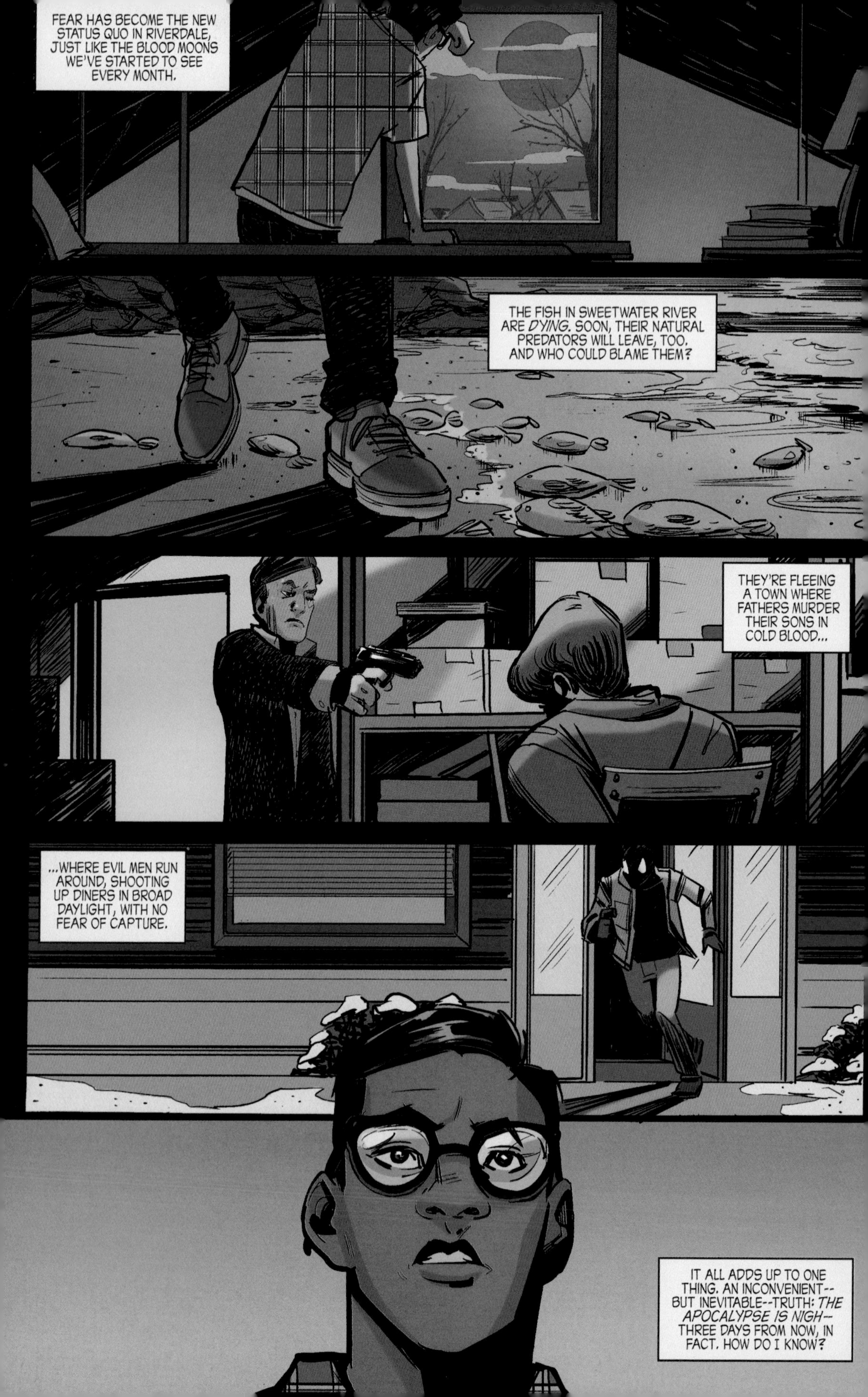
FEAR HAS BECOME THE NEW STATUS QUO IN RIVERDALE, JUST LIKE THE BLOOD MOONS WE'VE STARTED TO SEE EVERY MONTH.
THE FISH IN SWEETWATER RIVER ARE *DYING*. SOON, THEIR NATURAL PREDATORS WILL LEAVE, TOO. AND WHO COULD BLAME THEM?
THEY'RE FLEEING A TOWN WHERE FATHERS MURDER THEIR SONS IN COLD BLOOD...
...WHERE EVIL MEN RUN AROUND, SHOOTING UP DINERS IN BROAD DAYLIGHT, WITH NO FEAR OF CAPTURE.
IT ALL ADDS UP TO ONE THING. AN INCONVENIENT--BUT INEVITABLE--TRUTH: *THE APOCALYPSE IS NIGH*--THREE DAYS FROM NOW, IN FACT. HOW DO I KNOW?

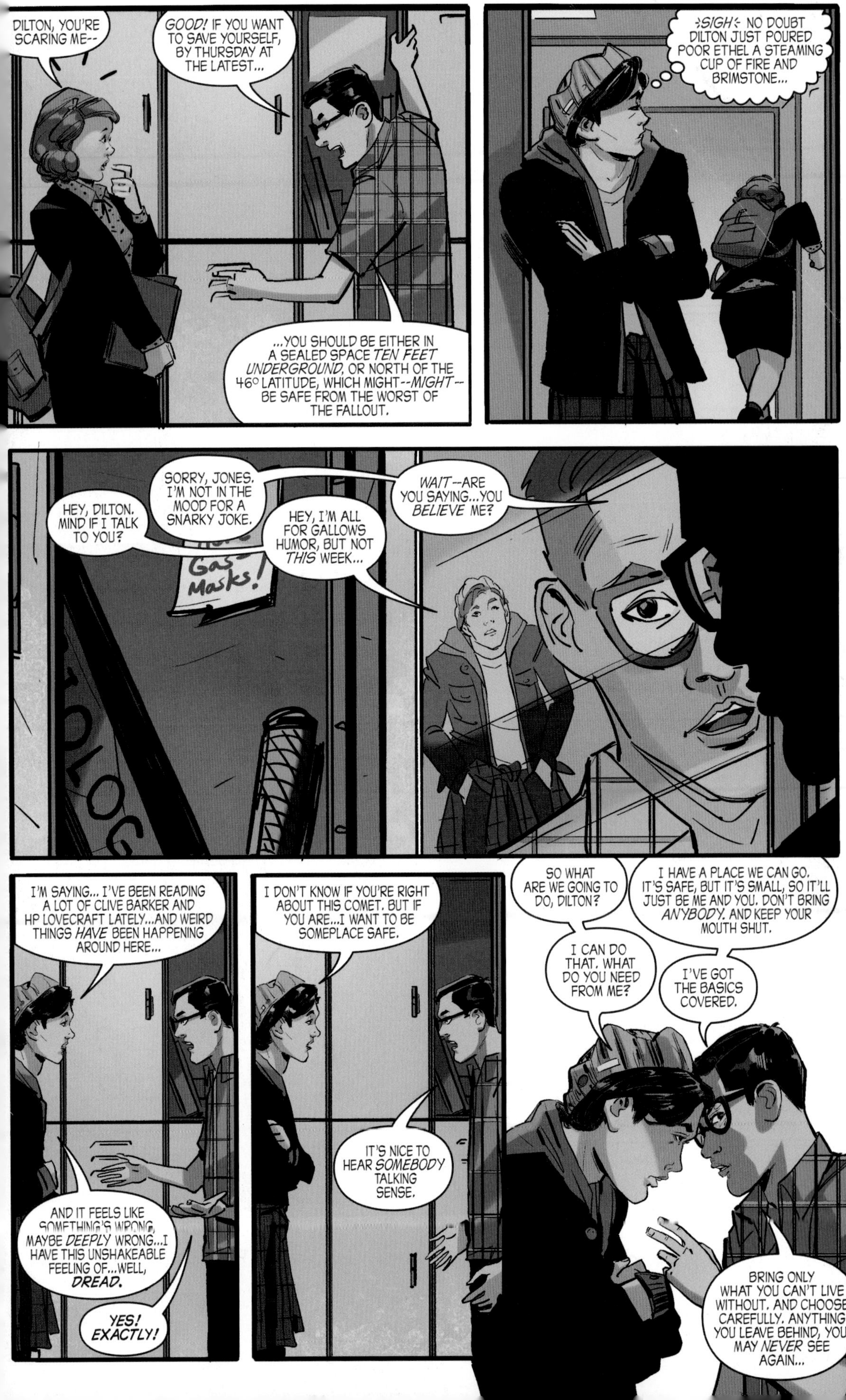
DILTON, YOU'RE SCARING ME--
GOOD! IF YOU WANT TO SAVE YOURSELF, BY THURSDAY AT THE LATEST...
...YOU SHOULD BE EITHER IN A SEALED SPACE TEN FEET UNDERGROUND, OR NORTH OF THE 46° LATITUDE, WHICH MIGHT--MIGHT--BE SAFE FROM THE WORST OF THE FALLOUT.
SIGH NO DOUBT DILTON JUST POURED POOR ETHEL A STEAMING CUP OF FIRE AND BRIMSTONE...
HEY, DILTON. MIND IF I TALK TO YOU?
SORRY, JONES. I'M NOT IN THE MOOD FOR A SNARKY JOKE.
HEY, I'M ALL FOR GALLOWS HUMOR, BUT NOT THIS WEEK...
WAIT--ARE YOU SAYING...YOU BELIEVE ME?
Gas Masks!
I'M SAYING... I'VE BEEN READING A LOT OF CLIVE BARKER AND HP LOVECRAFT LATELY...AND WEIRD THINGS HAVE BEEN HAPPENING AROUND HERE...
AND IT FEELS LIKE SOMETHING'S WRONG, MAYBE DEEPLY WRONG...I HAVE THIS UNSHAKEABLE FEELING OF...WELL, DREAD.
YES! EXACTLY!
I DON'T KNOW IF YOU'RE RIGHT ABOUT THIS COMET. BUT IF YOU ARE...I WANT TO BE SOMEPLACE SAFE.
IT'S NICE TO HEAR SOMEBODY TALKING SENSE.
SO WHAT ARE WE GOING TO DO, DILTON?
I HAVE A PLACE WE CAN GO. IT'S SAFE, BUT IT'S SMALL, SO IT'LL JUST BE ME AND YOU. DON'T BRING ANYBODY. AND KEEP YOUR MOUTH SHUT.
I CAN DO THAT. WHAT DO YOU NEED FROM ME?
I'VE GOT THE BASICS COVERED.
BRING ONLY WHAT YOU CAN'T LIVE WITHOUT. AND CHOOSE CAREFULLY. ANYTHING YOU LEAVE BEHIND, YOU MAY NEVER SEE AGAIN...

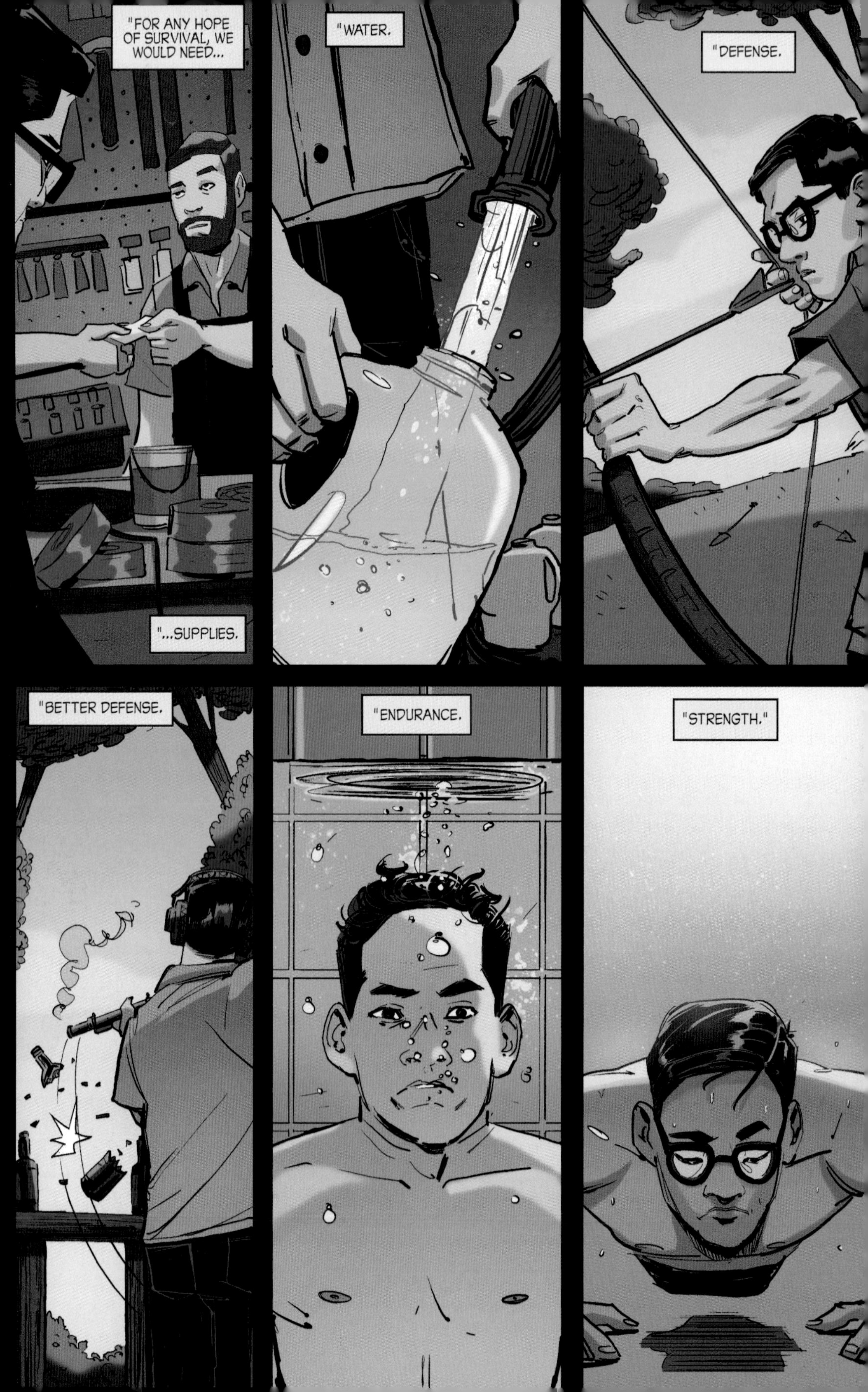
"FOR ANY HOPE OF SURVIVAL, WE WOULD NEED...
"...SUPPLIES.
"WATER.
"DEFENSE.
"BETTER DEFENSE.
"ENDURANCE.
"STRENGTH."

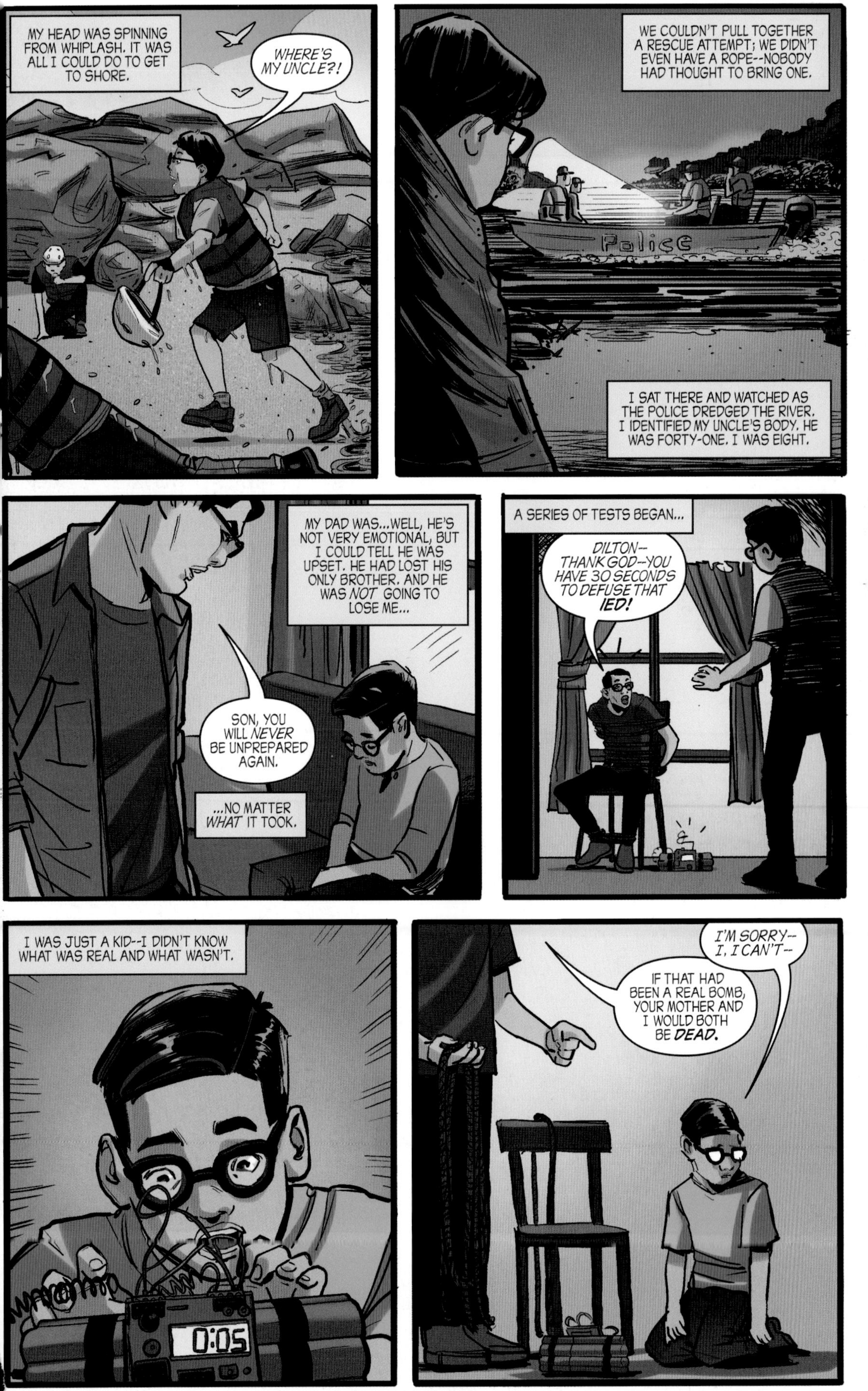
MY HEAD WAS SPINNING FROM WHIPLASH. IT WAS ALL I COULD DO TO GET TO SHORE.
WHERE'S MY UNCLE?!
WE COULDN'T PULL TOGETHER A RESCUE ATTEMPT; WE DIDN'T EVEN HAVE A ROPE--NOBODY HAD THOUGHT TO BRING ONE.
POLICE
I SAT THERE AND WATCHED AS THE POLICE DREDGED THE RIVER. I IDENTIFIED MY UNCLE'S BODY. HE WAS FORTY-ONE. I WAS EIGHT.
MY DAD WAS...WELL, HE'S NOT VERY EMOTIONAL, BUT I COULD TELL HE WAS UPSET. HE HAD LOST HIS ONLY BROTHER. AND HE WAS NOT GOING TO LOSE ME...
SON, YOU WILL NEVER BE UNPREPARED AGAIN.
...NO MATTER WHAT IT TOOK.
A SERIES OF TESTS BEGAN...
DILTON-- THANK GOD--YOU HAVE 30 SECONDS TO DEFUSE THAT IED!
I WAS JUST A KID--I DIDN'T KNOW WHAT WAS REAL AND WHAT WASN'T.
0:05
I'M SORRY-- I, I CAN'T--
IF THAT HAD BEEN A REAL BOMB, YOUR MOTHER AND I WOULD BOTH BE DEAD.

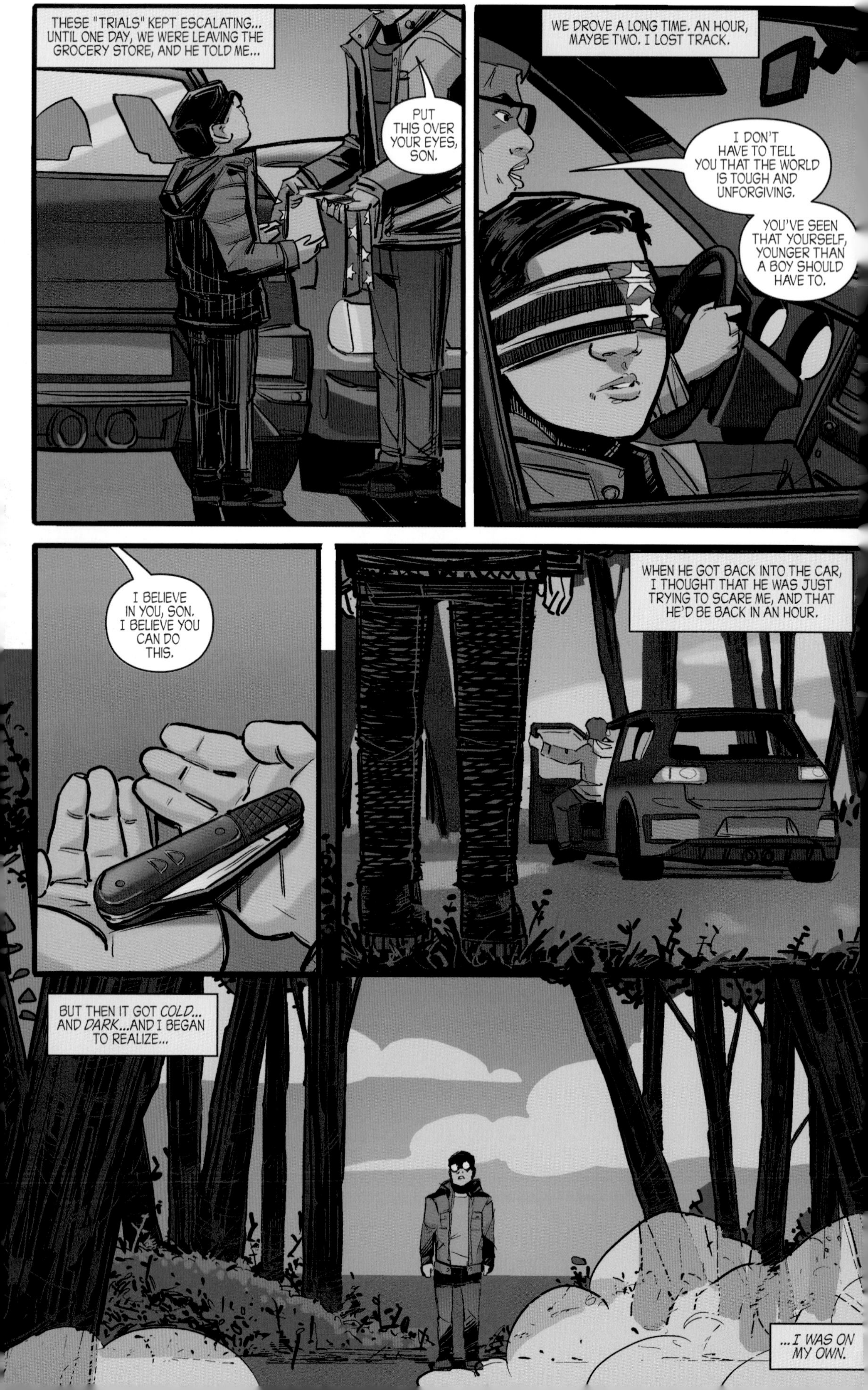
THESE "TRIALS" KEPT ESCALATING... UNTIL ONE DAY, WE WERE LEAVING THE GROCERY STORE, AND HE TOLD ME...
PUT THIS OVER YOUR EYES, SON.
WE DROVE A LONG TIME. AN HOUR, MAYBE TWO. I LOST TRACK.
I DON'T HAVE TO TELL YOU THAT THE WORLD IS TOUGH AND UNFORGIVING.
YOU'VE SEEN THAT YOURSELF, YOUNGER THAN A BOY SHOULD HAVE TO.
I BELIEVE IN YOU, SON. I BELIEVE YOU CAN DO THIS.
WHEN HE GOT BACK INTO THE CAR, I THOUGHT THAT HE WAS JUST TRYING TO SCARE ME, AND THAT HE'D BE BACK IN AN HOUR.
BUT THEN IT GOT *COLD*... AND *DARK*...AND I BEGAN TO REALIZE...
...I WAS ON MY OWN.

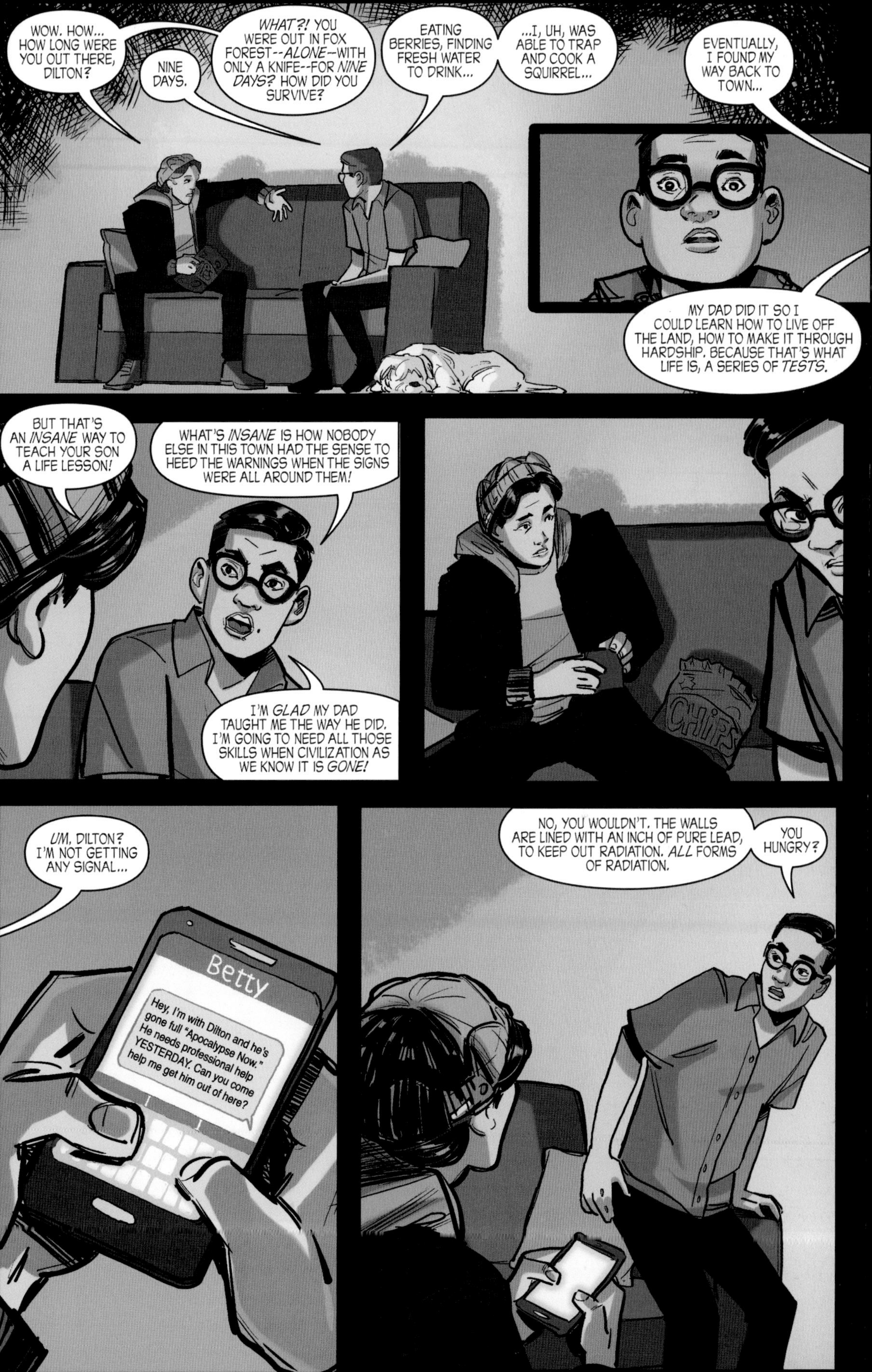
WOW. HOW... HOW LONG WERE YOU OUT THERE, DILTON?
NINE DAYS.
WHAT?! YOU WERE OUT IN FOX FOREST--ALONE--WITH ONLY A KNIFE--FOR NINE DAYS? HOW DID YOU SURVIVE?
EATING BERRIES, FINDING FRESH WATER TO DRINK...
...I, UH, WAS ABLE TO TRAP AND COOK A SQUIRREL...
EVENTUALLY, I FOUND MY WAY BACK TO TOWN...
MY DAD DID IT SO I COULD LEARN HOW TO LIVE OFF THE LAND, HOW TO MAKE IT THROUGH HARDSHIP. BECAUSE THAT'S WHAT LIFE IS, A SERIES OF TESTS.
BUT THAT'S AN INSANE WAY TO TEACH YOUR SON A LIFE LESSON!
WHAT'S INSANE IS HOW NOBODY ELSE IN THIS TOWN HAD THE SENSE TO HEED THE WARNINGS WHEN THE SIGNS WERE ALL AROUND THEM!
I'M GLAD MY DAD TAUGHT ME THE WAY HE DID. I'M GOING TO NEED ALL THOSE SKILLS WHEN CIVILIZATION AS WE KNOW IT IS GONE!
CHIPS
UM, DILTON? I'M NOT GETTING ANY SIGNAL...
Betty
Hey, I'm with Dilton and he's gone full "Apocalypse Now." He needs professional help YESTERDAY. Can you come help me get him out of here?
NO, YOU WOULDN'T. THE WALLS ARE LINED WITH AN INCH OF PURE LEAD, TO KEEP OUT RADIATION. ALL FORMS OF RADIATION.
YOU HUNGRY?

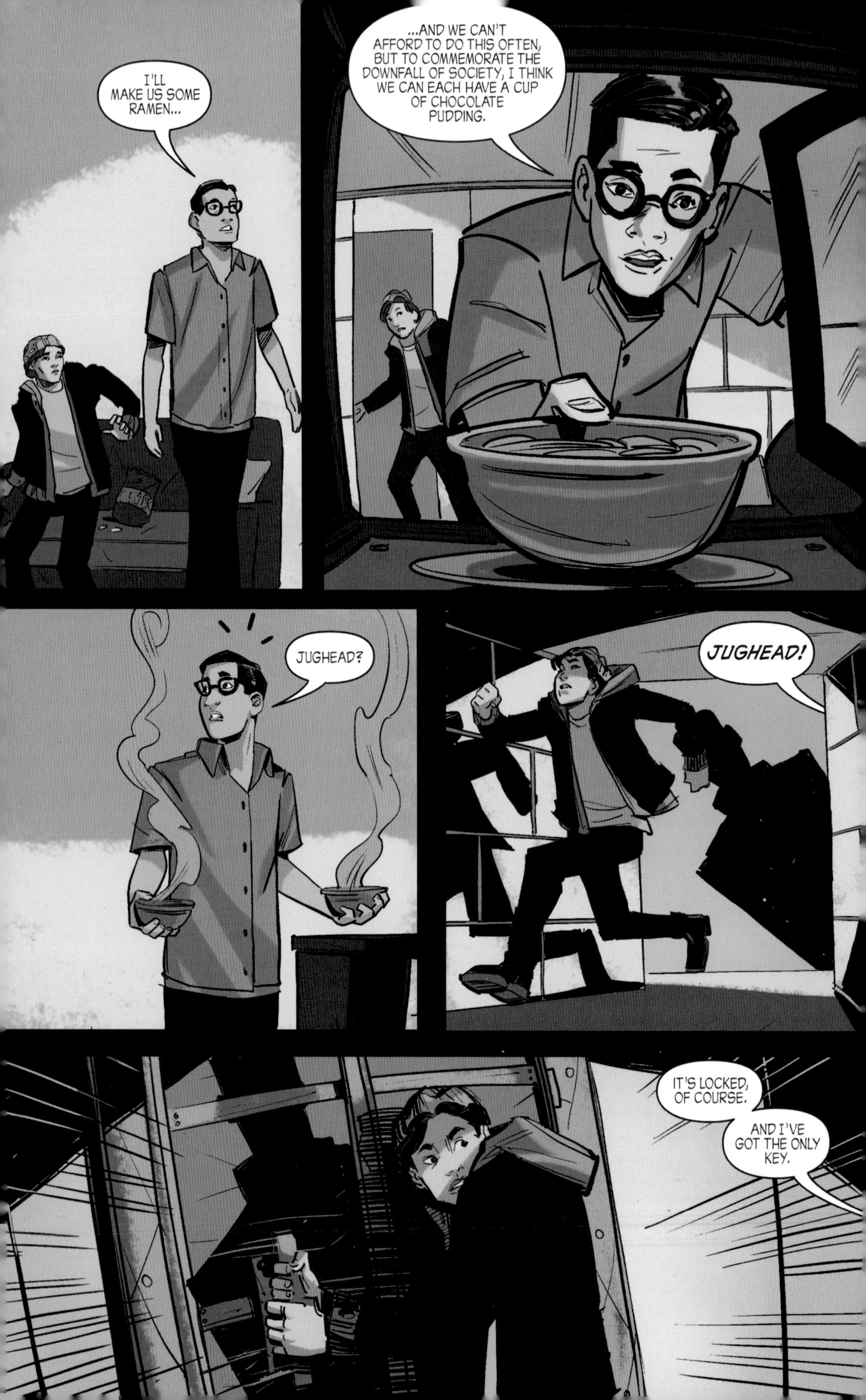
I'LL MAKE US SOME RAMEN...
...AND WE CAN'T AFFORD TO DO THIS OFTEN, BUT TO COMMEMORATE THE DOWNFALL OF SOCIETY, I THINK WE CAN EACH HAVE A CUP OF CHOCOLATE PUDDING.
JUGHEAD?
JUGHEAD!
IT'S LOCKED, OF COURSE.
AND I'VE GOT THE ONLY KEY.

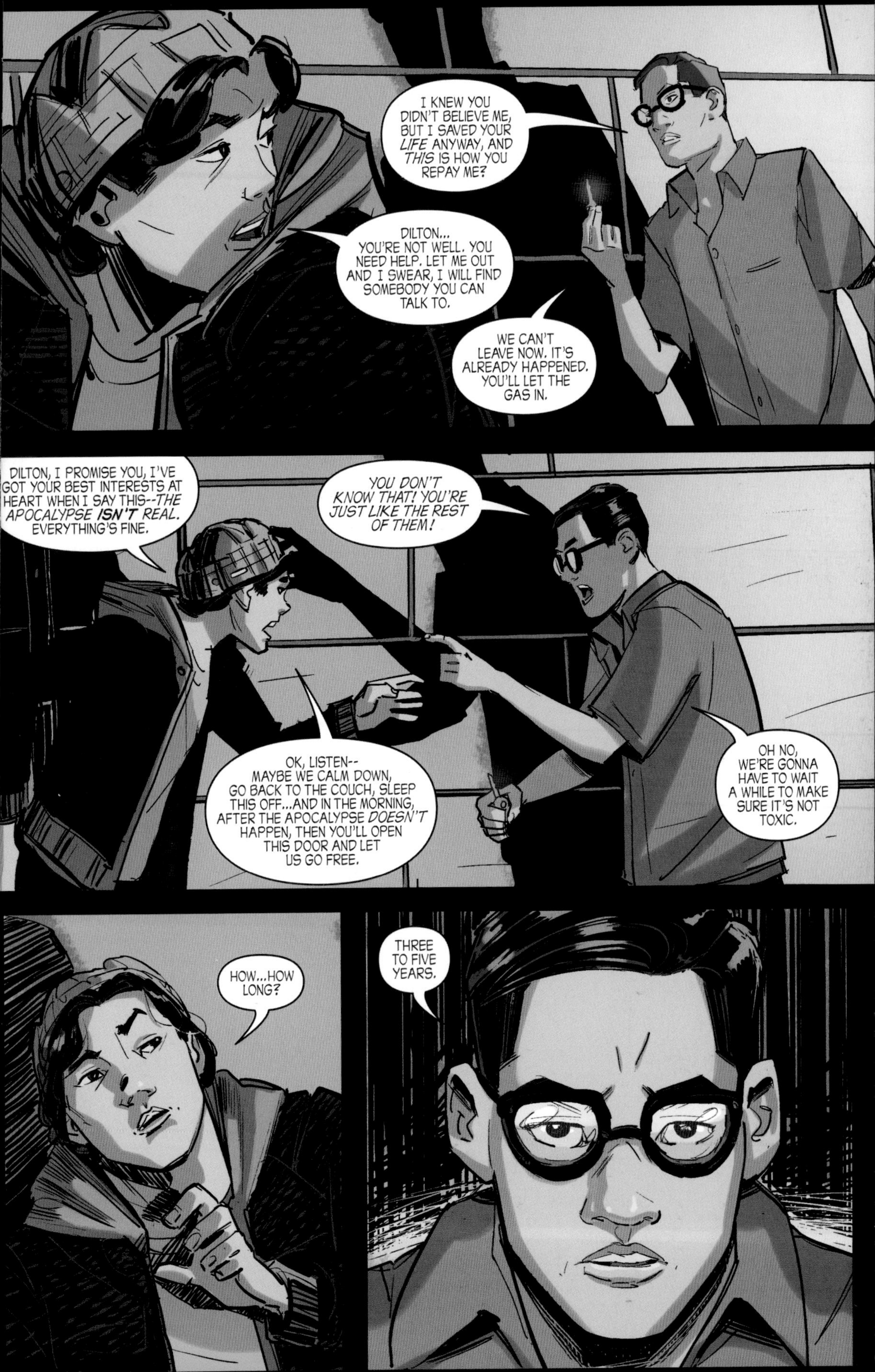
I KNEW YOU DIDN'T BELIEVE ME, BUT I SAVED YOUR *LIFE* ANYWAY, AND *THIS* IS HOW YOU REPAY ME?
DILTON... YOU'RE NOT WELL. YOU NEED HELP. LET ME OUT AND I SWEAR, I WILL FIND SOMEBODY YOU CAN TALK TO.
WE CAN'T LEAVE NOW. IT'S ALREADY HAPPENED. YOU'LL LET THE GAS IN.
DILTON, I PROMISE YOU, I'VE GOT YOUR BEST INTERESTS AT HEART WHEN I SAY THIS--*THE APOCALYPSE* ***ISN'T*** *REAL*. EVERYTHING'S FINE.
YOU DON'T KNOW THAT! YOU'RE JUST LIKE THE REST OF THEM!
OK, LISTEN-- MAYBE WE CALM DOWN, GO BACK TO THE COUCH, SLEEP THIS OFF...AND IN THE MORNING, AFTER THE APOCALYPSE *DOESN'T* HAPPEN, THEN YOU'LL OPEN THIS DOOR AND LET US GO FREE.
OH NO, WE'RE GONNA HAVE TO WAIT A WHILE TO MAKE SURE IT'S NOT TOXIC.
HOW...HOW LONG?
THREE TO FIVE YEARS.

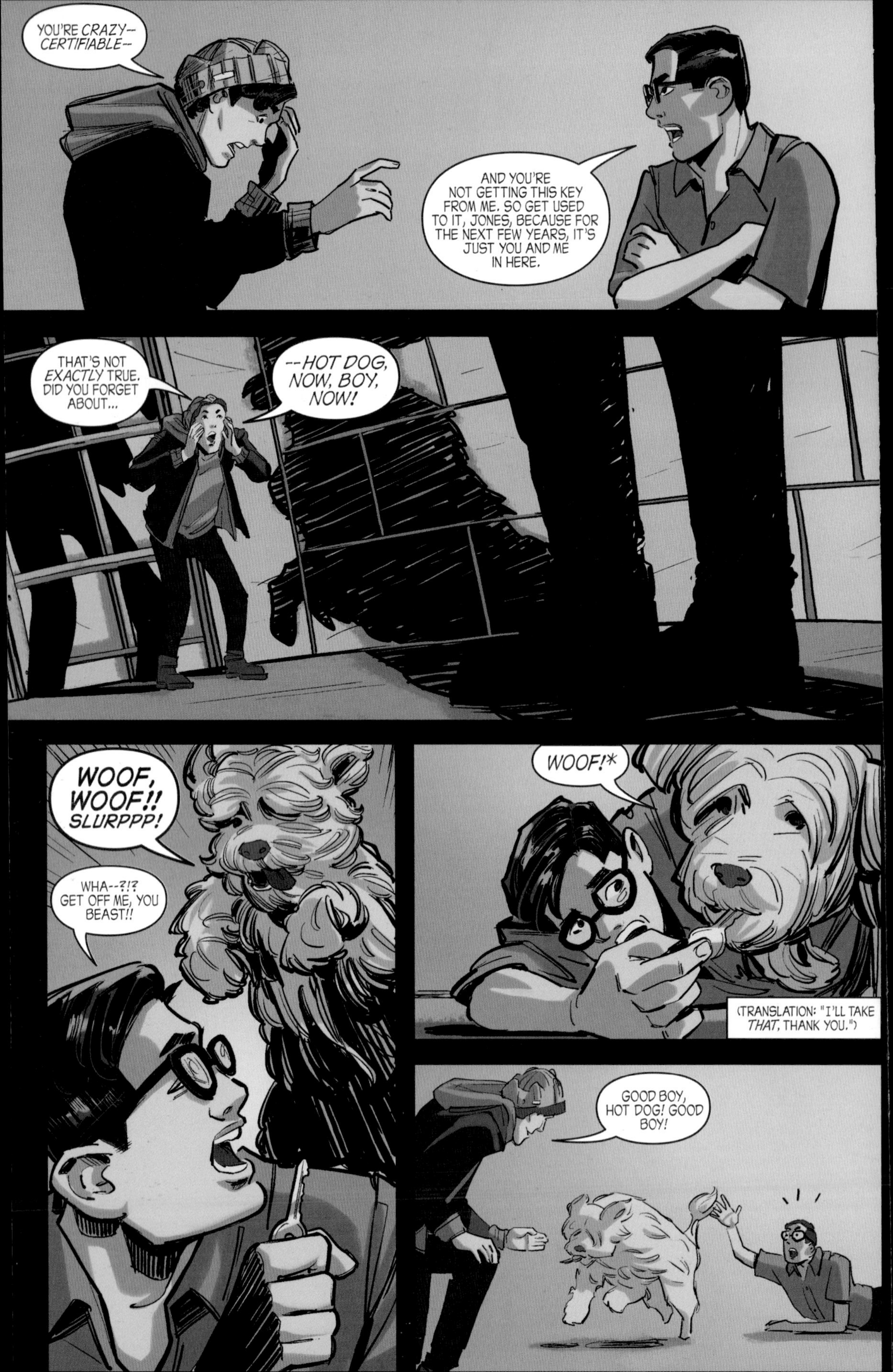

YOU'RE CRAZY-- CERTIFIABLE--
AND YOU'RE NOT GETTING THIS KEY FROM ME. SO GET USED TO IT, JONES, BECAUSE FOR THE NEXT FEW YEARS, IT'S JUST YOU AND ME IN HERE.
THAT'S NOT EXACTLY TRUE. DID YOU FORGET ABOUT...
--HOT DOG, NOW, BOY, NOW!
WOOF, WOOF!! SLURPPP!
WHA--?!? GET OFF ME, YOU BEAST!!
WOOF!*
(TRANSLATION: "I'LL TAKE THAT, THANK YOU.")
GOOD BOY, HOT DOG! GOOD BOY!

DINER

ISSUE EIGHT

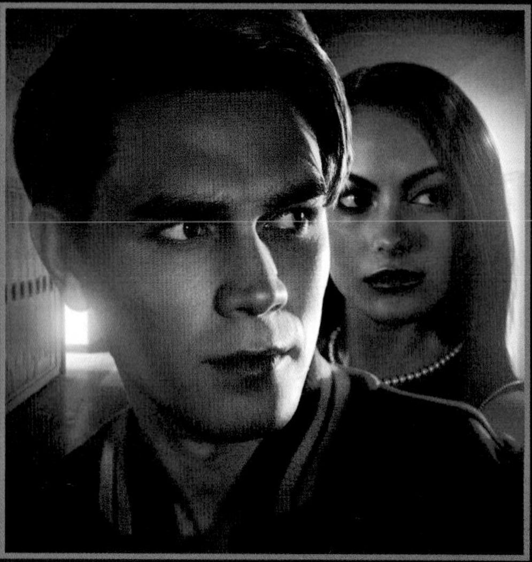

METROPOLITAN

WRITER:
WILL EWING

ART:
THOMAS PITILLI

COLORS:
ANDRE SZYMANOWICZ

LETTERS:
JOHN WORKMAN

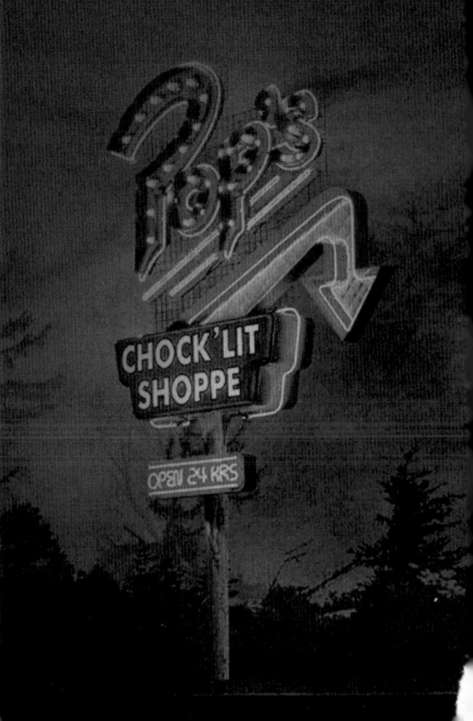
Pop's
CHOCK'LIT
SHOPPE
OPEN 24 HRS

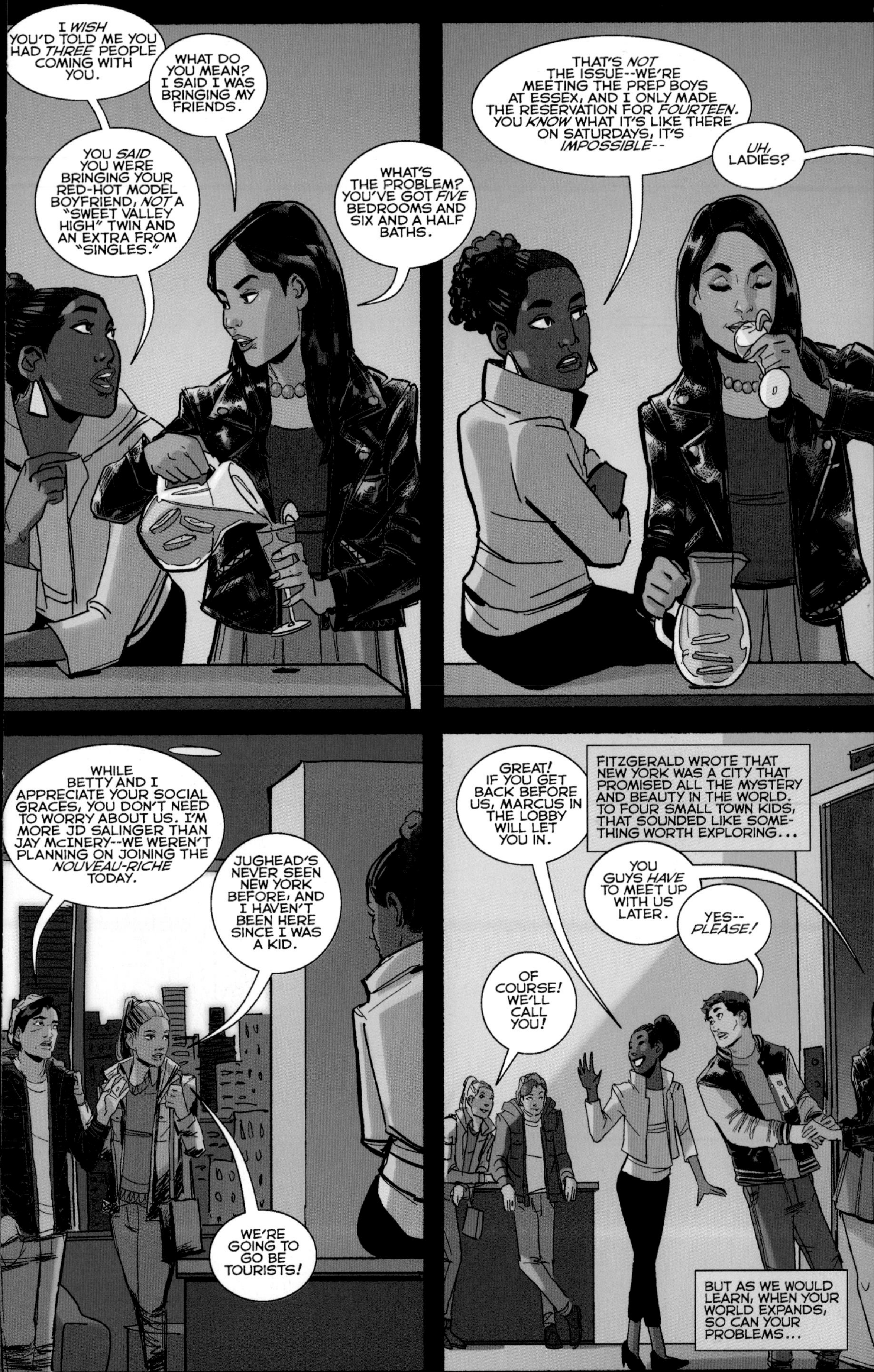

I *WISH* YOU'D TOLD ME YOU HAD *THREE* PEOPLE COMING WITH YOU.
WHAT DO YOU MEAN? I SAID I WAS BRINGING MY FRIENDS.
YOU *SAID* YOU WERE BRINGING YOUR RED-HOT MODEL BOYFRIEND, *NOT* A "SWEET VALLEY HIGH" TWIN AND AN EXTRA FROM "SINGLES."
WHAT'S THE PROBLEM? YOU'VE GOT *FIVE* BEDROOMS AND SIX AND A HALF BATHS.
THAT'S *NOT* THE ISSUE--WE'RE MEETING THE PREP BOYS AT ESSEX, AND I ONLY MADE THE RESERVATION FOR *FOURTEEN*. YOU *KNOW* WHAT IT'S LIKE THERE ON SATURDAYS, IT'S *IMPOSSIBLE*--
UH, LADIES?
WHILE BETTY AND I APPRECIATE YOUR SOCIAL GRACES, YOU DON'T NEED TO WORRY ABOUT US. I'M MORE JD SALINGER THAN JAY McINERY--WE WEREN'T PLANNING ON JOINING THE *NOUVEAU-RICHE* TODAY.
JUGHEAD'S NEVER SEEN NEW YORK BEFORE, AND I HAVEN'T BEEN HERE SINCE I WAS A KID.
WE'RE GOING TO GO BE TOURISTS!
GREAT! IF YOU GET BACK BEFORE US, MARCUS IN THE LOBBY WILL LET YOU IN.
FITZGERALD WROTE THAT NEW YORK WAS A CITY THAT PROMISED ALL THE MYSTERY AND BEAUTY IN THE WORLD. TO FOUR SMALL TOWN KIDS, THAT SOUNDED LIKE SOMETHING WORTH EXPLORING...
YOU GUYS *HAVE* TO MEET UP WITH US LATER.
YES-- *PLEASE!*
OF COURSE! WE'LL CALL YOU!
BUT AS WE WOULD LEARN, WHEN YOUR WORLD EXPANDS, SO CAN YOUR PROBLEMS...

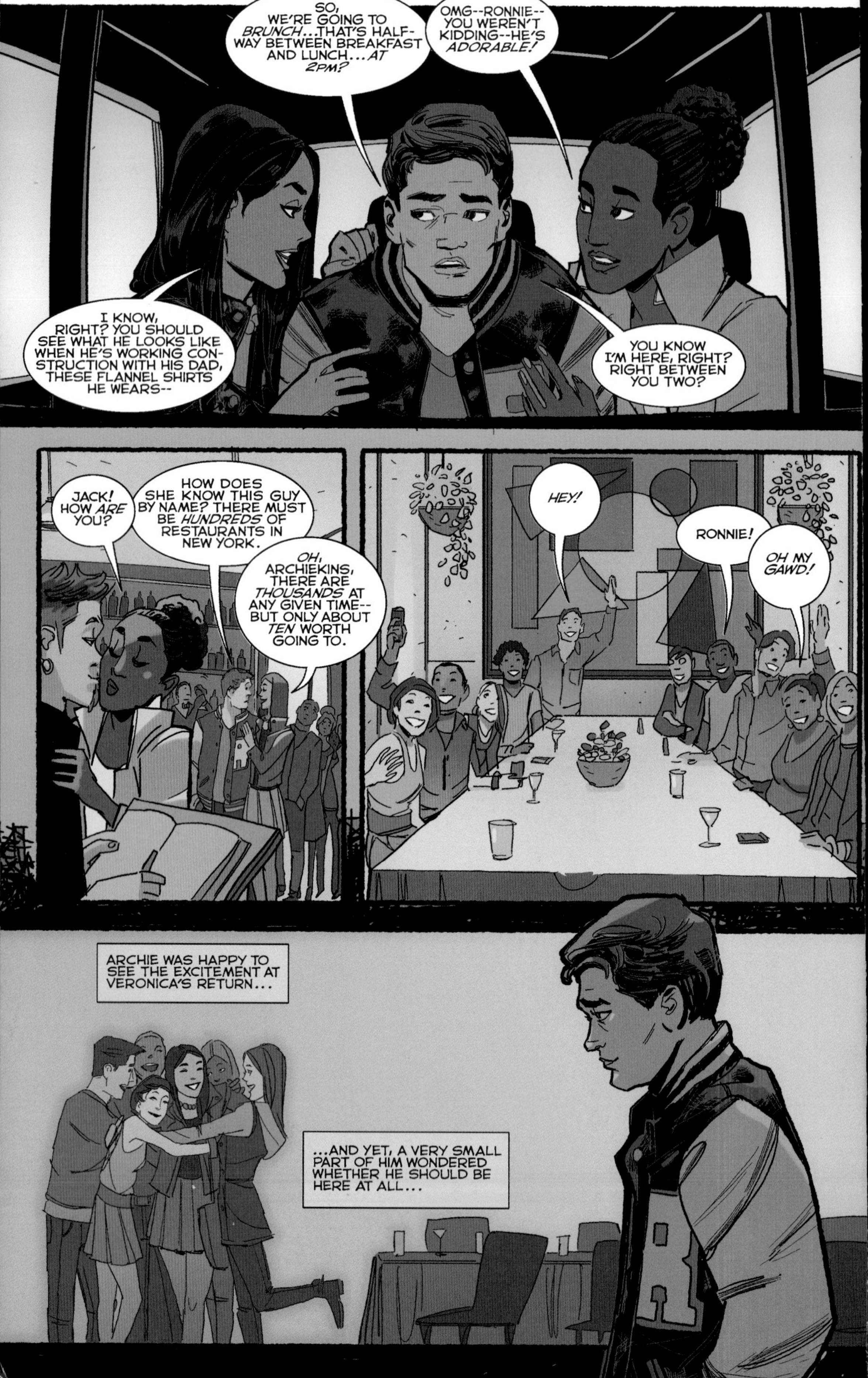

SO, WE'RE GOING TO BRUNCH...THAT'S HALF-WAY BETWEEN BREAKFAST AND LUNCH...AT 2PM?
OMG--RONNIE--YOU WEREN'T KIDDING--HE'S ADORABLE!
I KNOW, RIGHT? YOU SHOULD SEE WHAT HE LOOKS LIKE WHEN HE'S WORKING CONSTRUCTION WITH HIS DAD, THESE FLANNEL SHIRTS HE WEARS--
YOU KNOW I'M HERE, RIGHT? RIGHT BETWEEN YOU TWO?
JACK! HOW ARE YOU?
HOW DOES SHE KNOW THIS GUY BY NAME? THERE MUST BE HUNDREDS OF RESTAURANTS IN NEW YORK.
OH, ARCHIEKINS, THERE ARE THOUSANDS AT ANY GIVEN TIME--BUT ONLY ABOUT TEN WORTH GOING TO.
HEY!
RONNIE!
OH MY GAWD!
ARCHIE WAS HAPPY TO SEE THE EXCITEMENT AT VERONICA'S RETURN...
...AND YET, A VERY SMALL PART OF HIM WONDERED WHETHER HE SHOULD BE HERE AT ALL...

RIVERDALE®

SPECIAL FEATURES

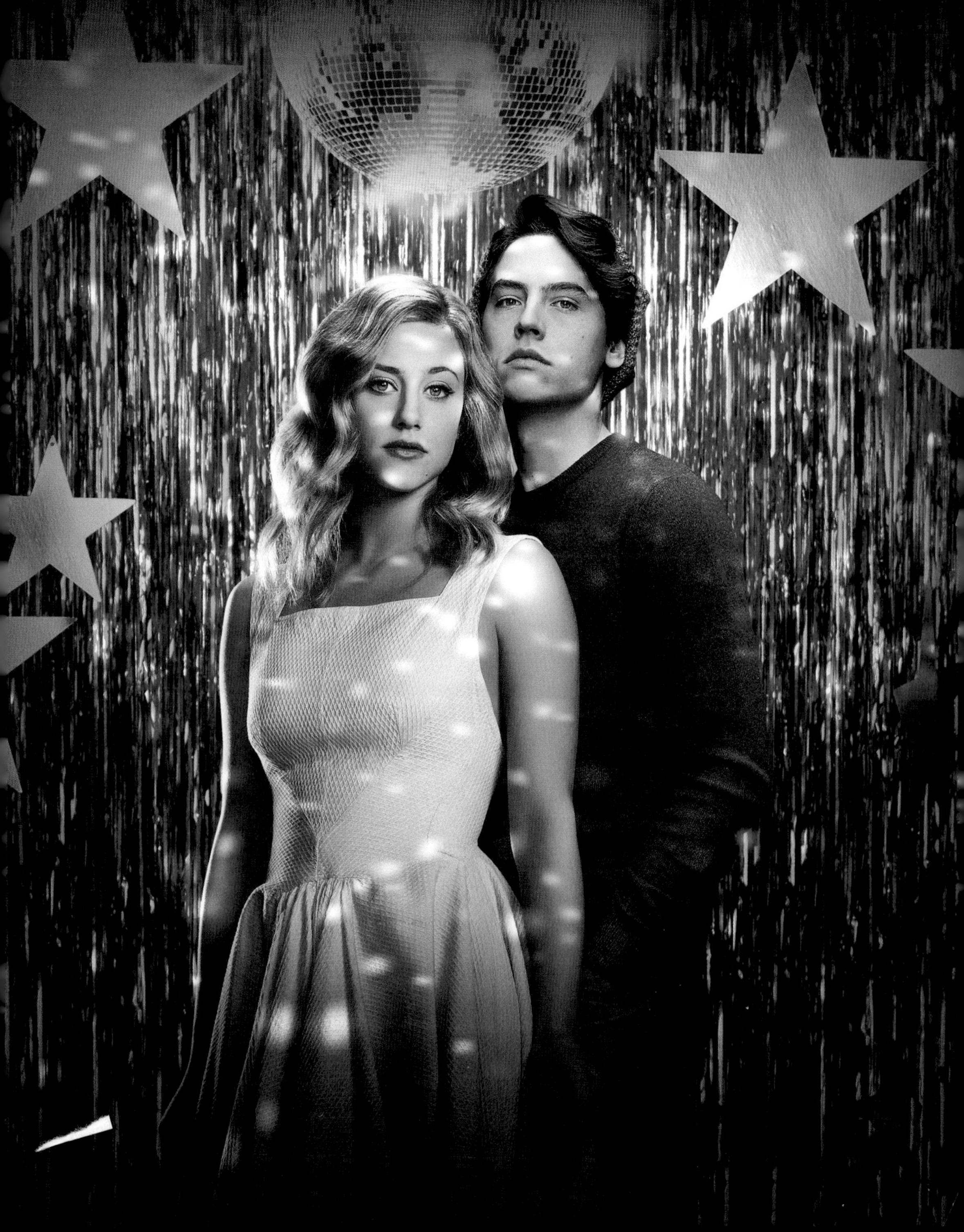

RIVERDALE®

COVER GALLERY

Take a look at our eye-catching main and variant covers for the five issues included in this graphic novel collection. These are comprised of some gorgeous artwork from our talented artists along with some high quality promotional photos of the The CW's *Riverdale* cast courtesy of The CW/Warner Bros.

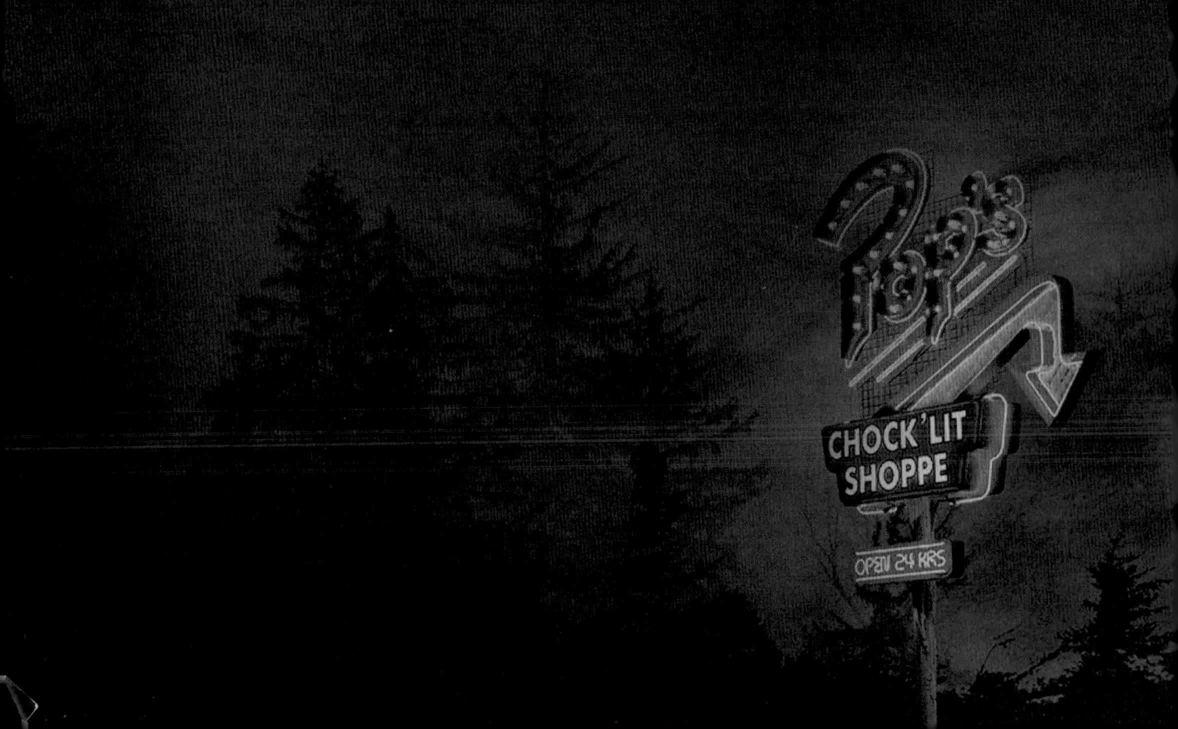
CHOCK'LIT
SHOPPE
OPEN 24 HRS

ISSUE FOUR

1
FRANCESCO FRANCAVILLA

2
ROBERT HACK

3
T. REX

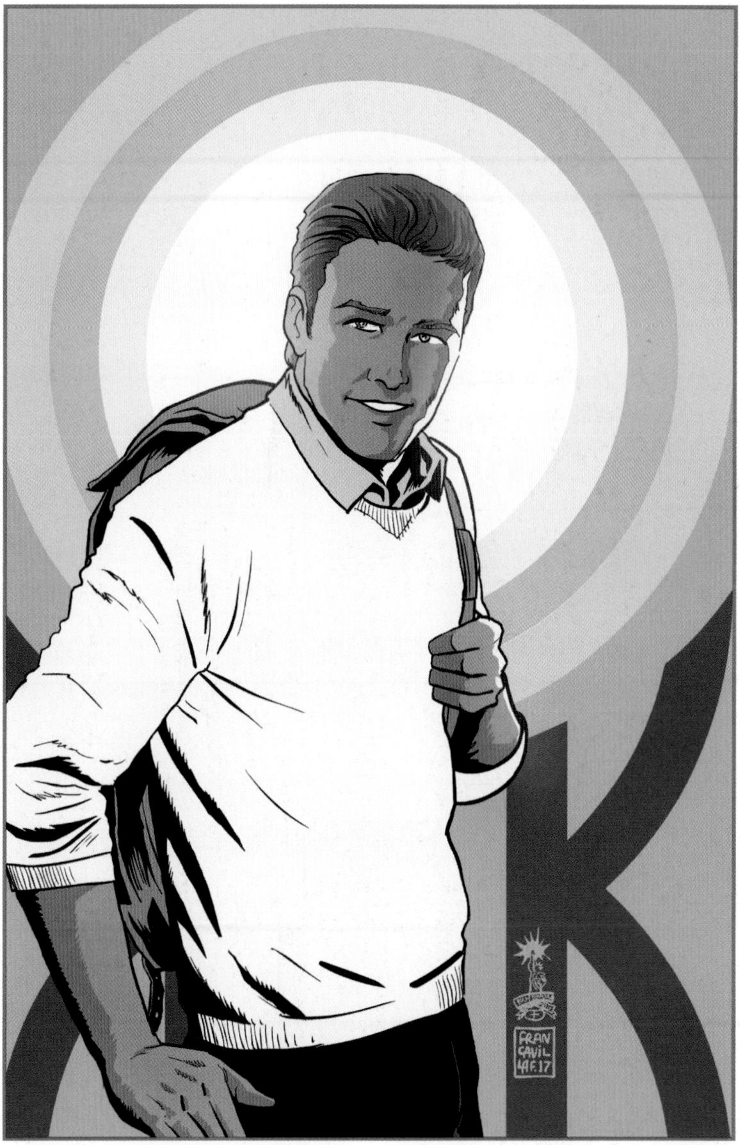

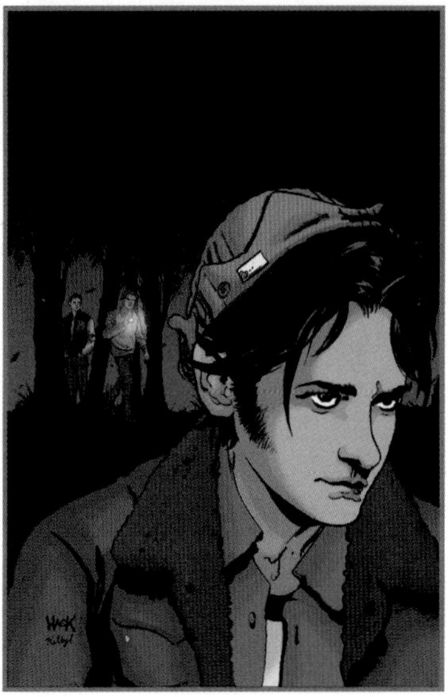

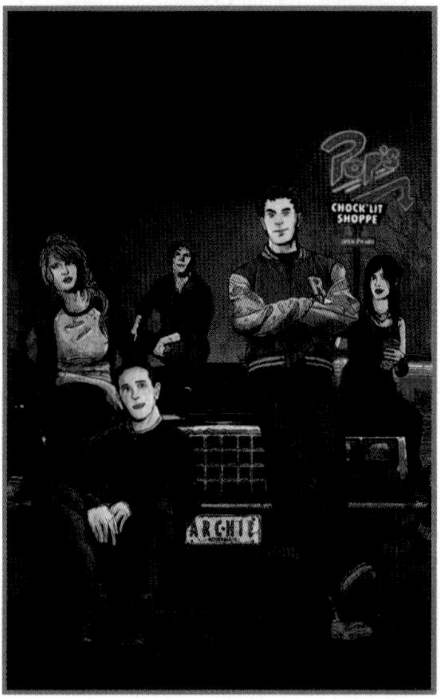
CHOCK'LIT SHOPPE
ARCHIE

ISSUE
FIVE

1
FRANCESCO FRANCAVILLA

2
MATTHEW DOW SMITH

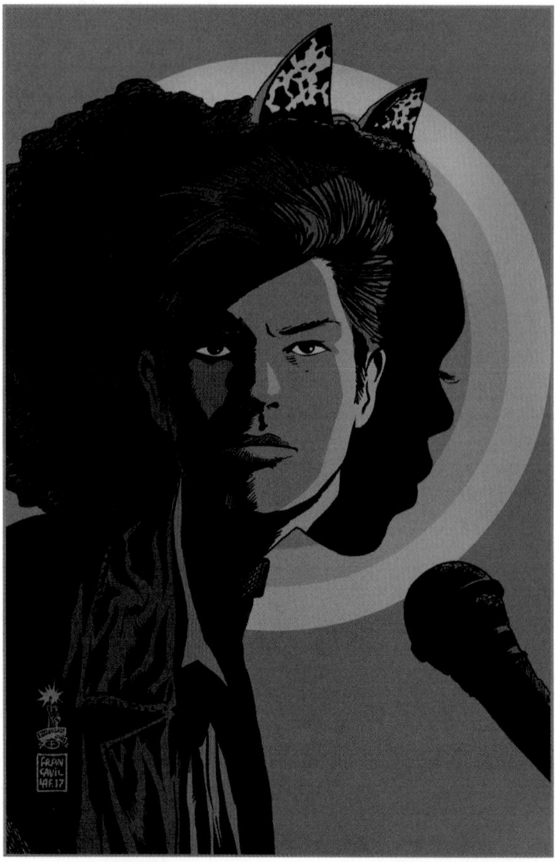

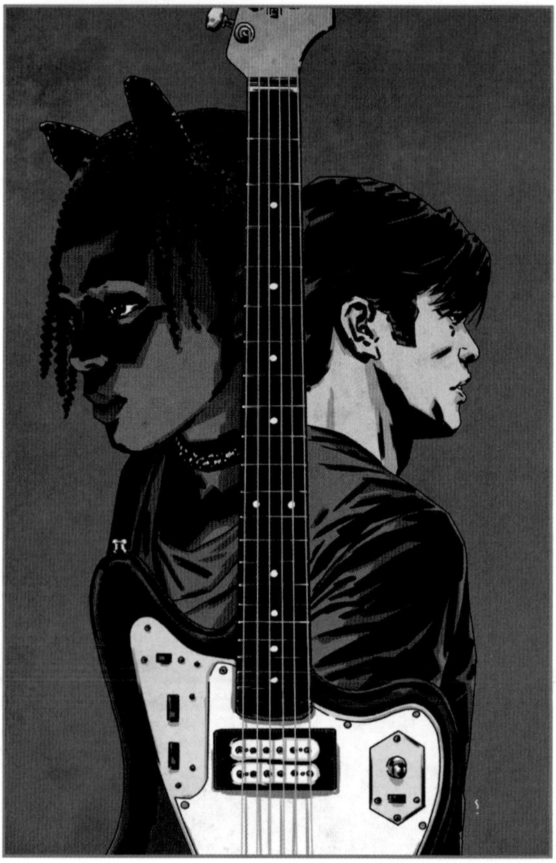

ISSUE
SIX

1

PHOTO COVER
ARCHIE: KJ APA

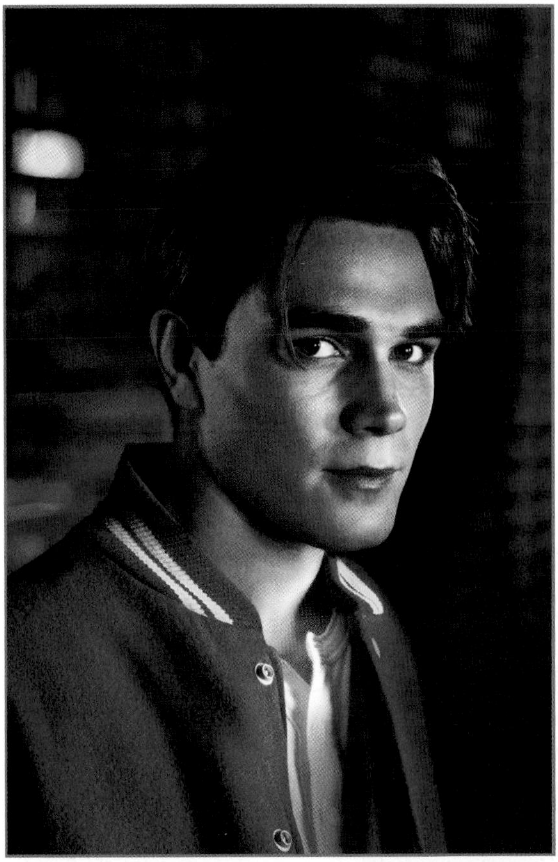

2

FRANCESCO
FRANCAVILLA

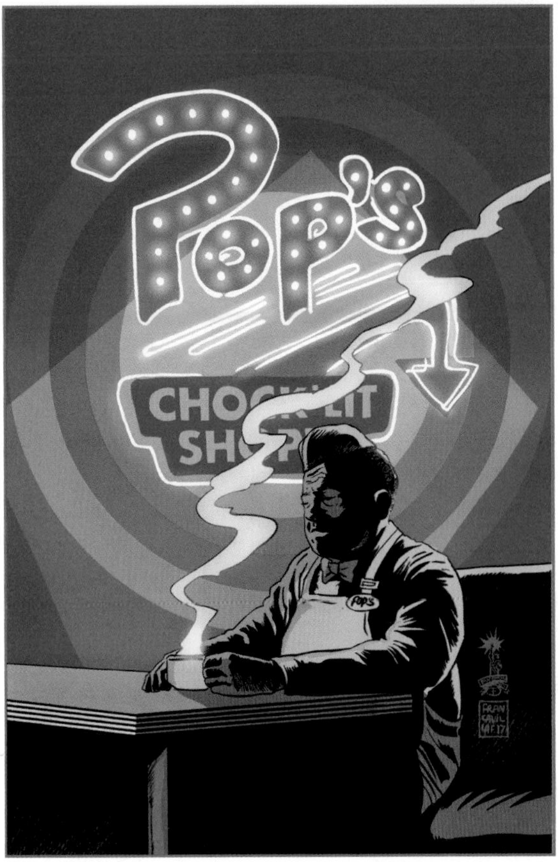
Pop's
CHOCK'LIT
SHOPPE
POP'S

ISSUE
SEVEN

1

**PHOTO COVER
JUGHEAD:
COLE SPROUSE**

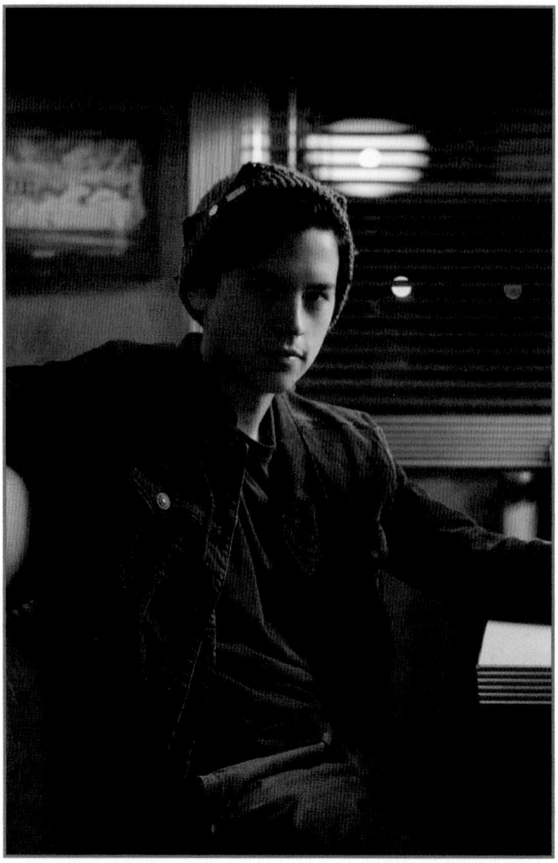

2

**FRANCESCO
FRANCAVILLA**

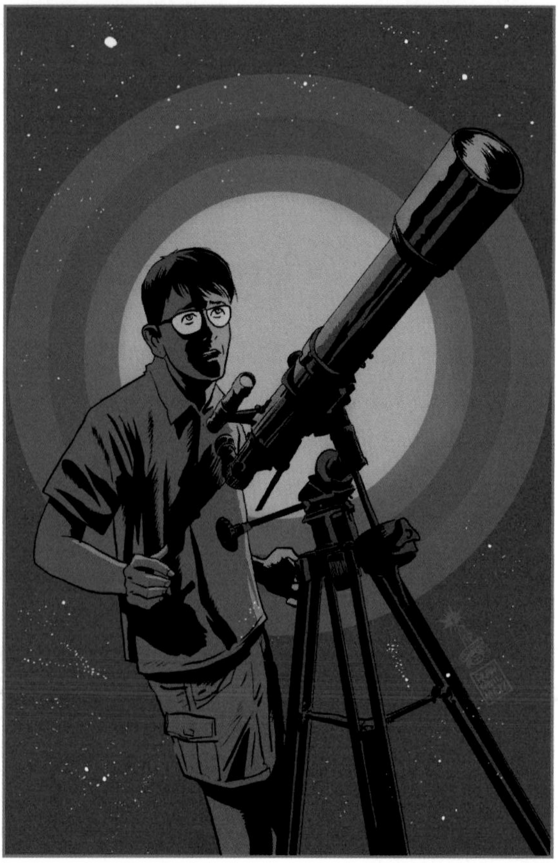

ISSUE
EIGHT

1

PHOTO COVER
BETTY:
LILI REINHART

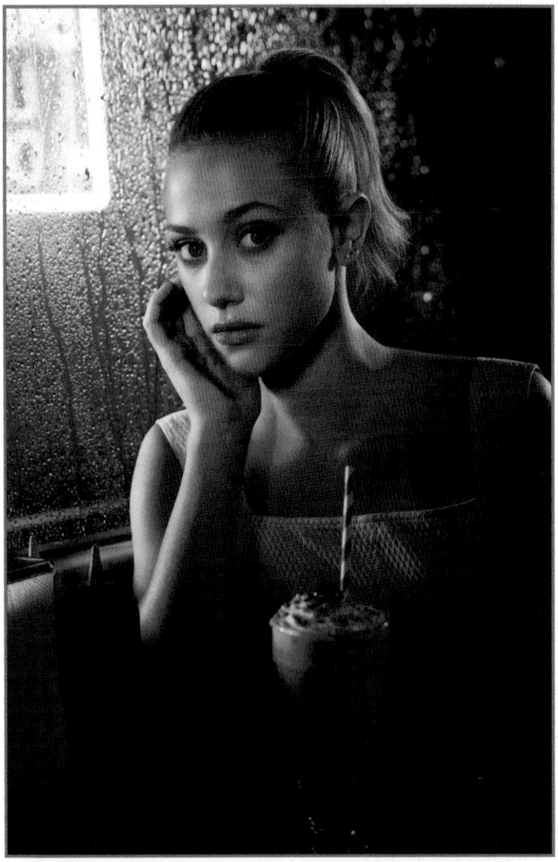

2

PHOTO COVER
VERONICA:
CAMILA MENDES

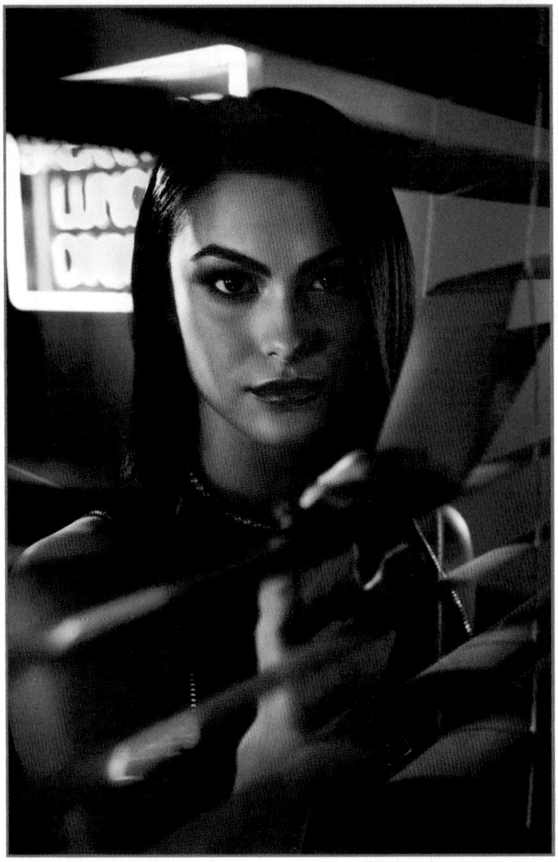

RIVERDALE

SEASON TWO: EPISODE THREE
THE WATCHER IN THE WOODS

Archie took inspiration for his "Red Circle" group of vigilantes from an old comic book that he finds in his garage. The Red Circle superhero characters first appeared in the 1930s and 1940s and have been around since before Archie Andrews. These characters include The Shield, The Web, The Comet, The Black Hood, and many others. They've had multiple incarnations throughout the decades that followed, including a recent reinvention under the Dark Circle Comics imprint in 2015.

The Black Hood has been part of Red Circle Comics since its early days and the most recent version came in 2015 as Officer Gregory Hettinger was wounded in the line of duty after stumbling upon a fight involving the original Black Hood. After struggling with addiction and being framed by corrupt officials, he dons the mantle of the Black Hood in his vigilante quest for justice. His story is collected in THE BLACK HOOD VOLUME 1 - THE BULLET'S KISS graphic novel.

Toni Topaz first appeared in JUGHEAD DOUBLE DIGEST #176 in 2012 as a foil for Jughead. She has recently been featured as a supporting character in the new ARCHIE series by Mark Waid and attends Riverdale High in the comics alongside the core characters.

One of the coolest parts of watching Riverdale is finding all the easter eggs and callbacks to the classic comics put there by the show's writing team. Whether it's an old comic book title getting used in a line of dialogue or Archie's fake ID having the name of a classic comic book character, there's always something new to find if you're looking close enough!

— RON CACACE **Digital Marketing Manager**

SEASON TWO: EPISODE FOUR
THE TOWN THAT DREADED SUNDOWN

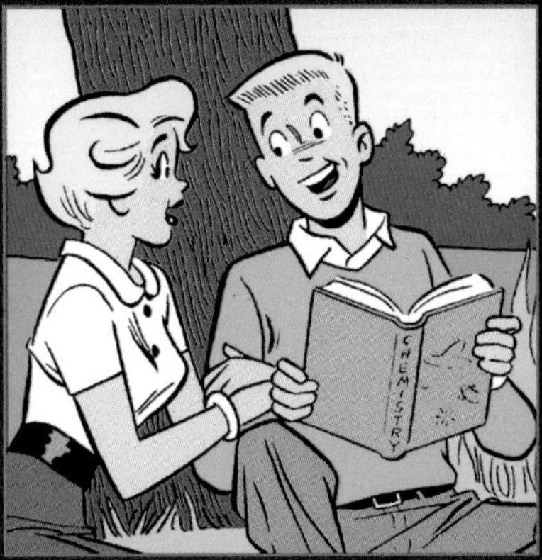
CHEMISTRY

Wilbur Wilkins was a character that debuted before Archie Andrews in 1944 and was published by MLJ Comics (which later became Archie Comics). Wilbur first appeared in ZIP COMICS #18 and some of his classic stories are reprinted in the pages of the various Archie Comics Digests, which are available on newsstands, grocery store check-out lines, and in comic shops.

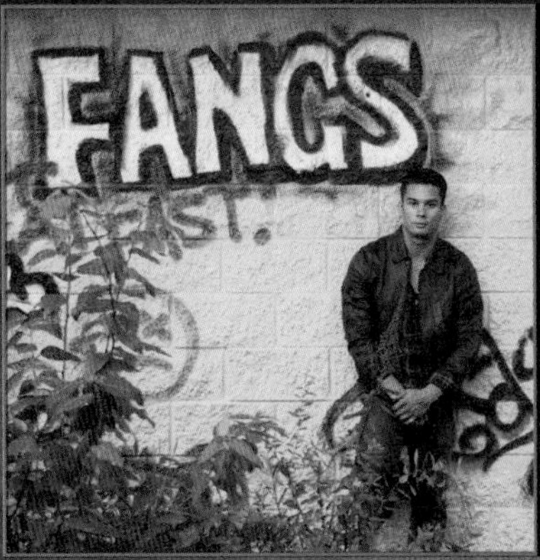
FANGS

Fangs Fogarty is from the Little Archie comics, which featured Archie and the gang as young children, and was a bully to Archie, Jughead, and Reggie.

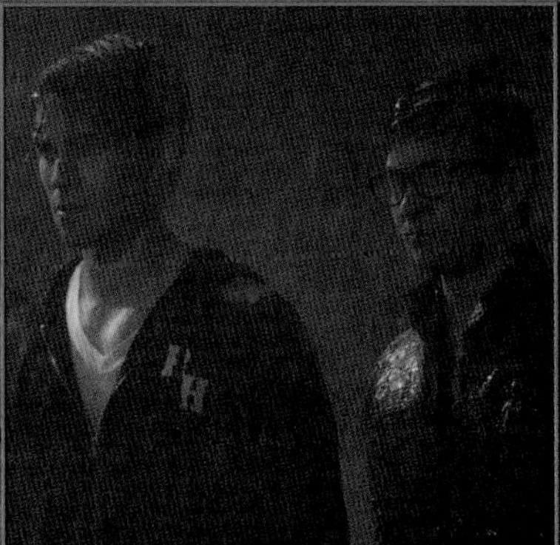

Dilton Doiley recommends that Archie prepare for the worst-case scenario of encountering the Black Hood and encourages him to buy a weapon. In the seventh issue of the RIVERDALE tie-in comic, Dilton is revealed to be a meticulous planner, including having a bunker prepared in case of the apocalypse. Dilton was a scientist and inventor in the original Archie Comics and his obsession in the show has changed to be that of a hardcore survivalist.

SEASON TWO: EPISODE FIVE
WHEN A STRANGER CALLS

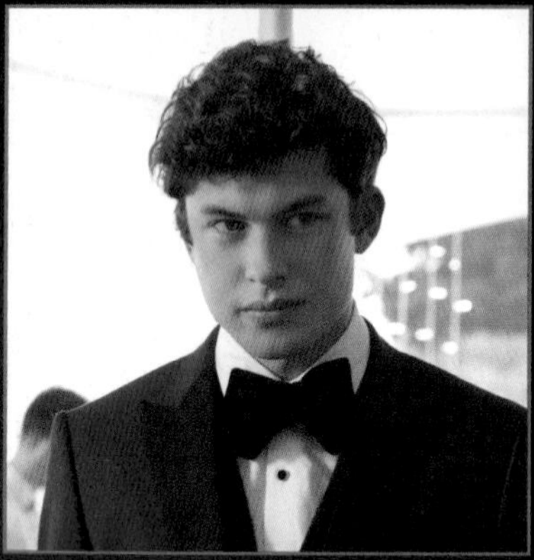

Nick St. Clair first appeared in Archie Comics in 2007 in the Archie New Look series, "Bad Boy Trouble"—although his character was a bit different from the show's version.

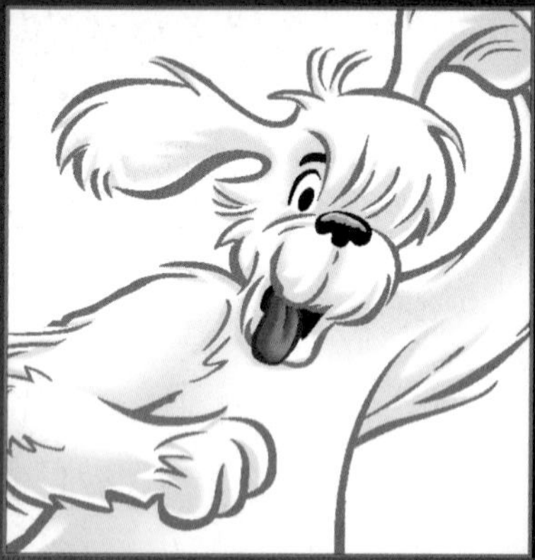

Hot Dog first appeared in *The Archie Show* during the 1960s and later debuted in the comics. His first appearance in the comics was actually as Archie's dog—he later became Jughead's. Hot Dog's thoughts are usually displayed for the reader—he even had his own series at one point, which can be read on the Archie Comics App.

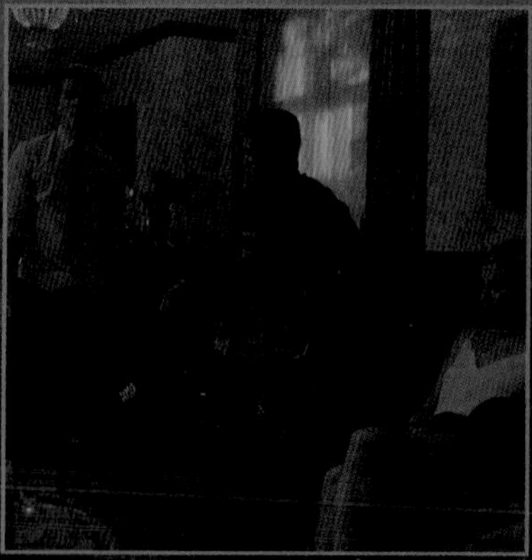

The Reggie/Josie hookup at Nick's party was foreshadowed by the fifth issue of the RIVERDALE tie-in comic which focused on Reggie's attempts to take Josie on a date and Josie's rebuking of him.

CHAPTER ONE: BRUISING

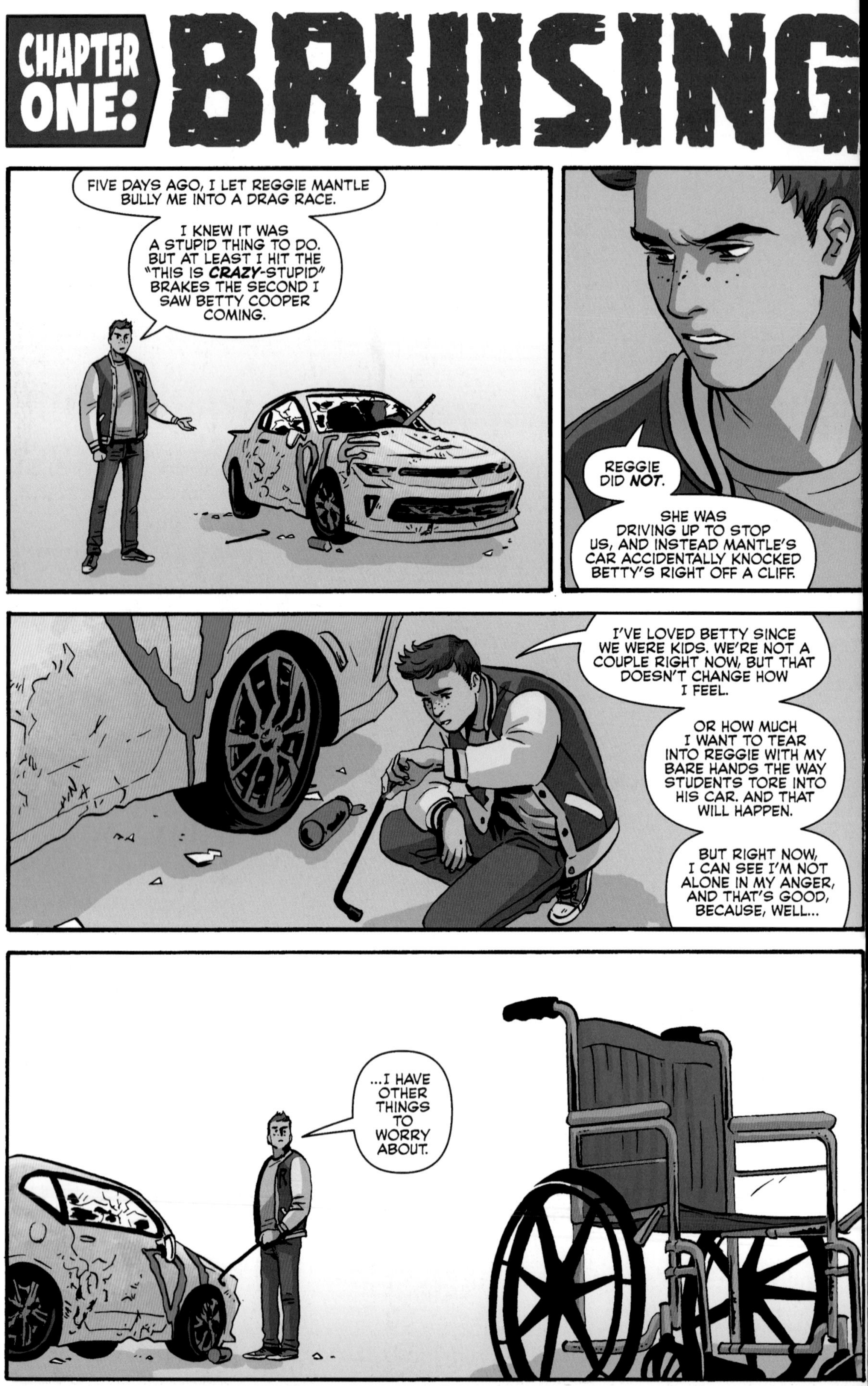
FIVE DAYS AGO, I LET REGGIE MANTLE BULLY ME INTO A DRAG RACE.
I KNEW IT WAS A STUPID THING TO DO. BUT AT LEAST I HIT THE "THIS IS CRAZY-STUPID" BRAKES THE SECOND I SAW BETTY COOPER COMING.
REGGIE DID NOT.
SHE WAS DRIVING UP TO STOP US, AND INSTEAD MANTLE'S CAR ACCIDENTALLY KNOCKED BETTY'S RIGHT OFF A CLIFF.
I'VE LOVED BETTY SINCE WE WERE KIDS. WE'RE NOT A COUPLE RIGHT NOW, BUT THAT DOESN'T CHANGE HOW I FEEL.
OR HOW MUCH I WANT TO TEAR INTO REGGIE WITH MY BARE HANDS THE WAY STUDENTS TORE INTO HIS CAR. AND THAT WILL HAPPEN.
BUT RIGHT NOW, I CAN SEE I'M NOT ALONE IN MY ANGER, AND THAT'S GOOD, BECAUSE, WELL...
...I HAVE OTHER THINGS TO WORRY ABOUT.

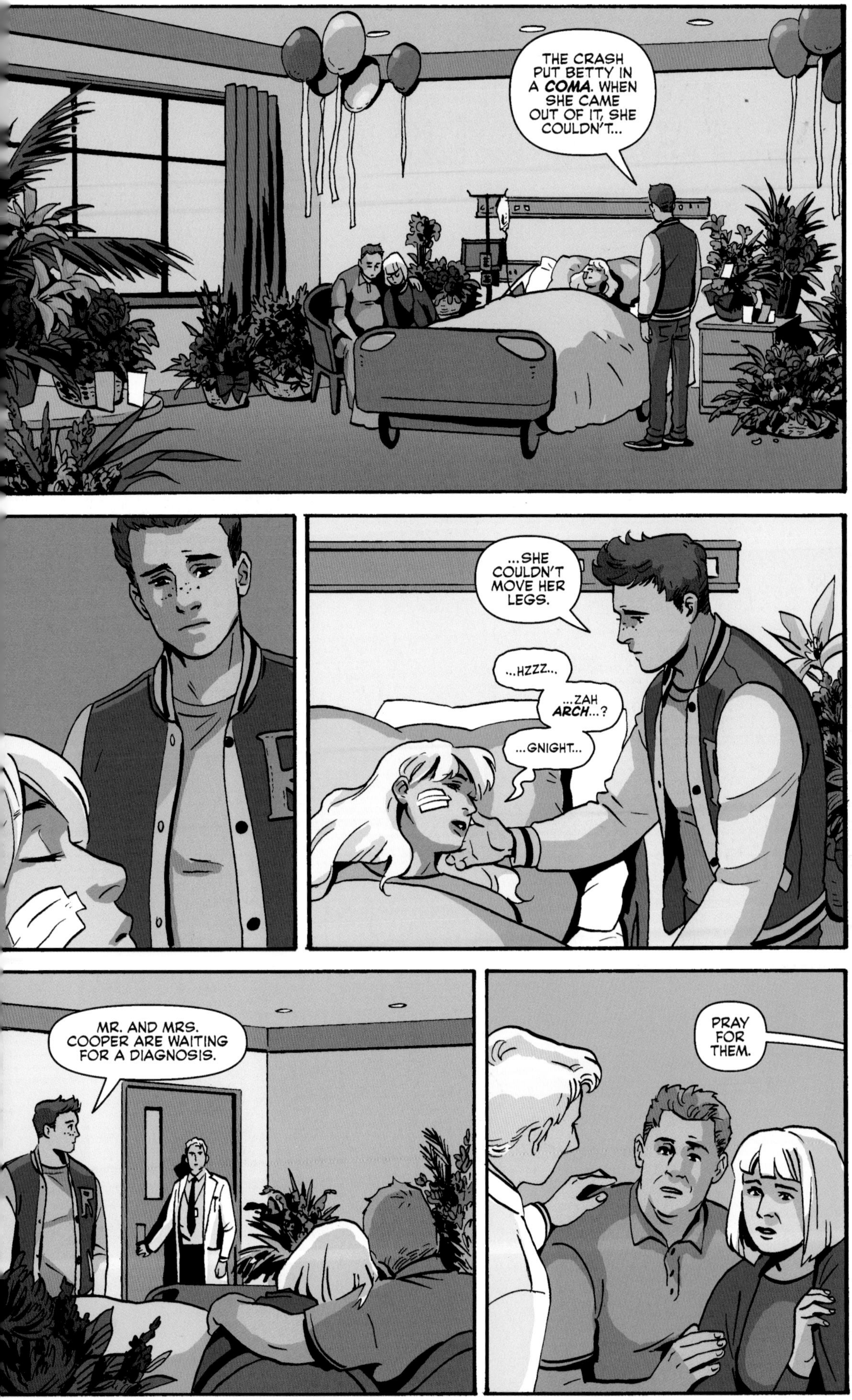
THE CRASH PUT BETTY IN A *COMA*. WHEN SHE CAME OUT OF IT, SHE COULDN'T...
...SHE COULDN'T MOVE HER LEGS.
...HZZZ...
...ZAH *ARCH*...?
...GNIGHT...
MR. AND MRS. COOPER ARE WAITING FOR A DIAGNOSIS.
PRAY FOR THEM.

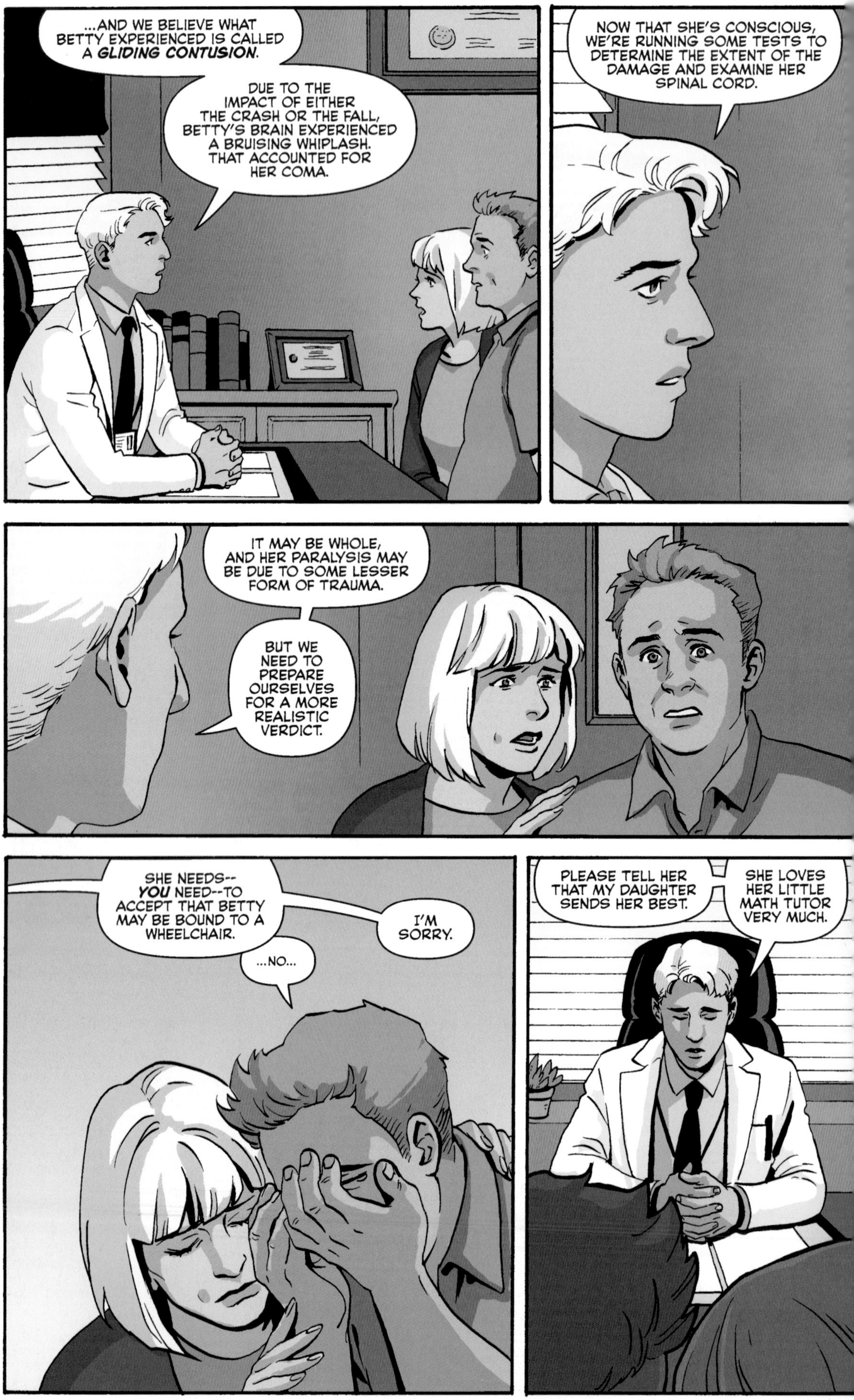
...AND WE BELIEVE WHAT BETTY EXPERIENCED IS CALLED A *GLIDING CONTUSION*.
DUE TO THE IMPACT OF EITHER THE CRASH OR THE FALL, BETTY'S BRAIN EXPERIENCED A BRUISING WHIPLASH. THAT ACCOUNTED FOR HER COMA.
NOW THAT SHE'S CONSCIOUS, WE'RE RUNNING SOME TESTS TO DETERMINE THE EXTENT OF THE DAMAGE AND EXAMINE HER SPINAL CORD.
IT MAY BE WHOLE, AND HER PARALYSIS MAY BE DUE TO SOME LESSER FORM OF TRAUMA.
BUT WE NEED TO PREPARE OURSELVES FOR A MORE REALISTIC VERDICT.
SHE NEEDS-- *YOU* NEED--TO ACCEPT THAT BETTY MAY BE BOUND TO A WHEELCHAIR.
I'M SORRY.
...NO...
PLEASE TELL HER THAT MY DAUGHTER SENDS HER BEST.
SHE LOVES HER LITTLE MATH TUTOR VERY MUCH.

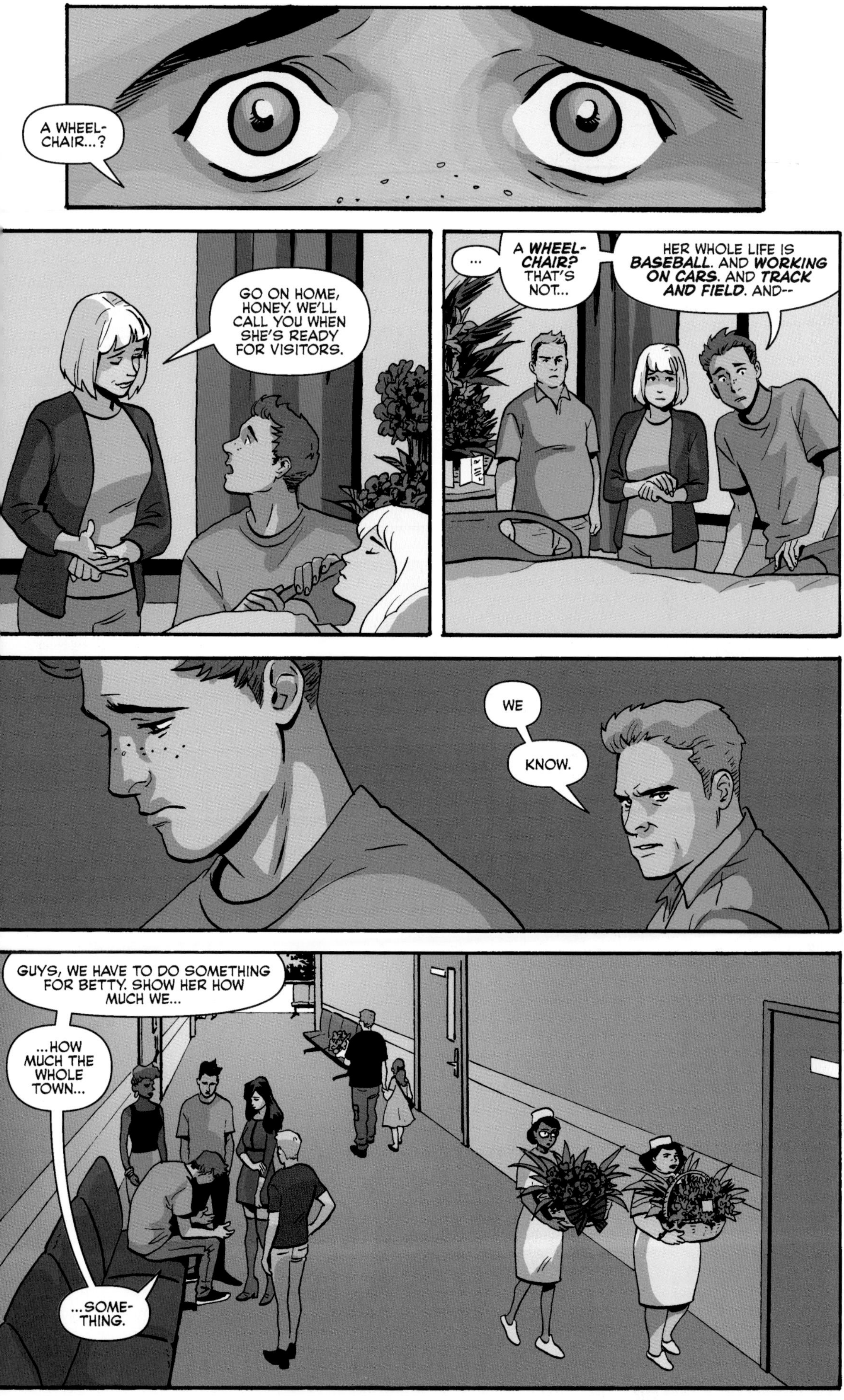
A WHEEL-
CHAIR...?
GO ON HOME, HONEY. WE'LL CALL YOU WHEN SHE'S READY FOR VISITORS.
...
A **WHEEL-CHAIR?** THAT'S NOT...
HER WHOLE LIFE IS **BASEBALL**. AND **WORKING ON CARS**. AND **TRACK AND FIELD**. AND--
WE
KNOW.
GUYS, WE HAVE TO DO SOMETHING FOR BETTY. SHOW HER HOW MUCH WE...
...HOW MUCH THE WHOLE TOWN...
...SOME-THING.

CHAPTER TWO: LIKE e-MAILS

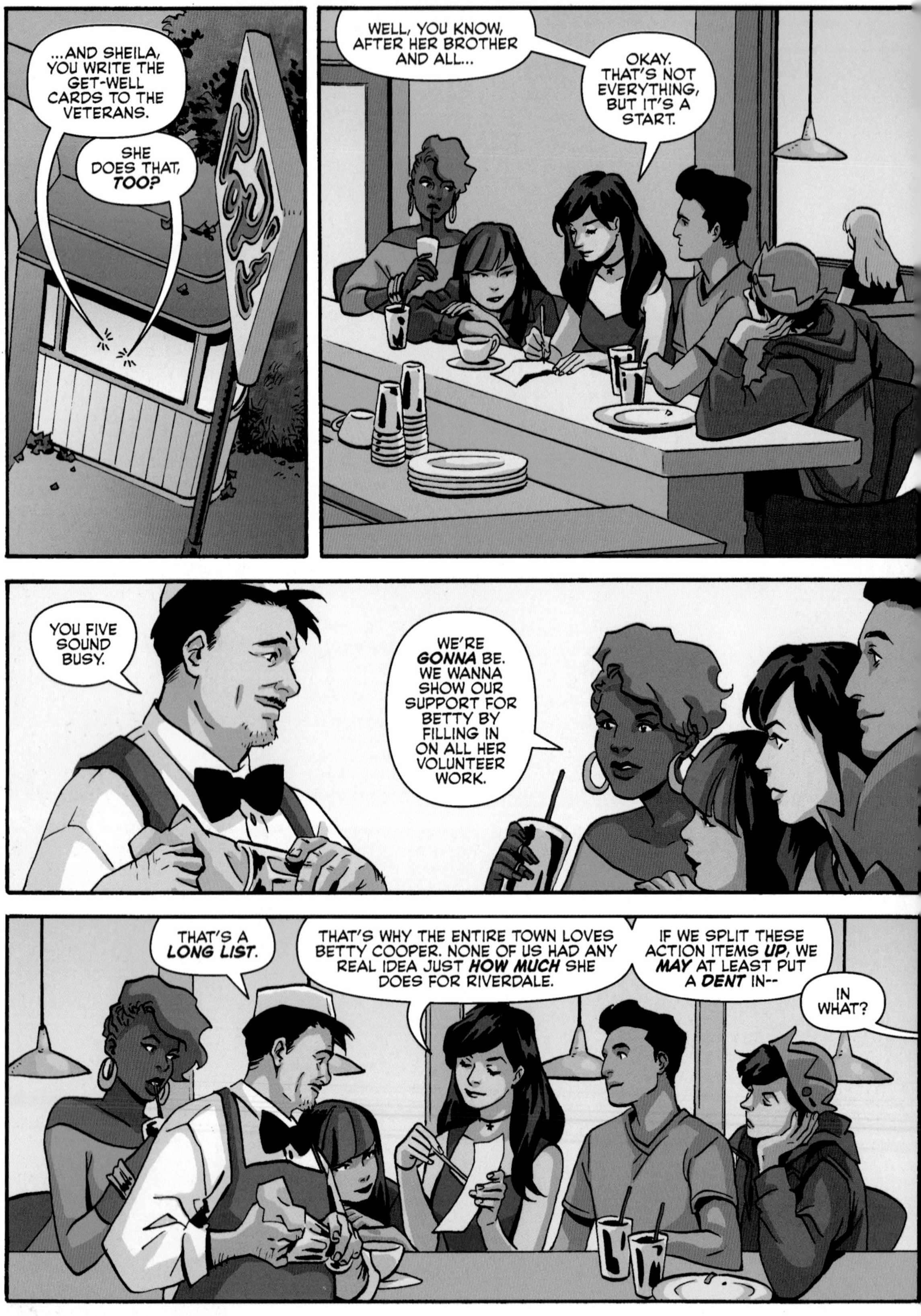
...AND SHEILA, YOU WRITE THE GET-WELL CARDS TO THE VETERANS.
SHE DOES THAT, TOO?
WELL, YOU KNOW, AFTER HER BROTHER AND ALL...
OKAY. THAT'S NOT EVERYTHING, BUT IT'S A START.
YOU FIVE SOUND BUSY.
WE'RE GONNA BE. WE WANNA SHOW OUR SUPPORT FOR BETTY BY FILLING IN ON ALL HER VOLUNTEER WORK.
THAT'S A LONG LIST.
THAT'S WHY THE ENTIRE TOWN LOVES BETTY COOPER. NONE OF US HAD ANY REAL IDEA JUST HOW MUCH SHE DOES FOR RIVERDALE.
IF WE SPLIT THESE ACTION ITEMS UP, WE MAY AT LEAST PUT A DENT IN--
IN WHAT?

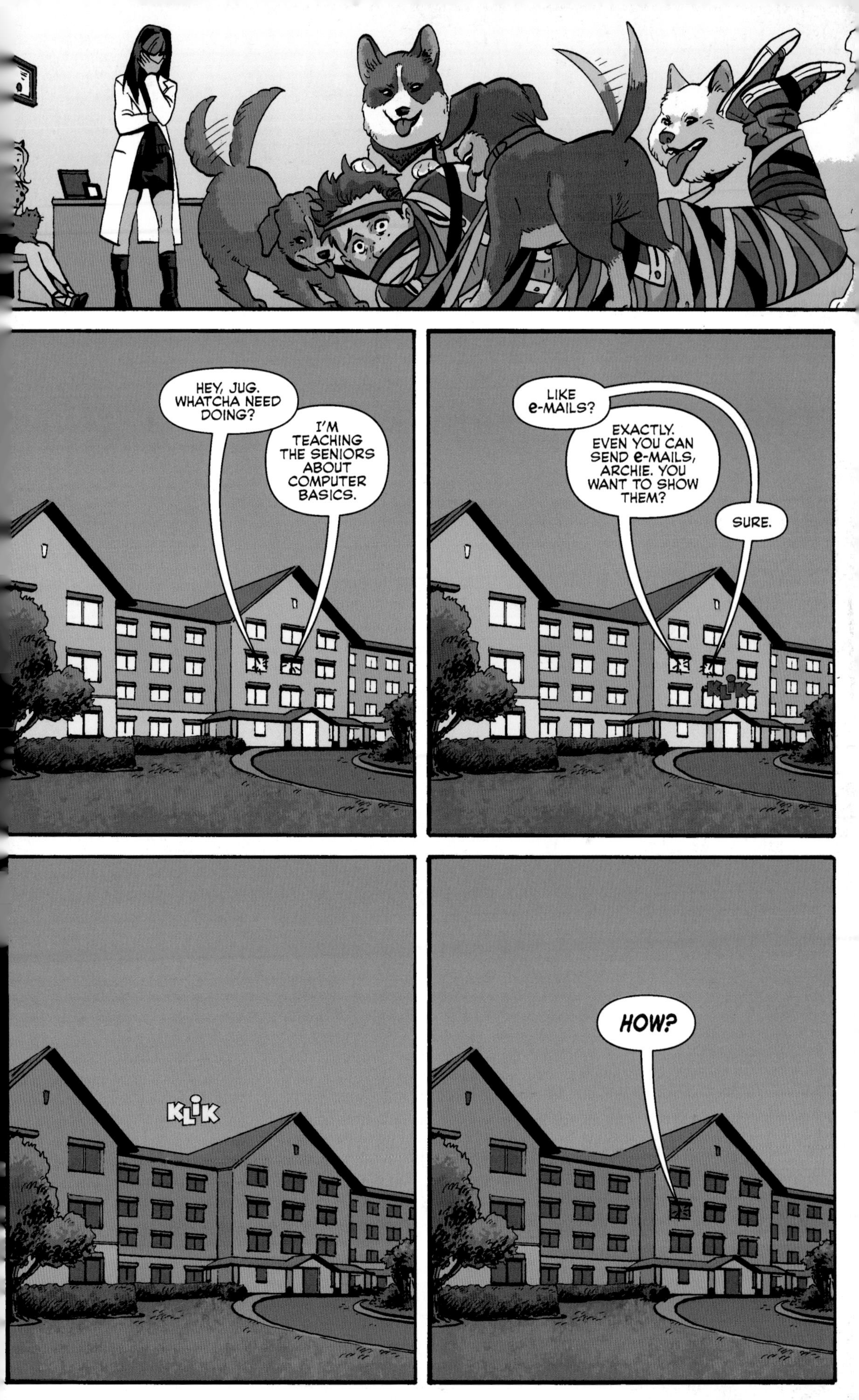
HEY, JUG. WHATCHA NEED DOING?
I'M TEACHING THE SENIORS ABOUT COMPUTER BASICS.
LIKE e-MAILS?
EXACTLY. EVEN YOU CAN SEND e-MAILS, ARCHIE. YOU WANT TO SHOW THEM?
SURE.
KLIK
KLIK
HOW?

CHAPTER THREE: HURRY.

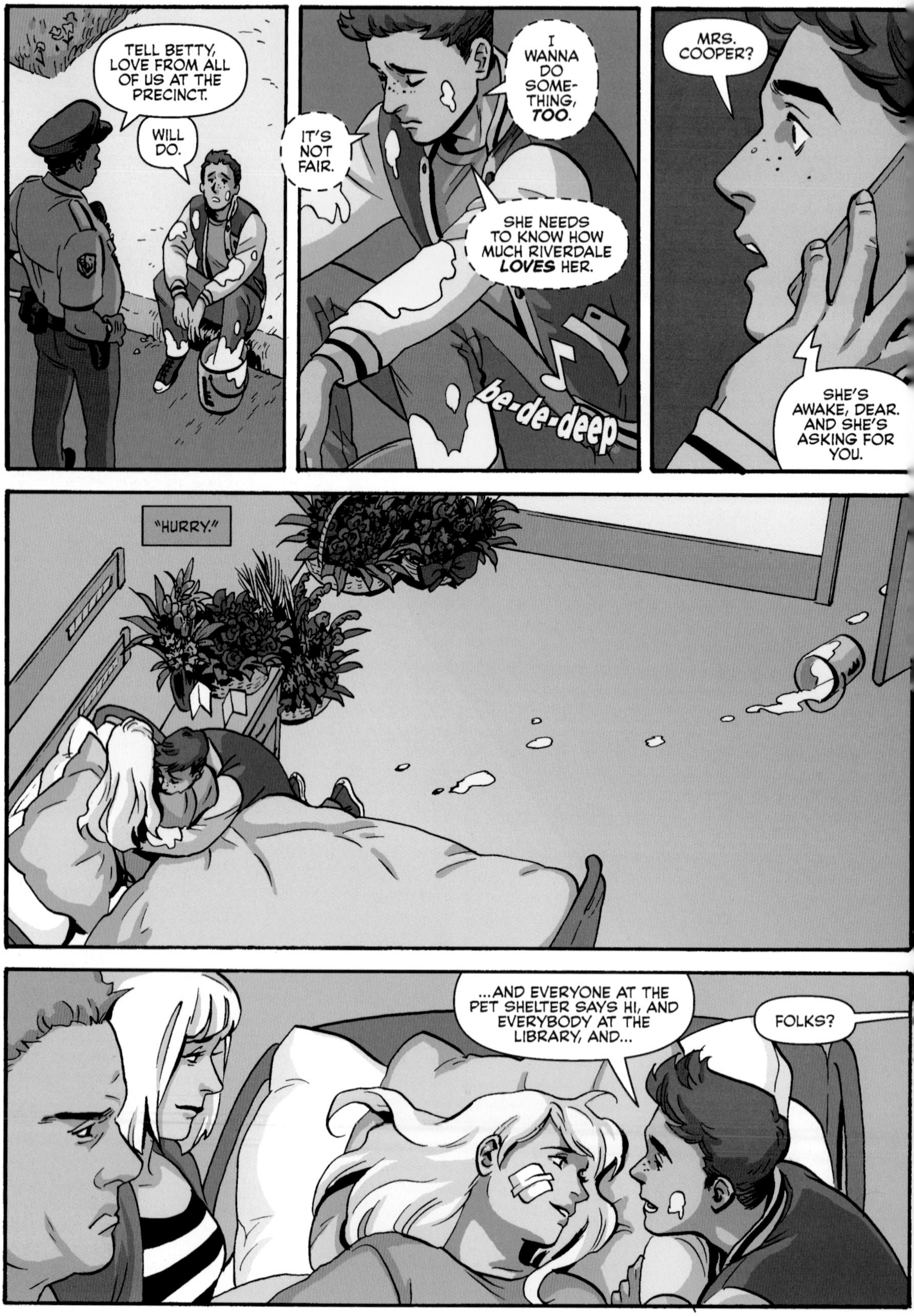
TELL BETTY, LOVE FROM ALL OF US AT THE PRECINCT.
WILL DO.
IT'S NOT FAIR.
I WANNA DO SOME-THING, TOO.
SHE NEEDS TO KNOW HOW MUCH RIVERDALE LOVES HER.
be-de-deep
MRS. COOPER?
SHE'S AWAKE, DEAR. AND SHE'S ASKING FOR YOU.
"HURRY."
...AND EVERYONE AT THE PET SHELTER SAYS HI, AND EVERYBODY AT THE LIBRARY, AND...
FOLKS?

CHAPTER FIVE: THE HEART OF RIVERDALE

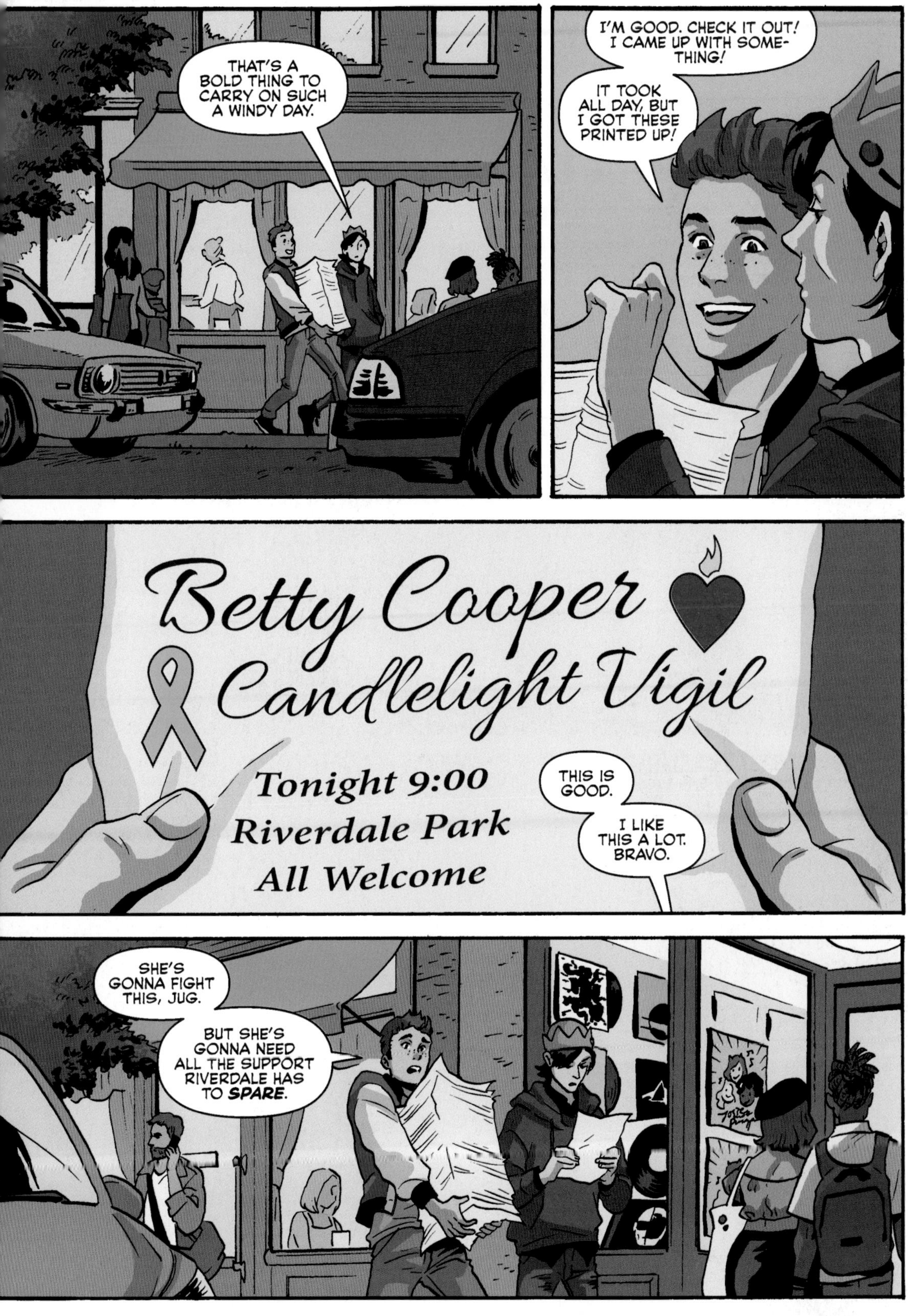

THAT'S A BOLD THING TO CARRY ON SUCH A WINDY DAY.
I'M GOOD. CHECK IT OUT! I CAME UP WITH SOMETHING!
IT TOOK ALL DAY, BUT I GOT THESE PRINTED UP!
Betty Cooper Candlelight Vigil
Tonight 9:00
Riverdale Park
All Welcome
THIS IS GOOD.
I LIKE THIS A LOT. BRAVO.
SHE'S GONNA FIGHT THIS, JUG.
BUT SHE'S GONNA NEED ALL THE SUPPORT RIVERDALE HAS TO SPARE.

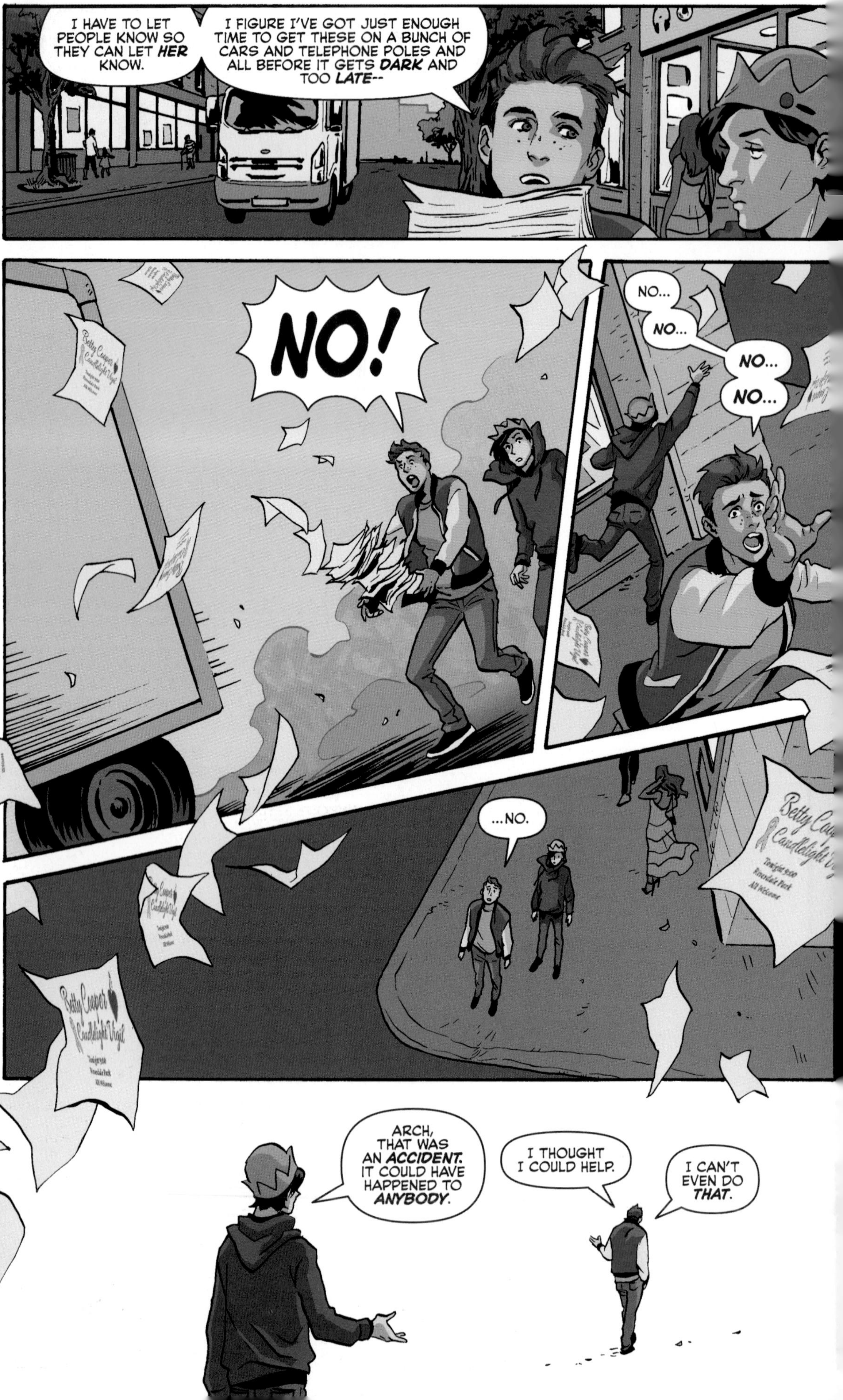
I HAVE TO LET PEOPLE KNOW SO THEY CAN LET HER KNOW.
I FIGURE I'VE GOT JUST ENOUGH TIME TO GET THESE ON A BUNCH OF CARS AND TELEPHONE POLES AND ALL BEFORE IT GETS DARK AND TOO LATE--
NO!
NO...
NO...
NO...
NO...
...NO.
Betty Cooper Candlelight Vigil
ARCH, THAT WAS AN ACCIDENT. IT COULD HAVE HAPPENED TO ANYBODY.
I THOUGHT I COULD HELP.
I CAN'T EVEN DO THAT.

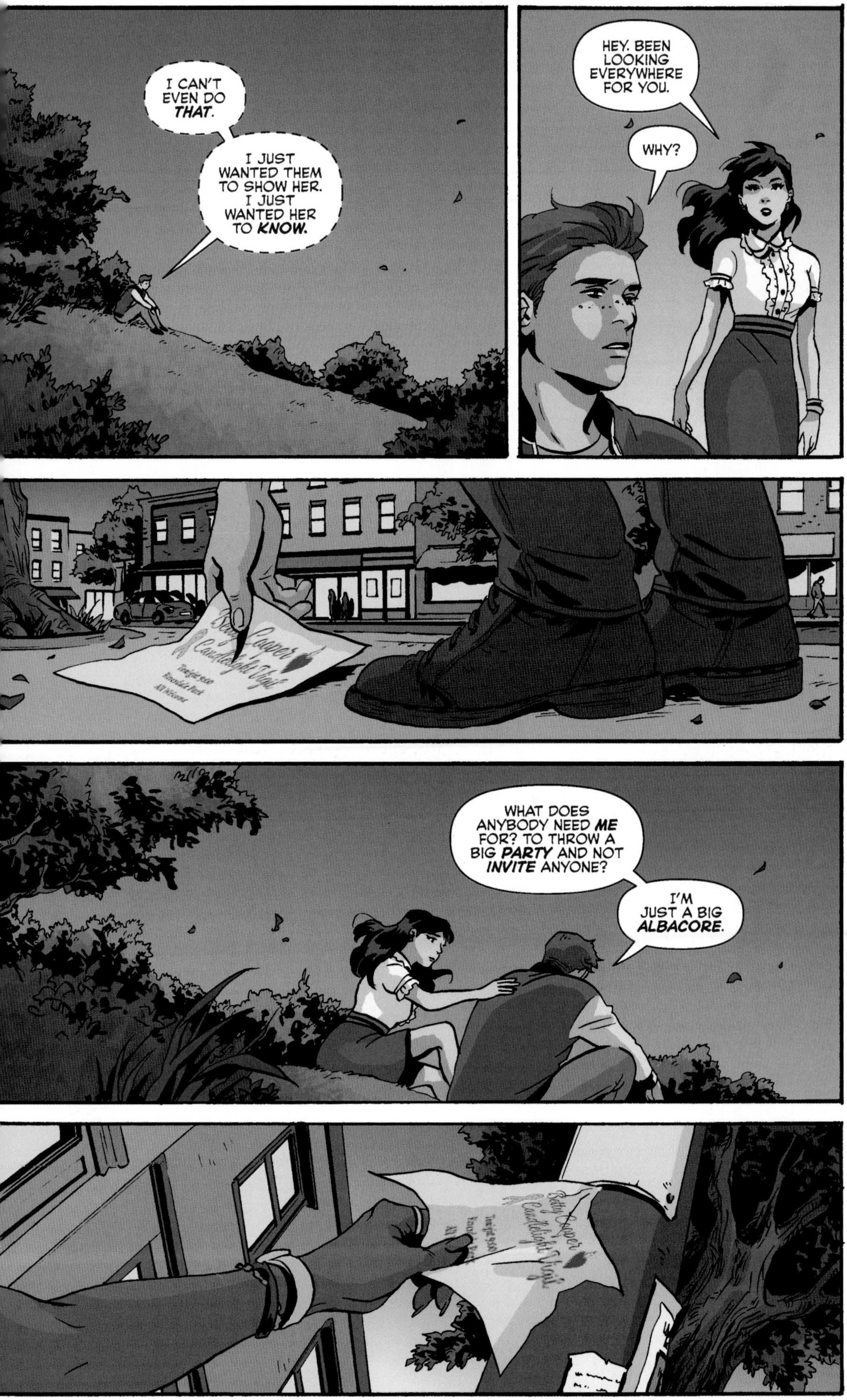
I CAN'T EVEN DO *THAT*.
I JUST WANTED THEM TO SHOW HER. I JUST WANTED HER TO *KNOW.*
HEY. BEEN LOOKING EVERYWHERE FOR YOU.
WHY?
Betty Cooper
Candlelight Vigil
WHAT DOES ANYBODY NEED *ME* FOR? TO THROW A BIG *PARTY* AND NOT *INVITE* ANYONE?
I'M JUST A BIG *ALBACORE*.
Betty Cooper
Candlelight Vigil

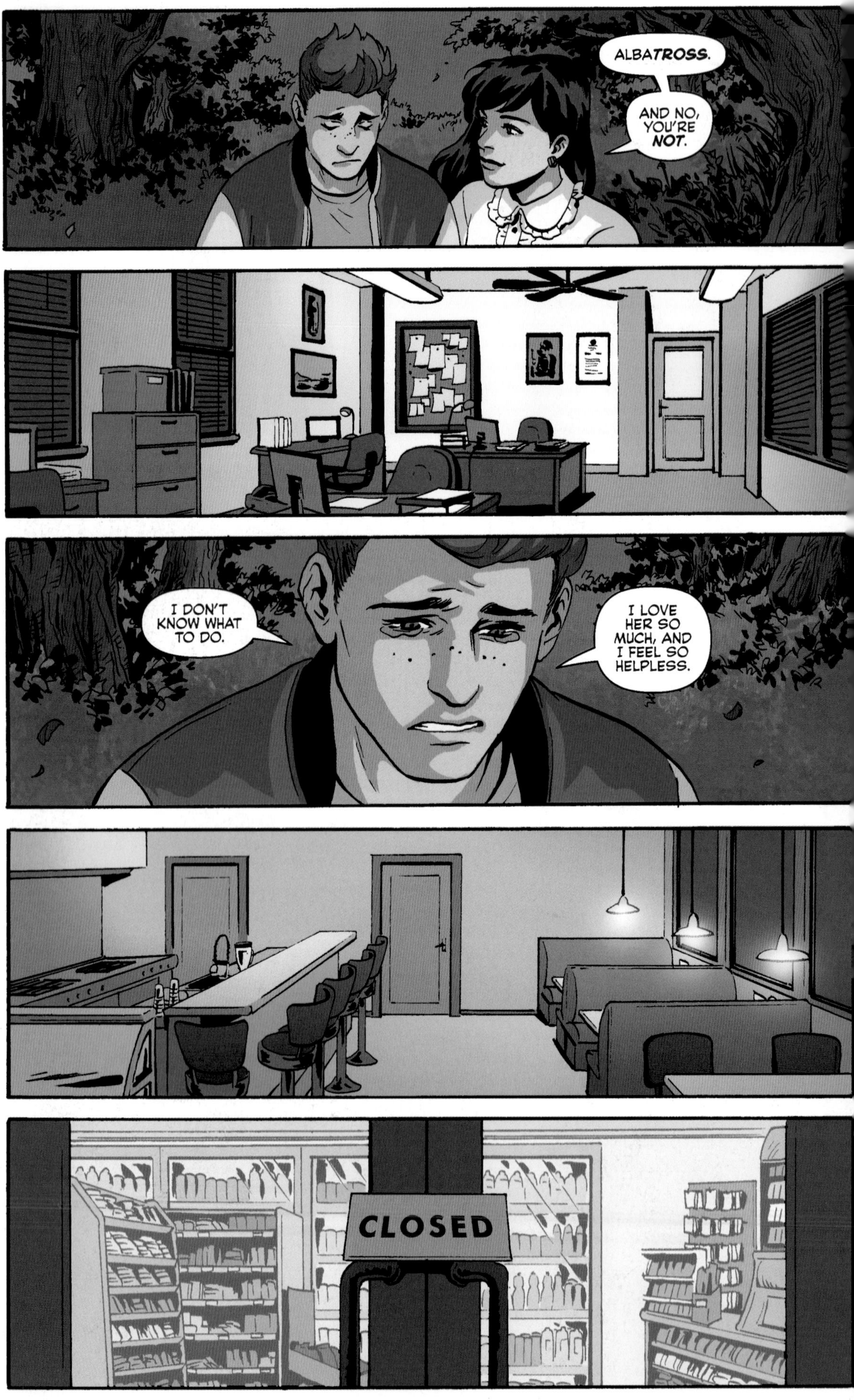
ALBATROSS.
AND NO, YOU'RE NOT.
I DON'T KNOW WHAT TO DO.
I LOVE HER SO MUCH, AND I FEEL SO HELPLESS.
CLOSED

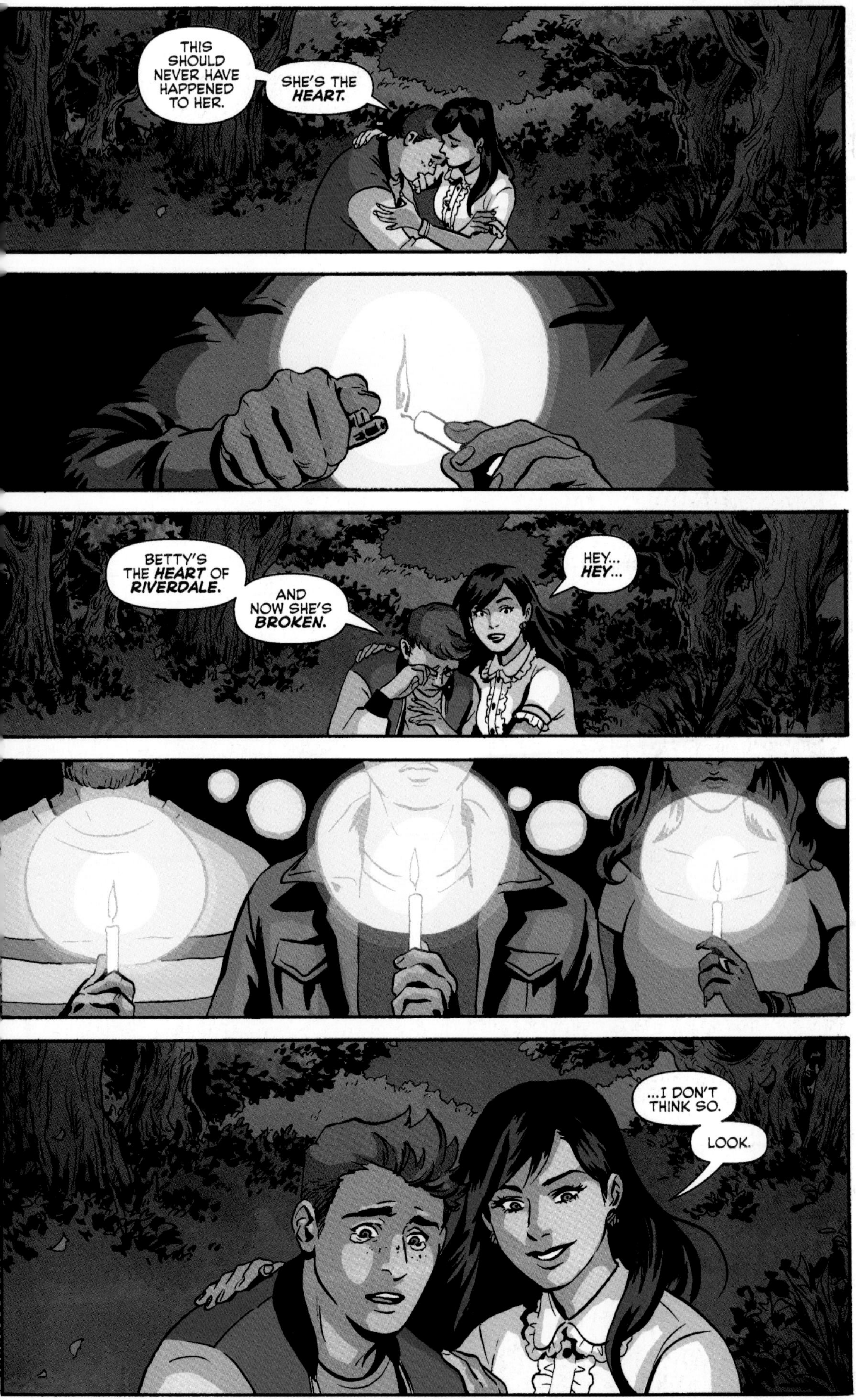
THIS SHOULD NEVER HAVE HAPPENED TO HER.
SHE'S THE *HEART.*
BETTY'S THE *HEART* OF *RIVERDALE.*
AND NOW SHE'S *BROKEN.*
HEY... *HEY...*
...I DON'T THINK SO.
LOOK.

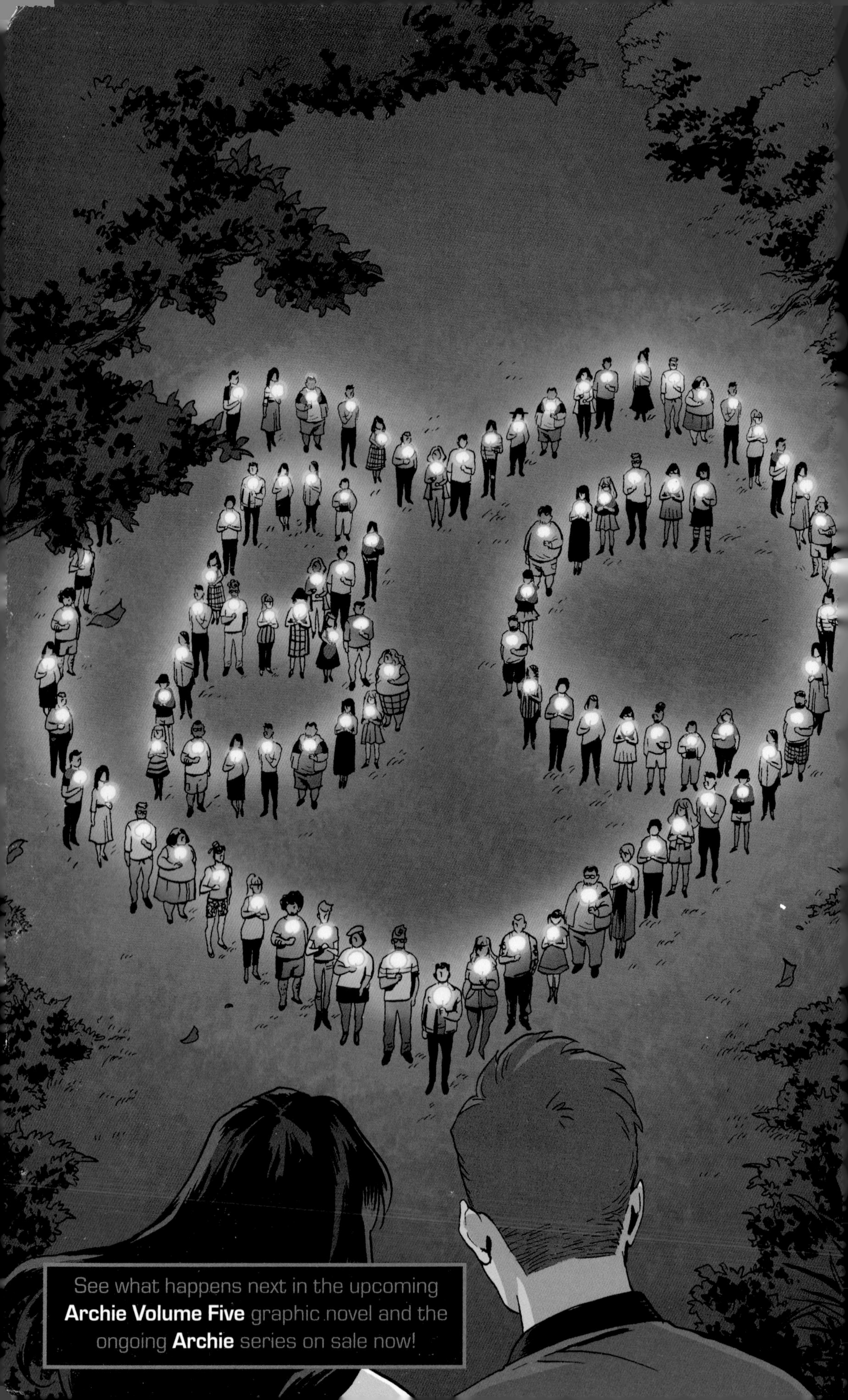
See what happens next in the upcoming **Archie Volume Five** graphic novel and the ongoing **Archie** series on sale now!